# GRIDIRON GOURMET

**SPORT, CULTURE & SOCIETY**

DAVID K. WIGGINS, SERIES EDITOR

## OTHER TITLES IN THIS SERIES

*The Olympic Movement in the Making of Latin America and the Caribbean*

*New Orleans Sports: Playing Hard in the Big Easy*

*Moving Boarders: Skateboarding and
the Changing Landscape of Urban Youth Sports*

*Defending the American Way of Life: Sport, Culture, and the Cold War*

*New York Sports: Glamour and Grit in the Empire City*

*LA Sports: Play, Games, and Community in the City of Angels*

*Making March Madness: The Early Years of the NCAA, NIT,
and College Basketball Championships, 1922–1951*

*San Francisco Bay Area Sports: Golden Gate Athletics,
Recreation, and Community*

*Separate Games: African American Sport behind the Walls of Segregation*

*Baltimore Sports: Stories from Charm City*

*Philly Sports: Teams, Games, and Athletes from Rocky's Town*

*DC Sports: The Nation's Capital at Play*

*Frank Merriwell and the Fiction of All-American Boyhood:
The Progressive Era Creation of the Schoolboy Sports Story*

*Democratic Sports: Men's and Women's College Athletics
during the Great Depression*

*Sport and the Law: Historical and Cultural Intersections*

*Beyond C. L. R. James: Shifting Boundaries of Race and Ethnicity in Sports*

*A Spectacular Leap: Black Women Athletes in Twentieth-Century America*

*Hoop Crazy: The Lives of Clair Bee and Chip Hilton*

# GRIDIRON GOURMET

## Gender and Food
## at the Football Tailgate

**Maria J. Veri and Rita Liberti**

The University of Arkansas Press • Fayetteville • 2019

ISBN: 978-1-68226-101-9
eISBN: 978-1-61075-671-6

23  22  21  20  19     5  4  3  2  1

Designer: Bookmobile Design & Typesetting Services

∞ The paper used in this publication meets the minimum
requirements of the American National Standard for
Permanence of Paper for Printed Library Materials
Z39.48-1984.

Library of Congress Cataloging-in-Publication Data

Names: Veri, Maria J., 1970– author. | Liberti, Rita, author.
Title: Gridiron gourmet : gender and food at the football tailgate / Maria J.
    Veri and Rita Liberti.
Description: Fayetteville : The University of Arkansas Press, 2019. | Series:
    Sports, culture, and society | Includes bibliographical references and index. |
Identifiers: LCCN 2019000681 (print) | LCCN 2019002186 (ebook) | ISBN
    9781610756716 (electronic) | ISBN 9781682261019 (cloth : alk. paper) | ISBN
    9781610756716 (ebook)
Subjects: LCSH: Tailgate parties—Social aspects—United States. |
    Football—Social aspects—United States. | Football fans—United
    States—Social life and customs. | Sex role—United States.
Classification: LCC GV1472.3.U6 (ebook) | LCC GV1472.3.U6 V47 2019 (print) |
    DDC 642.3—dc23
LC record available at https://lccn.loc.gov/2019000681

*For my Dad, Vince Veri, with love.*

*—mjv*


*Dedicated to the memory of Christina I.
Liberti, née Tabone (1940–2018).*

*—rl*

# CONTENTS

Acknowledgments ix

Series Editor's Preface xiii

Introduction 3

1. "As Welcome as Lunch at the Ritz": Episodes in the History of Tailgating 15

2. Cooking Steak with a Hatchet and a Hubcap: Spectacle on the Blacktop 49

3. "We're in the Steel Business, There's Not A Lot of Vegetarians": Meat in Tailgate Culture 71

4. 'Ethnic Edibles' and 'Hindu' Spices: Racial and Ethnic Representation in Tailgate Cookbooks 95

5. Culinary Community on the Blacktop 125

Conclusion 145

Notes 153

Bibliography 181

Index 187

# ACKNOWLEDGMENTS

When we first set out to write about tailgate culture, we were excited about a project that would meld food and sport but did not necessarily see a book in our future. After a presentation at the 2010 NASSS conference, colleagues and friends started to share their tailgate stories with us, send us photos of tailgate scenes, and alert us to topical news stories. We quickly realized there was more material to cover, and that tailgating was growing into a bigger and bigger cultural phenomenon, so we decided to dive deeper. The development of this book has been a nearly decade-long process and there are many people to thank. We are grateful for all of the feedback and encouragement we received from our colleagues at NASSS, our respective departments and universities, and especially at NASSH as we progressed with our research. When colleagues started to ask us if a book was in the works, we figured that eventually the answer could be yes.

It was our great fortune that we initially approached Dave Wiggins, editor of the Sport, Culture, and Society series for The University of Arkansas Press, with our idea for a book proposal. We couldn't be more appreciative of his support, guidance, and enthusiasm for our project. We would also like to thank the anonymous reviewers from The University of Arkansas Press and editor-in-chief David Scott Cunningham for their careful, constructive engagement with the initial drafts of our manuscript. The final product benefitted immensely from their comments and suggestions. Thank you also to our copy editor, Molly Rector, for her thoughtful review of our completed manuscript, and to editorial assistant Jenny Vos for shepherding us through the publication process in such a genial way.

Our research took us to blacktops across the country, where we had the pleasure of watching some real gridiron gourmets in action and enjoyed tasting the samples of their culinary creations they generously offered us. We are indebted to the 3rdRail9ers, Black Pot Mafia, Mitch, Bill, and Mike, and the numerous other individuals and groups who took the time to speak with us and share their tailgating experiences. This book is much richer for their contributions, and we hope we have done them justice in these pages.

Thank you to Glenn Brewster, at California State University, East Bay media and academic technology services, for his technical acumen and assistance on everything from conference presentations to image reproduction throughout this project. Thanks also to CSU East Bay library staff member Paul MacLennan for his help in tracking down key definitions and sources. We are grateful for the research assistance provided by San Francisco State University Kinesiology students Michelle Kim, Mikaela Amble, and especially Jeffrey Dean. We would be remiss not to mention our own cheerleader and personal reference librarian extraordinaire, Trudy Toll. Her continued enthusiasm and support for this project has made working on it that much more fun and rewarding.

We are indebted to the Department of Kinesiology at CSU East Bay for its generous financial support of all of our indexing and image permission costs. These costs represent a significant burden to authors who publish with academic presses; that CSU East Bay understands and values the humanities within Kinesiology is significant and greatly appreciated.

—mjv & rl

A decade ago, if someone had suggested that a project—much less a book-length project—on the culture of football tailgating was in my future, I would have thought them daft. But somehow when I first chatted with Maria about the topic, the idea of studying the intersection of food and sport was not only made plausible, but began to seem filled with so many rich possibilities. Researching and writing *Gridiron Gourmet* with her has been very enjoyable. Especially memorable were our "meat ups" to discuss the book. Everything, it is said, is better with bacon. We were glad, in these work "meat ups," to test that theory.

For more than two decades my colleagues at CSU East Bay have sustained and inspired me. There are so many wonderful faculty, both within my department and across the campus, with whom I've had the pleasure to work. I am especially grateful to Eileen Barrett in the English Department and Linda Ivey in the History Department for their friendship.

And to Trudy, who upon reading an article in the *New York Times* about Food Network star Guy Fieri's new show, *Tailgate Warriors*, nine years ago commented, "You and Maria should write on that." Indeed. Her suggestion, like so many others, was right on the mark. She looks out for me at every turn. Everyone should be so lucky.

—rl

The inspiration for *Gridiron Gourmet* came about serendipitously. Like Rita, before this project began, I did not in any way anticipate that I would write a book about tailgating culture. But, after a *New York Times* profile with a local angle, a nudge from a partner and friend (the aforementioned Trudy Toll), a few conference presentations, and a well-timed sabbatical for me, there we were, making forays onto the blacktop and discussing the ways we could explore gender at the intersection of food and sport—often over burgers during our "meat-ups" across Oakland and other Bay Area locales. For all of that, plus an easy collaborative camaraderie with my coauthor, I am grateful. Writing and researching *Gridiron Gourmet* with Rita has been an immensely enjoyable and rewarding process.

I'm grateful to Becky Johnson and Pat Ash, Joy DeSensi, and Rosa Lopez for their hospitality while traveling to attend tailgates. The Johnson-Ash home, in particular, always provides a cherished respite, with the added bonus of Dino the wonder kitty. The Lopez-Ayala household offers a different kind of experience—one filled with hustle and bustle and the wonderfully fun kiddos Leo and Benjamín. For helping to propel me ever forward with great care over the last decade, a big thank you to Frances Fuchs. I have been blessed with some special friends over the years; the list is long, but in the acknowledgments for this book I'll highlight Trudy Toll, Ninfa Ortiz, and Dave Walsh. I am, quite simply, the better for their presence in my life.

I am privileged to work with some remarkable colleagues in the Department of Kinesiology and across the campus of San Francisco State University. Thank you to those who have provided inspiration, support, and oft-needed levity. You know who you are. Much appreciation to the College of Health and Social Sciences for a mini-grant that afforded me a bit of extra time to devote to this book during the fall 2016 semester.

During the researching of this book, two women dear to me passed. First, my aunt, Anne Marie Antonio. Her love, sustenance, and influence on my life were immeasurable. I miss her greatly. I am comforted that she knew about this project, but not having her here to proclaim upon publication—loudly, proudly, and often, I'm sure—that "my niece wrote a book!" tinges this accomplishment with sadness. Second, my friend and doctoral adviser, Dr. Joy DeSensi—a wonderful scholar, a masterful teacher, and a kind, caring, mentor. I carry her influence with me still.

To Xochitl, my love and best friend. She wanted me to write that though life with her can be challenging, I love her anyway. Maybe so on the challenging part (mostly in good ways), definitely on the loving her part. I am grateful for the wonderful life we are building together. Thank you for standing with me as this book moved into the home stretch, and for all that you have brought me.

Finally, for my dad, Vince Veri, to whom this book is dedicated. I struggle to find the right words to express all that he means to me. Importantly, he made good on a promise that a college education would be possible for me. As a result, I am a proud first-generation college graduate who then continued to stay in school for as long as I could. His affinity for and deep knowledge of sports, not to mention his appreciation for history, shape much of what I do. I am so happy that I can share the completion of this book with him.

—mjv

# SERIES EDITOR'S PREFACE

Sport is an extraordinarily important phenomenon that pervades the lives of many people and has enormous impact on society in an assortment of ways. At its most fundamental level, sport has the power to bring people great joy and satisfy their competitive urges while at once allowing them to form bonds and a sense of community with others from diverse backgrounds and interests and walks of life. Sport also makes clear, especially at the highest levels of competition, the lengths that people will go to achieve victory. Additionally, sport is closely connected to to business, education, politics, economics, religion, law, family, and other societal institutions. Sport is partly about identity development and how individuals and groups, irrespective of race, gender, ethnicity, or socioeconomic class, have sought to elevate their status and realize material success and social mobility.

*Sport, Culture, and Society* seeks to promote a greater understanding of the aforementioned issues and many others. Recognizing sport's powerful influence and ability to change people's lives in significant and important ways, the series focuses on topics ranging from urbanization and community development to biographies and intercollegiate athletics. It includes both monographs and anthologies that are characterized by excellent scholarship, accessible to a wide audience, and interesting and thoughtful in design and interpretations. Singular features of the series are authors and editors representing a variety of disciplinary areas and who adopt different methodological approaches. The series also includes works by individuals at various stages of their careers, both sport studies scholars of outstanding talent just beginning to make their mark on the field and more experienced scholars of sport with established reputations.

*Gridiron Gourmet: Gender and Food at the Football Tailgate* explores how sport and food intersect in popular culture. More specifically, authors Maria J. Veri and Rita Liberti analyze how masculinity plays out at the football tailgate. Through an examination of the lived experiences of veteran tailgaters and exploration of cookbooks, television shows, commercials, and movies, Veri and Liberti provide cogent and important insights into what takes place when men control a cultural space—in this case the preparation and serving of food—historically most closely associated with women. In all, it is a highly creative, imaginative, and multidisciplinary study that charts new terrain, delineating how masculinity is performed in the world of tailgating that attracts large numbers of participants in search of good food and drink and conviviality prior to the big game. Along the way, *Gridiron Gourmet* also accounts for important racial and ethnic differences and representation via the consumption of food and football and makes clear the seemingly universal quest that all people have for a sense of community.

*David K. Wiggins*

# GRIDIRON GOURMET

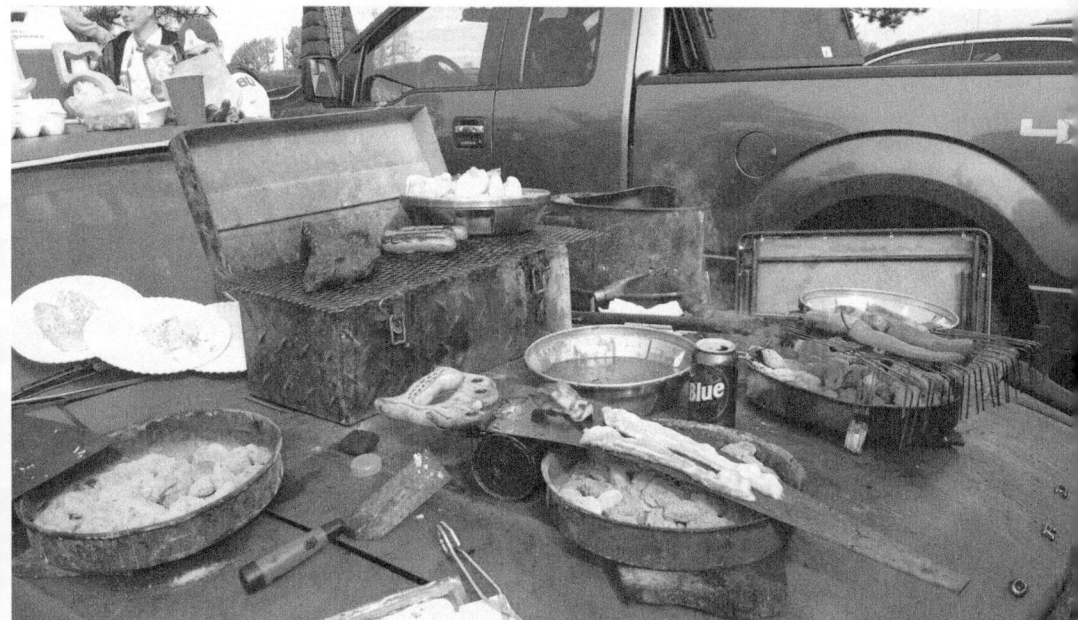

The hood-turned-cooktop of Pinto Kenny's defunct car, Buffalo.
*Courtesy of authors.*

# INTRODUCTION

*"We're not here for the game, the game is nothing . . . The real
reason we Americans put up with sports is for this . . . the tailgate party, the pinnacle of human achievement."*

—Homer Simpson

A stroll around any college or professional game day parking lot confirms
that Homer Simpson is not too far off the mark with this assessment.[1]
Whole roasted pigs, custom-made smokers, gourmet spreads, and state-
of-the-art RVs decked out in team colors testify to the creativity and
ingenuity of serious tailgaters. In Buffalo, there is Pinto Kenny, a longtime
Bills fan who has forsaken the usual tailgate trappings of grill and smoker
to create perhaps the most uniquely functioning feast on the blacktop.
Fans gather around the hood of Kenny's rusted-out, nonoperational red
Pinto to watch all manner of carnivorous fare being prepared over an
array of auto parts, tools, and toolboxes. One of the many innovations
on display involves sausage and peppers sizzling on a lawn rake strategi-
cally placed over an old hubcap filled with hot coals. Mark, a professor
of mechanical engineering based in Albany, New York, and a veteran of
Kenny's crew, drives four-and-a-half hours for every Bills home game to
deep fry chicken wings in a repurposed World War II helmet. The devices
in use and the commitment of the guys in Kenny's crew not only indicate an investment in their craft but also in masculinity, with gendered
markers on clear display.

In San Francisco, in a lot at Levi's Stadium, the guys of the 3rdRail9ers
tailgate crew set up an outdoor cooking station for 49ers home games
that rivals those of any professional catering operation and go about the
task of producing pregame food that surpasses the quality of most restaurants. Fans and friends clamor for Kimo's sesame chicken, Nick's specialty
bacon-infused macaroni and cheese, and George's grilled tri-tips. For
home games at the University of Tennessee, Herschel tows his custom-
built meat smoker and rotisserie to a prime spot in Circle Park, and he
and his tailgating partner Hank proceed to grill up one hundred pounds
of baby back ribs, chicken wrapped with bacon, and pulled pork. Their

weekly price tag for food and alcohol: $1500. For a group of Louisiana State University tailgaters from New Iberia, Louisiana, $2000 fills their forty-gallon gumbo pot with chicken, sausage, duck, and andouille, with assorted sides, appetizers, and beverages rounding out the menu. Then there are the names. Some tailgating crews operate as cohesive teams with a strong sense of identity behind names like Black Pot Mafia (at LSU), Los Malosos—loose Spanish translation for "Raiders"—(in Oakland), and the aforementioned 3rdRail9ers (drawn partly from the moniker of the punk metal band some members play in). These tailgating operations have evolved considerably from the early twentieth-century automobile picnics that dotted college campuses on fall Saturdays. Gone are the days of the quaint picnic basket and plaid blanket spread at the rear of the station wagon, where tailgaters ate sandwiches wrapped in wax paper and drank warm coffee from a thermos before heading into the stadium. In today's tailgate culture, food and cooking occupy a central role in a practice that is enjoyed by thousands and represented widely in popular culture. Whether in Louisiana, San Francisco, or upstate New York, tailgating is a significant aspect of the social spectacle of football, as well as a space saturated with clues about gender.

In part, it was this over-the-top spectacle that inspired us to write a book about tailgating. Another source of inspiration came in August of 2010, when we came across a *New York Times* profile of celebrity chef Guy Fieri.[2] The profile recounted Fieri's rise to fame on the Food Network and promoted his upcoming *Tailgate Warriors* series, produced by the Food Network in conjunction with the National Football League (NFL). *Tailgate Warriors*, hosted by Fieri, was billed as a show featuring "tailgate teams from around the country . . . dukin' it out to see who has the most killer grub in the game."[3] Each of the four episodes in the series featured two teams of four tailgaters in a structured, timed, judged, made-for-television cook-off. Teams were charged with preparing two appetizers, one entrée, two side dishes, and one dessert to be evaluated by the panel of judges. All episodes were taped at preseason NFL games.

After attending the taping of the show that took place in Oakland, CA, later that month and watching the subsequent episodes of *Tailgate Warriors* as they aired on the Food Network that fall, we were intrigued by the ways that food and sport intersect in popular culture, and also curious about what happens when men dominate a cultural space—the preparation and serving of food—that is traditionally associated with women. The historical legacy of male professional chefs is well known, but considerably less attention has been paid to men who cook in more everyday, noncommercial sites and how ideas about gender are constructed in those settings. Thus, we thought it would be interesting to explore how masculinity enters and is performed in this space that has been archetypally conceived as the realm of the feminine. Our curiosity led us to blacktops across the country, as well as to cookbook shelves, television shows, commercials, and movies to both learn about the lived experiences of seasoned tailgaters and to explore how tailgating has been represented across various forms of popular culture. Our research on the blacktop focused on those tailgaters who are serious about menu development, food preparation, and the quality of the dishes they serve to the football faithful on autumn weekends. Ultimately, we found that tailgating can at times reinforce stereotypical ideas about men and masculinity, yet in other ways the practices on the blacktop disrupt fixed cultural assumptions about gender.

As tailgating evolved from the early football picnics of the late nineteenth century to the grilling extravaganzas of today, performances of gender have always been central to the activity. Across the first few decades of the twentieth century, as college football grew in popularity, a steadily increasing number of fans extended game day gaiety by enjoying a pregame meal at the stadium. The planning, preparation, and serving of these meals was very much the domain of women.

By the 1960s, a rich tradition of tailgating had developed around American football at numerous universities across the United States. Fans and college students flocked to such noted venues as the Yale Bowl in New Haven, Connecticut and the Grove at Ole Miss on Autumn Saturdays to enjoy pregame revelry before the on-the-field battle in the stadium. As professional football gradually grew in popularity during this era, fans extended the tailgating ritual to the stadium parking lots of NFL teams on Sundays. By the later decades of the twentieth century, men assumed greater responsibility for the tailgate and the fare shifted from prepared-ahead cold dishes to meat-centric meals. Now, there is perhaps no more widely-practiced ritual than tailgating in American sport culture—"the action or practice of hosting or attending a party where food and drink are served at the tailgate of a motor vehicle before a sports event (typically a football game)."[4] Or, as Homer Simpson sees it, the opportunity for man "to stuff his guts with food and alcohol in anticipation of watching others exercise."[5] From hibachis on the beds of pickup trucks to professional-grade gas grills, football fans devote significant time, energy, and financial resources to the ritual of tailgating, making it an integral part of the sport's spectacle.

Yet, for all of its richness and its more than a century of history, there is only a small body of existing academic literature about tailgating.[6] When we began our research, we were repeatedly surprised to find that a cultural spectacle of such magnitude has received so little critical attention. This finding struck us as even more surprising as we immersed ourselves in the field of critical food studies. What better place to explore the marriage between sport and food, and to expand the already robust food studies literature on gender, identity, and culinary practices than tailgate culture?

As cultural studies scholars, we are guided by the imperatives to take popular culture seriously and to read the texts and practices of everyday life as meaningful cultural signifiers. Given football's deeply entrenched and highly valued cultural status in the United States, such a pervasive associated ritual as tailgating warrants our critical attention. The significance of the football spectacle, including its gendered dimensions, extends well beyond the four quarters of play on the field; for our purposes in *Gridiron Gourmet*, it begins in the space outside the stadium hours before kickoff and continues well past the final whistle.

According to Watson and Caldwell, "food is a universal medium that illuminates a wide range of other cultural practices."[7] A considerable amount of research in food studies has focused on the historical and cultural aspects of women's experiences with food, yet while recent years have seen increases, there remains a comparative dearth of research on men, masculinity, and cooking.[8] How food serves as a key site for the construction of femininity is well documented; less is understood, however, about what happens when men occupy the feminine-coded domain of cooking in nonprofessional settings. Even less has been written about the nexus of food and gender within the culture of sport.

In the United States, food media have influenced the way Americans shop for, prepare, and consume food, as well as shaped attitudes toward the meaning of food in everyday life.[9] As our initial point of entrée for *Gridiron Gourmet, Tailgate Warriors* led us to the food studies literature on the gendering of food and the evolution of food television.[10] Carol Adams' germinal work on the sexual politics of meat informed our analysis greatly. Adams theorized food as a key site for the social construction of gender, specifically positioning meat as a masculine food and meat eating as a male activity, two ideas which pervade Western culture.

Not only is there a culturally constructed expectation to eat meat—one that diminishes the status of noncarnivorous fare—but meat eating is viewed as a measure of one's virility. "Meat and potatoes men," Adams tells us, "are our stereotypical strong and hearty, rough and ready, able males."[11] On the other hand, vegetables and other nonmeat items are considered women's food, and to eat them is equated with femininity. Moreover, in a patriarchal society bound by a fixed gender binary, meat is a symbol of male dominance.

From the gendering of food, we delved into research on the evolution of food television and other forms of culinary-based media, believing it important to contextualize *Tailgate Warriors* in a broader history of televised cookery and the advent of the celebrity chef before moving into a gendered analysis of tailgate culture. Television has transformed interest in food into a cultural phenomenon, so much that cooking shows now proliferate and entire networks are devoted to food entertainment and cooking instruction—the Food Network the most notable among them.[12] The Food Network, founded in 1993, initially sought a domestic female audience with its programming, a marketing strategy that was both informed by and served to reify the already established cultural association between femininity and cooking.[13] Since its early days as a fledgling channel, the Food Network has transformed from an outlet for instructional, studio-bound shows hosted by classically trained chefs like Julia Child and Sara Moulton, to a spectacle preoccupied with the entertainment value of watching people cook food and the cult of the celebrity chef.[14] A prime example of this transformation is *Emeril Live!*. Chef Emeril Lagasse was liberated from the staid environment of his studio kitchen and placed in front of a live audience seated on bleachers, at small tables, and for a select few, at the bar-height counter in front of him as he cooked. The set resembled a late-night talk show more than a cooking program, but food preparation and consumption remained the central activities around which the entertainment was based. The success of *Emeril Live!* propelled Lagasse to chef stardom as the Food Network's first celebrity. Lagasse's blue-collar masculinity appealed to both male and female viewers, allowing him to connect with men in a way that cooking show hosts of the past had not, thus expanding the Food Network audience. At one point in its run, *Emeril Live!*'s largest demographic was men over thirty. Lagasse's star turn helped the Food Network transform "cooking from an essentially feminine chore to a glamorous hobby for men, women, and children."[15]

While showcasing the authority of male chefs in primetime enter-tainment slots provided a new wrinkle for the Food Network, male prowess had been exalted in food writing for decades, through the likes of early culinary celebrities James Beard and Craig Claiborne, and gas-tronomic advice for the midcentury bachelor set from male-oriented publications such as *Esquire* and *Playboy*.[16] The Food Network's daytime versus primetime programming scheme perpetuated the gendering of food authority and epicurean entertainment. The daytime block, "In the Kitchen," featured shows hosted by men and women. Those hosted by men presented cooking as a way to flex professional culinary muscles, while programs with female hosts were more likely to present cooking as domestic labor for family and friends. The advertising theme of the net-work's evening programming, "Way More Than Cooking," relied much more on the entertainment value of male hosts and often presented cook-ing in the format of a competitive contest.[17] At the peak of its run, *Emeril Live!* was the crown jewel of the Food Network's evening lineup.

Guy Fieri, who rose to fame on the heels of his victory on the Food Network's second season of the *The Next Food Network Star*, inherited Lagasse's masculine mantle. Fieri's first show as host, *Guy's Big Bite*, quickly resonated with the male viewers whom the Food Network was actively courting by the early 2000s. His set was replete with masculine signifiers, including a studio kitchen set up like a rec room with a full bar, pool table, racecar fridge, pinball machine, and giant television. His appearance screamed masculinity, too: spiky hair, goatee, multiple tat-toos, bowling shirts, studded bracelets. Susie Fogelson, the network's head of marketing, said of Fieri, "I haven't seen anyone connect to this range of people since Emeril . . . He really resonates with men."[18] Who better, then, to join the Food Network in a partnership with the NFL and take the helm of a tailgate-themed cooking series? In this sense, Fieri, like Lagasse before him, contributed to the re-gendering of food television and further drew men into the culture of cookery. The gendered perfor-mances of *Tailgate Warriors* were an extension of the Network's already established "Way More Than Cooking" theme. That program, and the many other texts that comprise the basis of our analysis, serve as rich sources of the various ways gender is socially constructed around the signifying practices of food and football.

Indeed, it is the food and cooking practices at the center of tailgating festivities that have captivated us the most as researchers. In the chapters to follow, we demonstrate how masculinity is understood, maintained,

Judges at work, *Tailgate Warriors* taping in Oakland, CA, 2010.
*Courtesy of authors.*

and challenged at the intersection of two of our most everyday—and thus often taken-for-granted—practices: food and football. In so doing, we hope to add to the understanding of the spectacle of football that occurs off the field, and to contribute a broader consideration of sport to the food studies literature that has been so instrumental in our own work.

This is not, however, a book about football; we are not interested in the action on the field, the numbers on the scoreboard, the prowess of certain players, or the strategic acumen of winning coaches (unless it relates to their culinary predilections). Nor is it a book about the best places to tailgate across the United States (though we're pretty sure we visited a couple). Rather, it is about a unique fan ritual with food at its center, and the various ways that ritual has been gendered. There are certainly important ways that football and tailgating are bound together. At times, it seems as if the composition of American football is perhaps less about athletic performance and more about social spectacle, to the extent that our preoccupation with what happens on the field serves simply as the foundation for the game's many associated rituals. "For the cultural scholar," historian Michael Oriard wrote, "football . . . can open a window into American culture in all its complexities and diversity."[19] Tailgating, as a key ingredient of the social spectacle of the game, appears as it does because of its relationship to football and all of its attendant meanings. Thus, tailgating offers an important site wherein we can analyze how gender is constructed and negotiated. Our aim is to provide a large, though by no means exhaustive, slice of tailgating history, along with a consideration of prominent themes in tailgate culture that partly make up the larger whole. Hegemonic understandings of masculinity run through themes of spectacle, meat, and community that are predicated on the culinary practices at the center of tailgating. Moreover, notions of race and ethnicity are constructed around food and sport on stadium blacktops, as well as in cultural representations of the ritual.

Food, like sport, is pervasive in Western popular culture. Various food-related issues regularly appear in news reporting—everything from food insecurity to agricultural policies to artisanal trends. We are in an era of the celebrity chef, food memoir, glossy cookbook, and of gastronomic glorification in television, film, and social media.[20] Tailgating is an extension of our cultural preoccupation with food that is intricately bound to our sporting practices. Tailgaters can be seen in any number of stadium parking lots and campus spaces, at levels of football ranging from high school to the NFL, while pop culture depictions of tailgating are seemingly limitless. In order to develop a critical examination that was both manageable and representative in scope, we selectively narrowed our focus to key texts and genres across the cultural spectrum and embarked on ethnographic research that took us to four NFL stadiums and five college campuses located in different regions of the country. In addition to dozens of conversations with tailgaters at those locations, we also conducted ten in-depth interviews with those who are significantly invested in tailgating. Throughout *Gridiron Gourmet*, we examine the intersection of food, football, and masculinity in popular culture representations of tailgating in forms ranging from cookbooks to commercials to television and film, and illuminate the gendered experiences of those who brave all manner of weather and team performance to do the tailgating. Examples from these varied sources are interspersed through-out the book.

Tailgate cookbooks presented us with a rich and relatively finite cate-gory of material. Cookbooks, it has been noted, do so much more than distribute recipes and coordinate the production of food; they are cultural tools that communicate ethnic and gender norms, and as food studies critic Sherrie Inness argues, are "rich, complex texts that reveal a great deal about a society and its changing mores, not just culinary ones."[21] These incredibly popular and now highly commercialized everyday texts help construct a sense of community, reinforce social identity, establish brands, and set culinary trends. Cookbooks are tangible, printed records that illuminate aspects of the past and present.[22] A close reading of the images, narratives, recipe instructions, and author notes therein yields information not only about food preparation, but also about those who cook, serve, consume, and read and write about it, as well as the occasions with which it is celebrated. We hope our analysis expands this body of research by demonstrating how tailgating cookbooks reflect and con-struct dominant views of gender, race, and ethnicity at the intersection of food and sport.

Forms of visual culture like film, television, and advertising—three media platforms in which tailgating is well-represented—occupy a central cultural role in everyday life and have the power to shape views, values, and consumer behavior.[23] Advertising, in particular, can influence our understandings of cultural practices like sport and cooking, as well as how gender is socially constructed within them. We concentrated our adver-tising analysis on contemporary television ads that feature tailgate scenes and were broadcast nationally in the United States from the mid-1990s to 2017, with most falling in the latter ten years of that range. Here we were able to build on advertising research in sport studies with an examination of how masculinity is constructed, reinforced, and contested through the visual and narrative content of the ads. Moreover, tailgating commercials provided us with another lens through which to view what is happening when men cook outside of the domestic space of the kitchen. The visual content of the ads we reviewed was dominated by masculine-identified brands and products. Tailgate-centric ads tend to fall into one of three categories: burgers and beer, trucks and SUVs, and outdoor cooking equipment like grills, charcoal, and generators, thus connecting tailgating to deeply coded masculine signifiers. In the majority of these ads, meat is central to the visual and scripted narrative. Though not the subject of our analysis, we would be remiss not to at least mention the centrality of beer to football culture, and alcohol more generally, and acknowledge its function as a gender signifier akin to red meat.[24]

Our approach to film and television portrayals of tailgating was similar. We identified situation comedies, sketch shows, and reality series that were either tailgate-themed or included a plotline devoted to tailgating. Our search led us to animated classics like *The Simpsons* and contemporary social parodies like *Portlandia*; we of course began with the *Tailgate Warriors* series that initially piqued our interest. The films cited in our analysis typically included a tailgate scene that was incidental to the main plot, and were usually in the sport film genre. Combined, the representations from these sources demonstrate how film and television can shape gender identities through messages about food and cooking, and indicate the broader cultural consciousness around tailgating and masculinity.[25]

While the book's central theme is gender, we are mindful of how constructions of masculinity intersect with race and ethnicity in tailgate culture. Thus, we draw explicit attention in *Gridiron Gourmet*, to issues of racial and ethnic identity on the blacktop. Our aim in offering up a more diverse range of examples is to deepen and complicate tailgating's gendered past and its present. Expanding our analysis to include race and ethnicity, for example, forces us to consider silences and omissions in communicating activity on the blacktop, as well as encourages us to consider how gender is conceptualized beyond a single axis frame.

We begin *Gridiron Gourmet* by providing a history of tailgating that details key episodes in the evolution of this practice as related to our themes of food and gender. Though by no means exhaustive, we have constructed a cultural history in which we explore how men and masculinities have been part of tailgating's past. Somewhat surprisingly for a practice that has, in recent decades, become dominated by and primarily associated with male sports fans, it was women who played a central role in tailgate culture throughout much of the twentieth century. Men might have been the more avid spectators, but it was women who orchestrated the tailgate. Thus, in a historical account of the gendered aspects of tailgating that focuses on men and masculinity, women merit—and are given—considerable attention. As we detail in chapter one, it was not until the late twentieth century that a shift to greater male control of cookery and more excess on the blacktop occurred.

In chapter two, we turn our attention to the spectacle itself, and the ways that masculinity emerges as part of the public spectacle and performance of tailgating. We consider the supersize grills, specialized cooking equipment, complex menus, and customized vehicles in use on the blacktop as aspects of the social construction of manhood around food and football. Mediated representations of tailgating tend to feature exaggerated versions of masculine signifiers, thus presenting "hyperbolic performance[s] of masculinity in everyday spaces."[26] These often excessive and loud public displays serve to distance cookery and the men who do it from the domestic, private sphere of day-to-day meal preparation in the home. Instead, culinary activities on the blacktop are cast as special and unique occasions in which men command attention and acclaim for their cooking skills.

Meat, the food commonly at the center of the tailgating spectacle, is the focus of chapter three. We detail the various ways that food serves as a signifier of gender, with red meat reigning as the ultimate masculine signifier and vegetables relegated to the second-class status of the feminine. Importantly, discourses around meat, as well as preparing and consuming animal protein, aid in fortifying notions of hegemonic masculinity. Men secure culinary capital when eating meat, and they enhance their status as men in the process.[27] Cookbook narratives, mediated cooking competitions, scenes in films and television shows, and the culinary action outside of football stadiums all reinforce the primacy of meat.

In chapter four, we explore racial and ethnic representation in tailgating cookbooks, noting how this genre has informed Americans' perceptions of ethnic foods and the cultural groups associated with them. Racialized relationships of power are also evident in cookbooks devoted to tailgate fare, with whiteness as the normative center around which narratives are constructed. In the pages of these texts, we see the dominant racial and ethnic stereotypes of the day reflected through images, explanations of ingredients, and descriptions of dishes, often resulting in ethnic othering, cultural misappropriation, and whitewashing of culinary traditions. The lack of diversity in the images and perspectives of these texts reinforces tailgating as a white cultural space—a dynamic that is mostly replicated in film and television representations of the practice. Yet on the blacktop, the degree of racial and ethnic diversity among tailgaters varies from location to location, as does the type of food cooked, sometimes reinforcing, and at other times complicating the whiteness of the spectacle.

Chapter five brings our analysis to a close with a discussion of culinary community on the blacktop. We consider how food functions in related aspects of this dynamic: competition, place identity, eating the other, spatial arrangements, and philanthropy. *Tailgate Warriors* dramatized competition and rivalry amongst tailgaters, but our ethnographic observations indicated that tailgaters also have a sense of camaraderie and cooperation on the blacktop. In many instances, local cuisine narrates a sense of place identity and collective belonging, and can, at times, be used to distinguish *us* from *them*. Creative tailgaters often cook and consume the culinary symbol of an opposing team's mascot as another manifestation of the competitive spirit. For example, when competing against the University of Oregon, tailgaters of the opposing team might smoke duck breasts. When space is limited or highly prized, we found that tailgaters will go to great lengths to secure their own territory in parking lots or on campus grounds. Finally, we see communal bonds reinforced through the philanthropic endeavors of male tailgaters. In this chapter, then, our focus rests with exploring how masculinities are constructed, expressed, and even contested within this seemingly oxymoronic space of competitive community on the blacktop.

Based on our analysis of the gendered dimensions of food and cookery, and the numerous masculine signifiers associated with tailgating, we argue that men enjoy a sort of *culinary cover* when they step up to the plate—or grill, or smoker, or rotisserie—on the blacktop. Tailgating's reliance on, and perpetuation of, traditional gender constructs provides a safe space in which men can engage in culinary practices, without worry about the "feminine taint" of the domestic kitchen. Men can compensate for doing work traditionally constructed as feminine by framing cooking as a hobby, performance, or form of leisure entertainment.[28] Sport, along with large slabs of meat, custom-built equipment, specialized cooking utensils, open flames in the elements, and the spectacle of public performance, provides the primary cover for men who cook at the tailgate, helping them to negotiate any perceived threats to their gender identity. With these qualifiers, when men cook, they are not less, but rather more masculine.[29] Even if meat and all its accoutrements are downplayed, the manliness of the gridiron assures men of their masculinity.

# 1.

# "As Welcome as Lunch at the Ritz"

## Episodes in the History of Tailgating

### Introduction

Recently blogger Matt Osgood wrote, "the beginnings of football tail-gating history are murkier than the dirty Solo cups at the end of a game."[1] His observation seems accurate, as many individuals and groups lay claim to being the first to partake in a pregame meal washed down with a favorite libation—usually off the back of a carriage or automobile. For example, some accounts suggest Yale fans in the nineteenth century who poured, by the thousands, into New Haven, overwhelming restaurants so much so the team's faithful took their sandwiches and coffee to the grassy areas just outside the stadium. It is also possible that the first foot-ball picnics were those hosted by Green Bay Packer fans who, in 1919, reportedly drove their cars into Hagemeister Park and right up to the field's boundaries, enjoying both their lunches and the game from vehicle tailgates.[2] This mystery of who first unwrapped boiled ham or sardine and butter sandwiches as part of football day festivities will not be solved in this chapter, or this book for that matter. What we do hope to offer are some observations about the history of tailgating—or, to use the more historically accurate phrase, the "football picnic."

Our more specific aim in this chapter is a turn toward history, which we present in loosely chronological episodes, to explore constructions of gender at the intersection of food and football. Tailgating in its present and past forms is many things, including a culinary space in which food is prepared and consumed. The feasting just before and after football con-tests, for over a century, is also highly gendered. Cookery, a traditionally feminine activity, is one of the elements at tailgating's core, and women, as we shall see, have consistently played a role in pregame culinary cus-toms. Yet football, the reason tailgaters are initially drawn to the space, has for over a century symbolized the embodiment of hyper-masculinity.

This juxtaposition raises a host of questions for us that we explore, in this, and subsequent chapters in *Gridiron Gourmet*. For example, how does food and cookery more generally inform changing gender relations in and around football stadiums over the course of a century? How have men and expressions of masculinities been part of tailgating's past? What insights about changing gender dynamics can be gleaned from an exploration of various episodes in tailgate history? How do masculine signifiers, like the automobile—which plays an enormous role in tailgate history—shape notions of gender on the blacktop and fields near to football stadiums? As this chapter argues, the football picnic, that "specialized variation" of the motor picnic that involves "picnicking beside your motorcar that is parked at a sporting event," has, from its murky origins, been fraught with gendered elements.[3] The automobile and then the recreational vehicle (RV), the picnic lunch, the cult of barbecue, and the reign of red meat have infused King Football with a social spectacle outside of stadiums to rival that which occurs on the gridirons of play.

## The "Most Manly Sport": The Growth of Early Football

It should be of little surprise, perhaps, that some of the more intriguing roots of tailgating's early history are found on the college and university campuses throughout the Northeast where football got its start in the latter decades of the nineteenth century. By the century's end the spectacle that was (and continues to be) football was far more than simply a game played by boys and young men on university campuses. The game's promoters and the ever-increasing throngs of spectators who enjoyed it did so, at least in part, because the game symbolized a particular understanding of manhood and masculinity.[4] Football's beginnings on elite college campuses advanced agendas uniquely important at this historical moment. The sport's violence and brutality assisted in undergirding an image of those who played it as rugged, virile, and manly. These qualities were seen as especially important to counter a perceived crisis of masculinity. Football was a strong antidote to those who believed that the virtues of a strapping masculinity were being lost in an increasingly modern world in which one's brain established itself as more significant and even more necessary than brawn.[5]

Gender unease around changing conceptions of masculinity was not the only identity marker of consequence to football promoters at the end of the nineteenth century. Fears and perceived threats to manliness were especially acute among those of the educated classes. Thus college football's growth among the largely upper class student bodies undercut images of the institution and its male inhabitants as places in which "esoteric knowledge and the egghead" dominated university spaces.[6] Class and gender intersected with race, as it was largely *white* educated men for whom the sport provided a laboratory through which participants advanced themselves and the racial status quo. According to Yale Professor Eugene Richards, "for a virile race, like the Anglo-Saxon the dangerous sports have always had the greatest fascination, because they call for just those qualities which make that race the dominant race of the world. Foot-ball is one of these sports."[7] Football was seen as an important location to hone the skills of white men of privilege as they prepared to take their rightful place as leaders atop various segments of society, with the result being the perpetuation of white supremacy. Bearing witness to expressions of masculinity on the field was just part of the gameday experience for gridiron enthusiasts.

Among Historically Black College and University (HBCU) football-playing institutions, the game was also used as a tool to build and promote particular understandings of manhood, but for reasons not shared with predominately white institutions. Athletic achievement was deployed as a strategy to advance race pride and the cause of racial equality. Excellence on the gridiron, to football supporters, was a very public way to demonstrate the embodiment of discipline, tenacity, and strength among African American men, challenging white assertions to the contrary. Discourses surrounding the game at HBCUs, like those of predominately white institutions, were forged upon traditional notions of gender.[8] Gender's central place, as enacted on the gridiron, is made clear in a 1911 black press report by the *Nashville Globe* as it stated hometown Meharry Medical College coach Ransom, "drills his men into manliness," in preparation for an upcoming football game.[9]

Across all of college football, in the sport's early decades, constructions of masculinity were built and framed in juxtaposition to femininity and womanhood.[10] It is "the pleasure" the black press' *Pittsburgh Courier* reminded readers, "of the maid and matron to snuggle near her big man and watch the gridiron encounter [and] gaze with admiration upon her hero."[11] Wherever the setting, whether at Harvard or historically black, Howard University, football was a proving ground for masculinity. Rugged athletic performances on the field underscored gender arrangements, as did the "lovely coed" who served to reinforce hypermasculinity.[12]

Part of the game's appeal lay in its reinforcement of gender ideologies, so that by the turn of the twentieth century, just decades removed from its origins, college football became the most prominent of the many activities on campuses across the country. Universities became *known*, not only to the thousands who might come to campus to watch a game, but the many more who read about the institutions and their athletic exploits in newspaper press reports. Full, front-page football news dominated big- and small-town papers, thereby selling the sport to many who were eager to consume it. The brutality and violence on the field certainly quieted enthusiasm for football in many circles, but by the end of the century its popularity on campus and beyond was hardly in doubt. Efforts to eliminate, control, or reform the game could not withstand the public's demand for football.[13] As a result, at the start of the twentieth century, campus and community enthusiasm for football reached unprecedented levels.

Campuses around the country were eager to maximize the economic benefits of football game days and a stadium building frenzy ensued over the course of the first two or three decades of the twentieth century. Harvard's 1903 stadium project could accommodate over twenty thousand spectators. The reinforced concrete structure was the first of its kind, revolutionizing the possibilities for football stadiums on other college campuses in the coming decades.[14] As the twentieth century progressed, schools worked to outpace and out build each other, making the Harvard stadium seem quaint. Built in 1913, the Yale Bowl's capacity for just over seventy thousand fans, who came by "every possible means of conveyance," including train, automobile, horse drawn carriage, and by foot to inundate New Haven.[15] This scene was replayed in many other parts of the country, including HBCU campuses, whose rich football history began in the late nineteenth century. By the 1920s Howard University, for example, spent over a quarter of a million dollars to build the "largest Negro stadium in America" to accommodate up to twenty thousand spectators.[16]

The convening of large crowds at football games forced structural engineers and urban planners to consider, well beyond the actual stadium, how best to accommodate the throngs of spectators. The "ceaseless stream of humanity" converging on the Yale Bowl, and many other football stadiums across the country, created the need for a complex logistical strategy around train schedules and roadway approaches to accommodate the tens of thousands of eager fans on any given Saturday.[17] Even as early as 1898 Yale officials announced that by the start of the following football season the roadway to the stadium would be re-graded. In addition, the construction of an "iron bridge built to carry two car tracks and two carriage tracks" was scheduled with the "car tracks extended to deliver passengers at the central Field gates."[18]

Popular Thanksgiving Day football contests tested the abilities of game day organizers to accommodate all of those fans who wished to see the game. Thanksgiving Day football games played in New York City, beginning in 1880, were often the most well publicized and attended, drawing tens of thousands of fans.[19] Press reports provide evidence of both the spectacle of gameday-related activities (including the game), as well as the complexity of hosting massive public entertainment events. In November 1891 *The Sun* newspaper in New York City highlighted the upcoming Thanksgiving Day game to be played in the city between Yale and Princeton. The game, according to the report, was to bring forty thousand fans to the stadium, creating a whole host of organizational challenges for event managers. Bleacher safety, monitoring ticket sales, parking (of horses/carriages), and crowd control were among the issues facing those in charge. Hoping to give everyone who wanted to see the game the opportunity to do so (and, invariably, to increase gate receipts), event planners got creative and decided to use a nearby hillside for 'standing room' only seating at the discount price of fifty cents per admission. However, game day organizers were forced to attend to one small detail in order for their plan to succeed; the livestock that freely roamed the hillside had to be removed. "Harlem goats will be excluded from this place for the day unless they, too, pay for standing room," the paper quipped.[20] As we will see, the tens of thousands of football fans (and a few goats) who flooded college towns and cities in the period were eager to partake in the many gendered spectacles both on and off the athletic field on game days.

## "Favorite Diversions": Early Football Picnic Lunches

Parades, dances, rallies, and picnics were among some of the festivities that encircled the actual football games on college campuses in the sport's early decades. By the last years of the nineteenth century football was equal parts "athletic contest" and "social event" to throngs of spectators.[21] A 1906 *New York Times* piece admitted that rooting for one's favorite team was only part of the attraction, as "interest in the scene" drew many others.[22] Fan enthusiasm was about the consumption of football as a massive public spectacle—not merely the result of the love of the game or team. The "manly" sporting skills displayed on the field were part of the attraction, as were any number of activities and special events that were associated with football on gameday or those days leading up to the contest. As we will see, simply getting to the game became part of the allure, infusing even more excitement in preparation for the competition on the field. Food also appeared to be an important part of the day's festivities, adding much to the convivial atmosphere among football fans. A 1912 illustration from the humor magazine *Puck* attests to the already established popularity of American football and the excitement of game days. In this early media depiction of Thanksgiving Day football games, we see that food was central to the festive atmosphere and that the few women in attendance were accompanied by men.[23] Gendered threads, woven tightly into football as an *athletic contest*, have long been a subject for our collective scholarly attention.[24] Here we extend this consideration to aspects of the game as a *social event*, including the pregame culinary feasts and cars on the grass or blacktop before football. These displays, we contend, are equally compelling and just as gendered.

*Puck* magazine illustration, 1912. The media popularized social aspects of the Thanksgiving Day football games, in this case at the expense of Native Americans. Courtesy of Library of Congress Prints and Photographs Division. LC-DIG-ds-03749

Food was a reoccurring element on football game days from the earliest years the sport was played in the United States. Occasionally, food seemed the reason *for* the athletic contest. A local Iowa newspaper, in commenting on a high school game in 1905, sheds light on food's fundamental place. The "boys were to have played football at the picnic at the Singmaster place near Keota last Saturday, but on account of the postponing of the picnic the game was spoiled."[25] At Yale University, in New Haven, Connecticut, gameday luncheons in the hours prior to the contest's start have been a special and publicized part of the school's storied football history for well over a century. Exceptions to male-only college spaces, including at Yale, were made on gameday, and food provided the reason. In 1902 the *Yale Daily News* alerted students that the "University Club will be open for members to bring ladies for meals" before the matchup with Harvard. This arrangement offers a window into gender relations and confirms Oriard's conclusion that women played a "crucial" role not in football as an athletic event, but as a social one.[26] The significance of food's place before football contests at Yale is captured in numerous news stories throughout the 1906 season. Planning, instruction, and strategy, similar to that given by a football coach to his charges, was necessary to successfully accomplish the "herculean task" of feeding several thousand people within time and space constraints of the University dining hall.[27] A "method of accommodation" was announced in the student newspaper outlining rules concerning luncheon tickets, time-tables, and general etiquette.[28] So popular were Yale gameday luncheons in the dining commons that souvenir china and menu postcards were sold to those who held dear the memories of boiled salmon and filet of beef with mushrooms.[29] University dining halls were far from the only place where food and football merged to heighten the festive atmosphere on game day.

Pregame football lunches hosted in private homes provided another space for revelers to cultivate a celebratory mood, and in the early decades of the twentieth century these activities were not always associated with the collegiate athletic scene. Beginning in the late 1890s, semipro and professional football existed in the United States. Though a good share of the game's formative influence was in the industrial and manufacturing sections of Pennsylvania and Ohio, football clubs and leagues could be found throughout several states across the nation. By the turn of the twentieth century, spectatorship of those in the professional ranks was small in comparison to collegiate football, but no less enthusiastic.[30] In Wisconsin, support for the upstart Green Bay Packers in 1924, just five years removed from the team's formation, provides a glimpse into the strength of the relationship between community and football team. The city "takes to its football team like Princeton does to its Tigers," the paper pronounced, making Green Bay one of the "greatest pigskin centers in the country."[31]

In Green Bay and other towns that were home to semipro and professional football teams, celebrating the hometown club sometimes centered on food, as was the case in and around college campuses. The local industrial teams of Fort Wayne, Indiana scheduled their first meeting on a Saturday September afternoon in 1919 where the athletes would "practice tricks and various maneuvers" of the sport. The event, a press report announced, "will be in a form of a picnic and fans from every factory or shop in the city are expected to attend."[32] Community wide enthusiasm for the game, as well as pre- and post- game activities, were points of pride, with food billed as part of the festivities. In Portsmith, Ohio "football is the password" on Sundays, where the "city has taken on a college atmospheric attitude," according to the local press. That "attitude" was fostered in and through food, as "bruncheon" parties, held in private homes, was one of the more well- liked social affairs of the day before fans headed to the game.[33]

Other pregame luncheons in the homes of football rooters were solely the province of women. Women's place in game day football rituals often centered on meals and picnics, rather than the actual athletic event which seemed to serve as a convenient backdrop for a social occasion involving food. A lengthy 1903 article in the women's magazine section of *The Philadelphia Inquiry* described an elaborate (five-course) luncheon hosted by a young woman for other women prior to a University of Pennsylvania football game. Luncheons such as this one, the paper noted, had become "favorite diversions," before games. The intricate place setting featured a "mini gridiron" including "little fitted sweaters on all the figures."[34] Female-only football luncheons, like the Penn affair, reinforced dominant gender arrangements of the period. Moreover, sex segregated football-related events blended seamlessly with more general Progressive era gender logic in which women's separation from men served to minimize the threat of feminine incursions in male sporting spaces. Women were welcome, but often only to partake in activities that reinscribed cultural gender norms and/or were sex segregated.[35] *The Lincoln Star* (Nebraska) reported in 1916, for example, that the University Girl's club was to hold a "football luncheon" just before Saturday's game against

Iowa State College. After the luncheon the paper noted the University of Nebraska "co-eds will march together to the game, sitting in a reserved section of the grandstand."[36] Sex segregation, it seemed, extended beyond afternoon tea with the girls to the field of play and the spectator stands surrounding it.

Pregame breakfasts and lunches that were so central to HBCU football contests throw into sharp relief both the gendered and classed arrangements at the intersection of sport and food. Social events, including breakfasts and lunches, that encircled football contests, especially the Thanksgiving Day Classic matchups between Howard and Lincoln in the 1920s, rivaled and surpassed enthusiasm for the game itself.[37] Those who took part in the activities around the game will "go happily to [their] social grave," one observer noted in 1922. Because, he adds, "there is nothing more to which to aspire. You have reached the point of social sublimation."[38] Often featured on women and society pages of the press, details of the breakfast dances and proms, as well as lunches and teas prior to football games offer clues that these spaces were locations where gender and class arrangements were reinforced. In the days preceding the Wilberforce versus Tuskegee game of 1929, the society pages of the *Chicago Defender's* society page reporter noted, a "younger group of girls" planned the "breakfast dance and many other delightful opportunities."[39]

The inaugural 1926 homecoming festivities of Haskell Institute, a Native American school located in Lawrence, Kansas, provide even more evidence of the unique cultural elements at the intersection of food and football in the sport's early decades. Interestingly, the powwow festivities that marked the days and hours prior to the Haskell versus Bucknell football game provided the members of the Institute and the many Plains' tribes who participated an opportunity to carve out a resistive and anti-assimilationist space. Some of the ten thousand people who attended the athletic contest were invited to the pregame barbecue, which featured buffalo meat that had been hunted the traditional way (with bows and arrows). The historically deep physical and spiritual connections between the Plains' Indians and the buffalo created "feelings of nostalgia and unity" among the Native Americans who participated.[40] Whether at a Native American college, an HBCU, or a predominantly white Ivy League institution, during the early decades of the twentieth century, foodways and football were strong threads creating community and identity.

When pregame meals for fans were not being held in college dining halls, private homes, or outdoor barbecue pits adjoining the stadium, local restaurants often struggled under the weight of tens of thousands of football fans descending on towns like New Haven and Princeton, among others. Restaurants and stores did their best to keep up with demand and to capitalize on the thousands of football fans eager to find a meal prior to the game, offering quick eat-in or take-out meals and snacks as folks made their way to the stadium. In 1902 a New York paper noted that everything was "favorable" at the Princeton versus Columbia football game, despite the "inconveniences of the small university town [Princeton]." The paper added that one of the "inconveniences" for some fans was finding someplace to eat, forcing a few unfortunate revelers "to go hungry because of the push at all of the town restaurants." The food-service industry that blossomed as a result of the massive football rallies spared those in need. Nearly all, the paper reassured, were "supplied with at least a sandwich from the army of imported 'lunch dispensers'" on hand to keep hunger at bay.[41] Crowd density at HBCU contests resulted in the same issues as those found at Ivy League institutions, as one fan noted just before the Howard versus Lincoln game in 1923, "we succeeded in getting something which the waitress called a meal after a wait of two hours. We watched the milling throng made up of hungry folks like ourselves."[42]

Ingenuity in satisfying the appetites and thirst of fans sometimes came from unlikely sources—but was no less successful. In their second year of professional football, the Green Bay Packers began to attract healthy crowds for their 1920 season. "Can you imagine it? Ice cold drinks at a football game," the *Green Bay Press-Gazette* read. That was "the order [of the day] at Hagemeister Park. The youngsters who were selling pop got rich quick in about an hour and a half."[43] As this example and others illustrate, the entrepreneurial culture that surrounded early football sometimes centered on food and beverage.

Indeed, if a pregame lunch could not be eaten indoors given the crush of fans, then restaurants encouraged food to go. In 1920, York Pharmacy in New Haven advertised, "with crowds here you will face a difficult problem in providing an enjoyable lunch for your guest," to which it supplied the answer. "Why not try a lunch composed of our choice variety of sandwiches, hot chocolate or coffee and a fresh fruit sundae?" the promotion suggested, adding that its service "provid[ed] a happy outcome for a disagreeable situation."[44] Other establishments followed, offering "[d]elicious sandwiches, cakes and cookies daintily put up in a trim box." Every box, the ad promised, was "full of goodies to surprise you when you open [it] at the field."[45] With few restaurant seats available for the hordes of football boosters, take-out became the order of the day. This trend continued in the early 1920s, as more New Haven restaurants joined in to aid those fans wishing to picnic as part of the day's entertainment, expanding markets and consumptive practices on football Saturdays. For those not able or wishing to lunch indoors, the Hotel Duncan announced an "assortment of candwiches [sic] will be ready for you to take out."[46] As the century progressed, football continued to grow in popularity, as did the picnic lunches, though the 1928 *Princeton Alumni Weekly* alludes to the fact that al fresco dining before games may not have been widely known. The *Weekly* instructed the school's fans, who were not in the know, that "a large proportion of the spectators on their way to the Stadium carry food with them and partake of a picnic lunch" on the grounds.[47]

The pattern of taking in a meal prior to the game was not solely the business of East coast schools. West coast institutions and their fans also understood that bringing food to a football game was a practical necessity, as well as an opportunity to extend the festive atmosphere on game day. In 1899 over sixteen thousand fans attended the (seventh) annual Thanksgiving Day matchup between the University of California at Berkeley and Stanford. Spectators who arrived at the San Francisco stadium early brought sustenance according to the local press, "with luncheons safely stowed in pockets or more pretentious refreshment in little baskets."[48] As these illustrations suggest, football picnics as the precursor to more modern day "tailgate parties" were likely born out of necessity as pregame luncheons soon spilled out of restaurants and dining halls.

## "Motor-Grid Hounds": Food, Football, and the Automobile

Getting to the game was often part of the day's appeal with food, at times, featured as an important element bound to the experience. "Few were able to get luncheon on the way [to the stadium]," said the *New York Times* of Yale football fans in 1906. "These [fans] gazed with envious eyes as they neared the field at small parties of automobilists eating tempting viands that had been brought in hampers spread out in picnic fashion on a table cloth laid upon the ground."[49] As this quote indicates, these early "tailgates" fused automobile touring and picnics, two popular pastimes among the elite in the early years of the twentieth century. Interestingly, each (automobiles and picnics) offers up a lens through which we can better understand gender within the larger frame of food and football.

The motor vehicle's relationship with pregame parties near to football stadiums just prior to kickoff is a long and important one that stretches to the present day. By 1906 there were eighty-two thousand automobiles in use in the United States.[50] On any given football Saturday in New Haven, for example, it seemed a good share of those vehicles were headed to the game, as the fields surrounding the Yale Bowl were, according to a 1906 *New York Times* article, "black with machines parked together in such a hopeless mass as to make it seem impossible for one ever to find his own once more."[51] As the most "powerful signifier of [male] identity and status," the automobile in the early twentieth century situated the driver as an "unfettered and self-directing agent."[52] Not surprisingly, perhaps, the automobile among east coast elites, and others, became a preferred mode of transportation to football games. Occasionally vehicles not only provided transportation to the field but also seating once there—a feature the press thought worthy of reporting. Without adequate facilities, spectators, including those at the 1910 Thanksgiving-day game between HBCU rivals Fisk and Meharry in Nashville, made due. Six thousand fans arrived in a "festive mood" via automobiles, carriages, and "vehicles of all kinds" and proceeded to create their own stadium by encircling the playing field with the means of transport that brought them there.[53]

Given the sport's close connection to narrow constructions of men and masculinity, the automobile blended perfectly with efforts to report on, and promote, football. "Football Owes [its] Place to Auto," read a 1926 *Oakland (CA) Tribune* headline. The article highlighted what football fans had known for over two decades, the game would not be the "magnet" it was without the automobile. The connection was a deeper one, however, according to the report, which claimed, "champion teams and players have shown preferences for the speed, beauty, and the champion qualities of the Buick automobile."[54] The favored method of transport to football contests was so tightly woven to the game's supporters that newspaper accounts coined the term "motor-grid hounds" to describe the "automobile football fan[s]." This particular kind of football support was so committed they "will not hesitate to follow the trail though it be covered with snow and ice for many long and dreary miles, to enthuse over the valorous deeds of moleskin attired huskies, is oiling up the derelict fliver [sic] and sumptuous limousine."[55]

Other 1920s newspaper articles and advertisements were just as explicit in linking football and automobiles (or automobiling) to men and masculinity. The Slautterback Motor Company of Michigan adver-

## Flasks and Bottles For the Big Game

IT may be cold Saturday—a cold wave is about due—and some warm or warming drink may prevent that chilly feeling that sometimes ends in pneumonia. A Thermos Bottle full of hot coffee will help out almost as much as a fur coat—and will cost lots less.

At this time of the year no auto ride of any distance should lack a Thermos Bottle. It makes a wayside lunch possible and palatable, and furnishes an antidote to the chilly breezes.

| THERMOS BOTTLES, | $3.00 up |
| POCKET FLASKS, | .75 up |
| LUNCH BASKETS, | 11.50 up |

### The John E. Bassett Co.
Ye OLDe HARDe-WARE STORE
754-758 Chapel & 314 State Streets

An early ad linking autos and football picnics, 1910. Copyright 2010 Yale Daily News Publishing Company, Inc. All rights reserved. Reprinted with permission.

tised "In Automobiles as in Football—'All-American' is the Word!" In promoting one of its vehicles the paper drew no distinction between man and machine. "Power . . . drive . . . speed . . . spirit . . . a thrilling change of pace" the newspaper opined. These qualities characterized both "America's gridiron stars . . . and this brilliant American car."[56] The game of football and the automobile were linked by the popular press, which helped to cement a structure in which masculinity was conceptualized and defined between the two as not only similar but symbiotic.

Newspaper accounts were eager to forge a relationship for the reader among the automobile, football, and food and picnicking by continually reminding fans of the automobile's primacy within the sport's culture. For example, the dailies were quick to remind observers of the many important persons traveling to the contests by automobile and their status as powerful and well-connected people. In describing the University of California at Berkeley versus University of Southern California matchup in 1923, the *Los Angeles Times* stressed the auto's important place in bringing "society and big business" together in "paying tribute to King Football." Class marked the event as the paper thought it "not extraordinary that the automobile reflected the quality and wealth of the assembled thousands."[57]

The periodical press constructed narratives that reinforced the links between automobility and football by highlighting the trials and tribulations encountered by the country's most well-known fans as they journeyed to the athletic event. President Roosevelt's daughter, Alice, the *New York Times* reported, was on her way to the 1904 Harvard versus Yale matchup when "the machine" she was riding in "dashed up an embankment and overturned." Despite the delay and clothing "badly soiled with grease and dirt," the Roosevelt party, the paper assured, did not miss the game.[58] The press noted that accidents were not the only impediment to being on time—speed traps set up by local police were another obstacle for those headed to the game. The "small army of automobilists" going to and from New Haven on game day provided local coffers with a boost.[59] Newspapers readily supplied any number of details about the fines and arrests for those speeding to the big game. Motoring "speed among elites" was after all a "marker of social power and distinction," and thus press reports reinforced class and gendered dynamics of those motoring (or being chauffeured) to early twentieth-century football.[60]

Once at the stadium, however, any inconveniences experienced en route to various Ivy League destinations were quickly forgotten as the picnicking began. The *New York Times* wrote in 1919, "by noon the campus choked with automobiles and these automobile parties opened up their hampers and were satisfied with a picnic lunch, for Princeton was swamped with the crowd and could not feed it. A cup of coffee and a sandwich were as welcome as lunch at the Ritz."[61] Amid the frequent prompts in the press it must have been difficult for fans to forget the relationship of food to football to motoring.

It is not surprising, perhaps, that meals served outdoors near to or at the stadium just prior to football games were an extension of motoring *and* picnicking, as the public seemed fascinated by both. One of the "greatest delights of motoring is the motor picnic" wrote the periodical *Truth* in 1907. The "old-time picnic," was a "delusion and a snare. The labor involved in conveying the provisions was out of all proportion to the realised delights. With the trusty motor available to convey unlimited quantities of provender . . . the [motor picnic] becomes another affair entirely."[62] The "affair" continued through the early decades of the century and became central to automobile marketing campaigns. In 1925, for example, a Ford Motors touring car advertisement tightly weaves the auto, leisure, and food, selling the activity as a "chance to get away into new surroundings every day—a picnic supper or a cool spin in the evening to enjoy the countryside or a visit with friends."[63]

Cars and culinary delights at the roadside provided a kind of freedom and escape from the constraints of early twentieth-century life. This carefree, spontaneous, and adventuresome spirit carried into football culture as well, as this 1928 *Chicago Daily Tribune* article about Yale fans detailed: "And down the road a piece, not far from the field house, there stands in orderly lines in a weedy lot several hundred concrete burial vaults, the current stock of a factory operating there. Motor parties arriving early for the games draw up at the roadside, dismount with their lunch hampers and spread picnic tables on the lids of the caskets."[64] Selling the game day experience as the sum of good food, automobiles, and football is captured in a 1938 article, "*Rah! Rah! Rah! Sis, Boom, Bah! We're Off To The Game!*" The drawing below the headline features a well-dressed couple beside their vehicle, with a caption, "a hot lunch on the way [to the game] starts the afternoon's fun." Written by a woman, presumably for other women, the article features picnic lunch recipes to bring along and enjoy at the roadside or stadium.[65]

The promotion of game day picnic merchandising had been part of football festivities for decades and these connections became more secure as the century advanced. A 1931 advertisement for a "Football Picnic Kit" serves as an example of the ways in which commercialization, albeit in its infancy, was part of the overall experience of football fandom. Game days are "usually scrambles when it comes to lunch," the promotion declared. Why not "pack your lunch inside [the kit] neatly, compactly—slip the kit in your car like a suitcase and forget the big crowds."[66] These details are a nod to a growing sophistication of the football picnic and not seen in earlier promotional material as they reinforce the triad of food, the automobile, and football. Saturdays offered interested fans an exciting outing, in which these three phenomena converged to help create individual adventures and enormous public spectacles.

Football picnics, clearly popular happenings, were about to undergo major changes as broader political and cultural forces reshaped pregame culinary customs in and around the midcentury point. America's fascination with motor touring and outdoor eating continued as the activities on the blacktops and grassy knolls outside of football stadiums grew much more elaborate and widespread. The automobile not only altered means of transportation to the game, but also transformed the way spectators ate and the type of food they enjoyed before kickoff. This transformation helped pave a gendered path in the direction of the tailgating spectacle as we know it today. Motor car picnics, as well as tailgates, featured mostly cold, pre-prepared food through the 1950s. As the motor picnic fused with the "pigskin picnic,"[67] both were significantly influenced by mid-century barbecue culture.

## The "Thrill of the Grill": Hot Coals and the Cold War

In the years just prior to and certainly after World War II, football's status in the United States as one of the premiere spectator sports, at both the college and even professional level, grew more secure. This growth, however, was far from linear as the influences of the Great Depression and World War II were enormous on all levels of the sport. Even as the country grappled with larger, more significant priorities associated with economics and war, football never completely left the nation's imagination.[68] Picnicking outside of stadiums prior to the start of the game flourished just as the athletic activity did on the field. As noted, food festivities before football were gendered, whether on lawns or parking lots outside the stadium, in private homes or restaurants, or public parks. Men's and women's roles and their understanding of what it was to be masculine and feminine infused and informed picnic lunches held by football fans. As the second half of the twentieth century progressed, grilling meat became a defining element of masculinity within society and eventually within the football picnic.

In the post-World War II United States, suburban grilling culture flourished and grew to embody American values and aspirations, especially with regard to gender. Moreover, the division of domestic labor in outdoor grilling clearly demarcated and stabilized Cold War gender roles, and the backyard patio activity grew into a symbol of nation and manhood. In 1950s America the grill and outdoor cooking became weapons in the cultural Cold War, where the "good life" was lived and achieved only in a democracy. Meat consumption and outdoor grilling fed a larger strategy of Cold War propaganda in which an abundance of food, a home (patio) in which to cook that bounty, and a family to share it was a "ritual that allowed postwar citizens to publicly perform Americanness."[69] US families were eager to take up this particular activity as their "patriotic duty" and moved enthusiastically, with spatulas in hand, to backyards and patios.[70]

Men's place in grilling and meat consumption, in the period, became a weapon to "reassert male primacy"[71] at home and at work—as it also fortified a nation's desire for supremacy on a global scale. Certifying men's unique expertise, the 1953 *Hungry Man's Outdoor Grill Cookbook* argues, "grill cookery is inventive—definitely a man's approach to food preparation."[72] Men were the grill masters whose creative public performance underscored not only a certain construction of masculinity, but also a particular understanding of the kind of life only lived and fostered in a democracy: an existence where leisure, joy, and abundance marked the parameters of life in America. While America was "bit[ten] by the barbecue bug" outdoor cookery's connection to men and masculinity did not begin in Cold War America—it simply heated up in that historical moment.[73] In 1940, for example, an *American Home* essay, "barbecue recipes to swell the male chest," was one among many prewar references in popular culture to a view of men's natural place firing up the grill.[74] The activity was pleasurable, unlike more ordinary, day-to-day cooking, seemingly because a man was involved. *LIFE* declared in the early 1950s that in recent years, "housewives discovered it was more fun to hang over an outdoor grill with a husband than over an indoor stove alone."[75]

No food represented rugged masculinity more than red meat, something men should hunt (and not shop for it at the grocery store), prepare, and eat. Outdoor cooking is "man's work and man-sized menus and portions should be the rule," wrote James Beard in 1941.[76] Men fortified themselves as men in cooking red meat and eating it, too. Beef will do what few other dishes do, according to a mid-1950s *LOOK* article, including "feed a man as well, fill him as full, and leave him with a great sense of well-being."[77] In this Cold War moment, the associations between meat and men took on even greater significance as links to strength and manliness reinforced messages about the nation's attributes as well.

America's preoccupation with meat and grilling was not simply a backyard suburban event (though it did have a stronghold there). Men were also encouraged to take their grilling show on the road. Portable grills had long been a feature of automobile touring and picnicking, but the nation's love affair with both reached new, sometimes creative, heights in the post-World War II era. *Popular Mechanics* proclaimed in 1946 that a new "Barbecue outfit" weighing only about 20 pounds "folds into [a] suitcase," ready to be taken wherever the grill master wished.[78] Just a year later *Popular Science* upstaged the suitcase grill with its own story of the "Rear-engine car [that] boasts [a] kitchen," complete with dinette, icebox, sink, stove, folding table, and dishes all hidden under the front hood.[79] Perhaps it is little wonder that within a decade the thirty million dollar outdoor cooking industry had become a "sizzling trade" and even, according to a front-page story in the *New York Times*, as popular as golf.[80] Regardless of the setting, be it the backyard, beach, or roadside, by the mid-1950s the "thrill of the grill" was an emphasized slogan directed squarely at men.[81] The masculinization of consumer identity accomplished through early twentieth-century automobile advertisements continued in barbecue promotions, with *LIFE* magazine noting of men, "gadget buying is man's meat."[82]

Cookbooks and the periodical press followed suit by instructing men on the fine points of creating the perfect backyard barbecue, from the purchasing of top-of-the-line equipment, to locating the best cuts of meat, to arranging the placement of food and guests. On the latter point, one source directed appetizer trays be placed accommodatingly so that guests would be out of the way of the grill man, but "close enough to appreciate his skill in grilling."[83] These sources, including John and Marie Roberson's 1951 volume, *The Complete Barbecue Book*, emphasized performance and acclaim and assured men in this mid-twentieth-century moment that "a little showmanship goes a long way."[84] Indeed, in a 1953 article, Sally Weiner of the *New York Times* declared, "barbecuing is becoming a year-round epicurean sport."[85] These mid-twentieth-century performative aspects of outdoor barbecuing helped to set the stage for the culinary spectacle of contemporary tailgating.

The links between grill portability and automobility related to tailgating culture were slow to develop, however, as pregame festivities remained largely a space where traditional gender arrangements were maintained. In women's tailgate participation during this era, we see an extension of femininely coded picnic responsibilities and domestic duties: women were the key players in preparing, transporting, and serving game day meals. Their roles, as they had for decades, mimicked and sustained those of broader society. The grill and a man's place behind it, attending to hot dogs and hamburgers, was not yet a fixture at football tailgates. In his romantic account of the football tailgate, Horace Sutton of *Sports Illustrated* provides a clear image of the activity, writing in 1954:

> The breeze is full of gusto, the air is full of festivity, the ladies are full of chrysanthemums, and the trees are beginning to share colored leaves with the Earth . . . By noon family Buicks are streaming like safari wagons . . . From the depths of the wicker, wrapped in cocoons

of waxed paper, come the hard-boiled eggs and deep fried chicken, and well mashed sandwiches . . . .Blankets are spread from hubcap to hubcap; the tailgates are down on the station wagons. Both are laden equally with cellophane bags of potato chips and plums and plates crowned with Himalayas of potato salad mixed by mama the night before.[86]

Traditional notions of family and love of nation join in this Cold War moment as the author adds that tailgating prior to football contests is a "prime [pleasure] of the *American* [italics added] autumn."[87] The idyllic images of football and food remained wedded to nation and the purported strengths of American democracy throughout the 1950s. *Sports Illustrated's* 1956 photo montage captures gridiron propaganda under the title, "Saturday Afternoon, U.S.A." Princeton Tiger fans enjoy a "Pregame Buffet on station-wagon tail gate," the caption reads to an image filled with smiles and plenty of food.[88]

## "Homemaker Turned Football Fan": Women's Work at the Tailgate

Through the 1950s and 1960s, those tasked with bringing smiles and plenty of food to the tailgate remained largely women, even as small shifts occurred in how that cuisine was prepared. Significant advances in portable grill technology enabled backyard barbecue enthusiasts easier and more numerous opportunities to broaden the culinary delights offered up before football games. More portable grill choices, including the Weber grill developed in the late 1950s, is reflected in football picnic descriptions near the end of the decade.[89] University of Illinois football fans in 1955 were the focus of this culinary transformation on the blacktop. Gone from football Saturday feasts were the boxed restaurant lunches of the 1920s, the local press reported. Rather "hamburgers cooked on portable grills alongside the owner's car," were now part of the football picnic buffet.[90] Articles promoted the idea of grilling meat at football picnics, but with an instructive tone for those unsure of or unclear about the latest trend in tailgate cookery. After all, the backyard cookout is one thing, but a parking lot outside of an athletic stadium is quite another. A fall 1958 *Sunset* article gave football partygoers several choices, with meals prepared on the "hibachi" or "reheated over a small camp stove" listed as the more "elaborate" of the options. The article cautioned that those interested in the charcoal broiled steak recipe should first "check your hibachi fire-lighting techniques" found in an earlier edition of the magazine.[91] Small charcoal fired grills dotted the football parking lot by the late 1950s, signaling a move from staples such as cold sandwiches and premade fried chicken, to other edibles. The red meat enjoyed in millions of backyard barbecues was on its way to stadium pregame festivities, though the road to grilling huge chunks of red meat on gigantic cooking appliances at football picnics was slow to develop as a common practice.

Though there were signs of change, for the most part, traditional gender arrangements that marked football picnicking in the post-World War II era continued into the decade of the 1960s, as promotional material and news of the activity were geared toward women. Organizing and executing an event with food at its core remained women's work. Though women were often the center of stories detailing football picnics, these accounts reinforced conventional ideas about femininity and womanhood.[92] Newspaper articles made clear who remained in charge of the culinary details of the day. According to the *Orlando Sentinel* in 1968, "the homemaker turned football fan takes the weather into account when she plans her menu."[93] Throughout the 1960s, when football picnic recipes or articles appeared on newspaper pages they often did so in sections with birth announcements, or advertisements for things like bras and girdles, thin spaghetti, and "push button" mustard.[94] Even into the early 1970s conventional gender arrangements around cookery remained intact for some tailgaters, including Tessie Rockmaker, part of the Penn State faithful. "I do all the work [food preparation]," Rockmaker concedes and adds, "but I do it because it makes Gordie [her husband] happy and he truly enjoys it. That give me lots of satisfaction."[95]

In many instances, women remained central as hostesses of the gameday picnics, wherever they were held. In what sounds remarkably similar to the early twentieth-century elaborate gameday luncheons, a 1969 article heralded the fun to be had in throwing a "pre-football picnic—indoors!" Found on a grocery special and recipe page of the paper, the audience was, presumably, women in this late 1960s moment. In addition to serving a "warming meal in a hospitable home," details for the luncheon might include "a tiny football 'tree', with miniature footballs dangling from little branches" presented as an "amusing centerpiece."[96]

The majority of activity, however, remained in the outdoors—in parking lots—where vehicles continued to be central to the evolution of the football picnic. America's fascination with the station wagon reached its peak in 1960, with fifteen percent of all sales in this vehicle category.[97] Postwar predilections for leisure and larger families resulted in the surge in station wagons on the road and consequently in stadium parking lots. The vehicle's structure, namely its downward swinging tailgate became the picnic table on which pregame meals were arranged and eaten. Initially, the name change required a descriptive qualifier be attached to "tailgate" parties or "tailgate" picnics so that readers could conceptualize the activity and avoid confusion. "Tailgate" parties, the *New York Times* wrote in 1964, are "outdoor picnics on station wagon tailgates before the game."[98] Consequently, the word "tailgate" picnic became the more common identifier for pregame stadium meals, replacing "football picnic" or "football lunch" by the end of the 1960s.

Stadium parking lots in the 1960s were populated with station wagons of every variety with traditional picnic food, prepared by women

Tailgaters at Milwaukee County Stadium, 1962.
*Courtesy of Wisconsin Historical Society. Image number WHi-27766.*

long before arriving to the blacktop, served off the tailgates. As tailgating cookbooks of the 1960s and early 1970s demonstrate, the suggested menus predominantly feature make-ahead dishes such as casseroles, dips, salads, and sandwiches.[99] This remained standard tailgate cuisine, with newspaper accounts suggesting the same, as charcoal grills were more of an anomaly than a routine fixture at tailgating activities. An observer of a 1971 Princeton tailgate noted that over the expanse of the parking lot area, "one group brought their charcoal grill for a proper barbecue."[100] Grilling culture and advanced forms of cookery more generally did influence the tailgater's approach to gameday fare, albeit gradually and with little indication of the grandeur to come. The "complicated" yet "fun" tailgates of the period were those that moved beyond traditional picnic victuals. A "spaghetti dinner with a kitchen set up in a camper," was the sophisticated exception to a more general rule that included a hamper and cold cuts.[101] But the rules were shifting, with hints of change in gender arrangements surrounding blacktop cookery, as well as organization and institutionalization in the increasingly widespread and respected football practice of tailgating.

By the late 1960s tailgating was an established and newsworthy ritual in football spaces around the country, as well as a space that, at times, nurtured homosociality among men. Media reports began to articulate the event's significance as a cultural form beyond the committed tailgaters who were already well aware of its importance. One noteworthy example of this shift in which men began to take center stage at a tailgate is a December 1966 *New York Times* article, "Jet Fans Hitch Their Chuck Wagons to Front-Office Stars." The large, above-the-fold photo includes a number of male New York Jets fans, all members of "the Jets Parking and Chowder Society," congregating around very large cooking pots that outsized the small charcoal grills on which they sat. Members made clear that their organization had "little purpose except camaraderie." However, what the Chowder Society lacked in organization, they made up for in clout, apparently, as Jets president David "Sonny" Werblin and head coach Weeb Ewbank were served up plates of food at the "open-air luncheon." Two years later, the *Times* again detailed the exploits of the "Chowderheads" (named for the "fine chowder" served at their tailgate gatherings). Jets leadership, once more was present at the parking lot party and head coach Ewbank even offered an apology to the Chowderheads for being tardy to the cake-cutting celebration of the team's Eastern Division title. Don Phelan, Jets fan and Chowderheads leader, recounted the impetus for the group's start. One week, hoping to create a community with other fans, Phelan "brought a hibachi and handed out hamburgers" to other likeminded Jets rooters on the stadium parking lot. He recalls, "the week after that, there were hundreds of people." The "Chowderheads" were football's "true believers," who comprised tailgating's present and its future.[102]

## "Here's the Beef": Men, Meat, and Masculinity

In the last decades of the twentieth century the popularity of tailgating at football contests continued to grow. It was both a cultural as well as increasingly commercialized force. By the end of the century, the activity was marketed more to men than to women, where expressions of masculinity took center stage in and outside the stadium. During the football season of 1980 journalist Jim Morris penned one among a growing nationwide body of articles about tailgating. Heightened awareness of the activity itself, among football followers and others, was not the only change afoot surrounding pregame feasting. In his survey of the various ways in which tailgate parties were executed, Morris claimed that except for margarine-maker Chiffon's tailgate party cookbook, the blacktop remained free from commercialization and all of its trappings. Seeming to contradict himself, Morris noted, in the same piece, that some colleges had recently "promoted the practice [of tailgating]" as a way to enrich university coffers.[103] Indeed, by the early 1980s, newspaper and magazine articles were reporting more widely on how the nationwide spectacle of tailgating was redefining football games. And if tailgating was not forcing fans to reconsider the game itself, it was forging change in that the activity, in some instances, became *the* reason why spectators went to the game in the first place. In 1978, for example, New York Giants fans placed a notice in the local paper's "want ads" asking to buy tickets to one of the home team's games so that fans could make it to the tailgate.[104] In a 1971 profile of Minnesota Vikings tailgaters, *Sports Illustrated* writer Jerry Kirshenbaum offered insight into the place of tailgating in football culture and in doing so sheds light on why New York Giants fans and so many others across the country were drawn to the party in the parking lot before the game as much as the game itself. Kirshenbaum writes, "in this smorgasbord on asphalt, the football is part of a hero sandwich: the festivities start in the morning and end well past dark, with the game buried in the middle."[105] The Vikings tailgate, according to the author, is similar to an Arctic street fair scene in which "the food is prepared with a care worthy of a Pillsbury bake-off."[106] Fans, insulated against the wintry elements in thermal layers, parkas, and the odd purple snowmobile suit, crowded into Metropolitan Stadium three hours before kickoff in cars, station wagons, mobile homes, campers, and even buses. Once at the stadium, they gathered around charcoal grills, the backs of vehicles, or for one group, a china-laden table to feast on everything from roasted buffalo to chicken Newburg, undeterred by the snow flurries and nine-degree temperatures.[107]

Tailgating's changing parameters in the 1970s and 1980s did not end with its growing popularity and clearer trends toward commercialization, but also included the kind of food served and those who prepared it at pregame festivities. Though the process was far from linear, the flavor of tailgating became more meat-centric and included more grill-specific interest and instructions, aimed increasingly at men. Grills, which seemed to undergo a supersizing of their own by the end of the century, became a more common sight across stadium parking lots in the 1980s. These changes reflect and reinforce broader shifts in gender relations happening well beyond the blacktop.

As we have seen, throughout much of the twentieth century tailgating was a culinary affair reflective of traditional gender roles, though there are clearly elements of change through this period as broader social forces altered cooking arrangements on the blacktop. Through much of the twentieth century, women handled most of the food preparation and packing at home and took charge of hosting and serving once at the stadium. Men drove to the stadium, and as barbecue culture increasingly influenced tailgating in the 1970s, they oversaw grilling on the blacktop— typically hot dogs and hamburgers on modest portable charcoal grills. The 1970s and 1980s are transitional decades for tailgating, as the practice continued to grow amid the cultural backdrop of significant social change in the United States. Notions of traditional masculinity and what it meant to be a man had been and continued to be challenged by the Civil Rights and Gay Liberation movements, as well as second-wave Feminism.[108] Feminism, in particular, challenged constructs of masculine identity as calls for gender equality inspired women to pursue higher education, careers outside the home, and political office in greater numbers. As Michael Kimmel argues, men were not necessarily receptive to the "rights" movements of the 1960s and 1970s. As a result, by the start of the 1980s Ronald Reagan's brand of rugged masculinity was welcomed by many who saw it as a salve to gender in crisis.[109]

Though a satirical look at manhood and the stereotypes associated with masculinity, Bruce Feirstein's 1982 monograph, *Real Men Don't Eat Quiche*, clearly underscores societal unease around changing gender constructions, as well as food as an identity marker. Sitting atop the bestseller list for nearly a year, the book is clear about how gender is made and remade through the food we eat. In a decade's time, Feirstein anxiously opined, the cultural artifacts society will be remembered by include, "frozen yogurt, 'Eight is Enough,' salad bars, cruise control, restaurants that spin, surf n' turf, and the Phil Donahue Show." We are, unfortunately, he claimed, "a nation of wimps, pansies, [and] quiche-eaters." Meat and potatoes were important anecdotes to the gendered ills plaguing men— not salmon, tofu, yogurt, rice pilaf, and arugula salad, among other food items, according to the author.[110]

In this moment, all-male spaces in which to socialize felt necessary for men who wanted to reclaim masculinity and reconstruct bonds with other men. Hunting trips, golf outings, and the increasingly male-dominated spaces on the blacktop before football games became those safe space havens for men. As women entered and thus altered the public sphere men, in turn, retreated to all-male spaces in which they could reclaim a rugged masculinity lost.[111] To do so however, required recoding cookery as an appropriate activity for men. The introduction, over the last couple of decades of the twentieth century, of supersized chunks of red meat and grills large enough to support those foods, are just two examples of how cooking and manhood began to be redefined to include men building "camaraderie around the chafing dish, the grill, the tailgate."[112] This process of men moving to the blacktop and codifying the space as male was less a sprint than a gradual trend in that direction. Just as more expansive societal gender arrangements appeared in flux, so too did the activities on the blacktop.

Women's presence in tailgate activities continued, albeit more often in tandem with their male partners. A *Time* magazine feature from 1973 on Minnesota Vikings fans sheds light on the popularity of tailgating among both men and women. Not even the decision to lift local television blackouts for that game could distract "a very special species of spectator" from making the pilgrimage to the stadium, according to the author.[113] Tailgaters Bernie and Lois Brodkorb were one among many husband-and-wife pairs featured in the article who participated in the blacktop affair described as "part block party, part fraternity beer bust, part Shriners' parade, and all Middle-American ritual." The Brodkorb's converted 1951 purple school bus, loaded with "two quarter-barrels of Grain Belt beer, 18 lbs. of roast beef, a ham, fish, potato salad and home-baked beans," was not the only reason the couple earned the title "flamboyant party [giver]."[114] The article notes that the couple also pulled in a flatbed truck each week that served as the stage for Joe Tomaszewski's six-piece Polish Show Band. Polka, in addition to food and libations, helped them secure and maintain their title.[115] The altered vehicle, the copious amounts of meat, and the centrality of liquor illustrate the masculinization of the tailgate during this period.

Though the party was cast as a "fraternity beer bust," women often remained central characters to the increasingly extravagant party on the blacktop. In the midst of the growing cavalcade of oversize vehicles in football stadium parking lots and despite the increased presence of meat on tailgate menus, much of the promotion for the activity continued to be directed by and at women in the 1970s. Tailgate cookbooks of this era were written mostly by women, and included mainly recipes for make-ahead salads, dips, and casseroles, seemingly presupposing a female readership.[116] A 1974 campaign by the San Francisco 49ers to spark greater fan participation focused on tailgating. Robin Mitchell, the newly appointed Director of Promotions for the 49ers, told the *New York Times*, "we encourage [fans] to come early and have 'tailgate' parties—barbecues and picnics—before the game. Last season we gave away recipe booklets written by the 49er wives."[117] A 1979 depiction of the Yale University tailgate scene similarly highlighted women's roles in gathering tailgate food, which mainly consisted of packaged and prepared items—wrapped sandwiches, clam chowder in a thermos, stuffed mushrooms, brownies, and molasses cookies. However, a young professor of plastic surgery and his wife, it was noted, entertained guests with "a pair of grills, one of which was kosher."[118]

Tailgating publications written by women for women remained common, as did the predilection to frame narratives within heteronormative boundaries. One 1984 newspaper article framed tailgating as an activity in which women grudgingly participated. The "idea behind a tailgate picnic is essentially to make bearable something that is essentially a dreadful idea." The writer continues, "spending a bone-chilling afternoon sitting out on some cold bleachers watching 22 fine young men bashing each other to bits is certainly not everybody's idea of a good time."[119] Wives and mothers are cautioned that despite "always looking for ways to make things easier on the feeding front, the tailgate picnic is not the place to hold back." Noting the conveniences afforded by tailgating from a vehicle, the writer of this article instructs women to use as many containers, thermoses, and coolers as needed, and to even pack real plates and silverware for the festivities. The menu ideas presented for readers remain centered on prepared-ahead dishes of some complexity. Moreover, readers are firmly advised, "tailgate food must always be hearty. Nobody wants to drive all the way out to some cold field to eat a carrot stick standing up." Here, it is women as family caretakers, charged with the planning and execution of a successful tailgate party, who are reminded to provide their guests with substantial fare. Not coincidentally, we would hazard, this article runs on the same page as a large "double coupons" ad for A&P grocery stores.[120]

The performance of traditional gender roles was also encouraged in tailgate cookbooks of the 1980s. Authors advise women on how to properly host tailgate parties, addressing them as the main preparers and servers of tailgate dishes. Tailgating tips directed at women (by women) were exhaustive, often including wide-ranging commentary on etiquette, as well as practical considerations when hosting this "new style show" sweeping the country.[121] Candy Coleman's *Pigskin Picnics*, published in 1980, is a great illustration of the ways in which dominant gender constructs are reinscribed in and through the pages of tailgate cookbooks of the period. Heteronormative ideologies, seen across the range of tailgate cookbooks, are in evidence in this book as well. According to Coleman: "One sure way of making the 'most appreciated list' of any [man] is to feed him well." The author adds, "when good food is combined with an interest in his favorite sport, you're sure to be a winner."[122]

Some cookbooks, such as the 1985 *Mid American Tailgaters Cookbook* even instruct women on how to dress for the occasion: "Just as you plan your food and drink down to the last detail, so must you plan your tailgate attire. Tailgating couture involves three vital considerations: fashion, comfort, and weather."[123] While the introduction to this book claims "fashion should always be in the back of a tailgater's mind," this exhortation is not one we have seen repeated in instructional publications directed at male tailgaters.[124]

In fact, tailgate publications directed at men are surprisingly rare until the 1990s. Newspaper and magazine photos provide evidence of men handling the grilling duties on the blacktop in the 1970s and 1980s, yet women remain a significant focus of many tailgater profiles. In an account of college football rivalries in Michigan, a Michigan State partisan proudly presented her green-food-themed tailgate menu of "celery, green peppers, honeydew melon and sour cream dip with chives."[125] Tailgater Susan Ward was credited with preparing one of the more traditional meals of a 1983 Yale Bowl matchup, "beginning with a beer and Cheddar-cheese soup, barbecued short ribs and chicken, warm German potato salad, cabbage and apple slaw, and assorted cheeses."[126] Two of Ward's contemporaries, it was noted, began offering cooking courses to help others meet the "endless challenges in preparing a successful and diverting tailgate picnic. Planning a tailgate picnic," those contemporaries said, "is not unlike designing football strategy for third down and short yardage: You want just enough flair and unpredictability to keep the other side guessing, but not so much fancy footwork that you risk a disaster."[127] The majority of articles about tailgating continued to reflect the style of women's cookbooks, with narrative content guided by the assumption that women were the ones responsible for the bulk of food preparation and cooking.

Clearly, however, there were emerging fissures disrupting gender arrangements across tailgate cookery activities. *Popular Mechanics*, a magazine distinctly geared to a male audience, promoted bigger, more complex tailgates in its October 1979 issue, indicating a shifting trend in tailgating practices. A feature article on West Point noted, "sandwiches 'n beer just aren't a class act at the stadium any more." Instructions for a build-it-yourself picnic kitchen and tailgate organizer—"a chuck wagon with a college degree"—are provided. The text accompanying photos of tailgate revelers claims, "for outscoring the opposition where it counts— the food and drink department—*PM*'s food and picnic chest is rated number one."[128] This article speaks not only to the primacy of tailgating in football culture and the turn toward a male audience, but also to a growing competitive spectacle within tailgate culture, with men as participants at its center.

Canisius College's tailgate party competition in 1984 underscored the changing dynamics around football picnics as commercialized, red-meat-centered contests. The College cosponsored a "Here's the Beef" competition with fast-food chain Wendy's, playing on that company's popular "Where's the Beef?" advertising campaign.[129] The beef, it appeared, was more likely than ever being grilled by men at tailgating events prior to football games throughout the nation.

A new product featured in a June 1980 sporting gear column in the *New York Times* is further evidence of increasing culinary sophistication among tailgaters and the marketing trends toward men. The "Trailcooker," billed as "a practical item for either camping or tailgate parties," includes a two-burner propane gas stove, running water, utility drawer, and a five-foot food preparation space, all of which folds up into a plastic case resembling a suitcase and weighing in at forty-seven pounds. The target market for this product appears to be men, and given the publication date (near father's day) and suggested retail price of $199.95, presumably fathers of upper middle-class financial means.[130] The "Trailcooker," like the *Popular Mechanics* picnic kitchen/tailgate organizer, presupposes a tailgate scene in which more complex food is prepared and cooked at the stadium. In these accounts we also see evidence of the value placed on the size and scope of one's tailgate. A 1981 article published in Auburn, NY's *The Citizen* declared of the tailgate party, "the bigger the better, the longer the better," and noted that "the football game, which started it all, is now something that's sandwiched between the double-ended parties, some starting before sun-up and lasting until the moon's over the mountain."[131] The ultimate tailgate machine, "an apartment-sized range with its bare, ugly back showing," dominated the VIP lot at the United States Military Academy. As tailgate parties grew more elaborate, "an observer left to munch a modest roast beef sandwich, an apple and a diet soda from the trunk of a car parked far, far away felt a little like Little Orphan Annie."[132] Increasingly, those tailgates taken to be the most serious had little space or tolerance for "modest" offerings, fruits, or diet drinks. Instead masculine excess was on the menu.

By the early 1980s, though still in the minority, more tailgating articles written by men for men were appearing in newspaper reports. Some of those entries, including a 1981 feature on Boston College "King of Local Tailgaters," Richard Carlson, expanded not only on his love of tailgating, but on his love of cookery. Carlson, the paper noted, begins preparing to feed dozens on football Saturday days before the event, planning the menu, shopping for food, and cooking. He arrives nearly five hours before kickoff and quickly begins to unpack coolers, grills, stoves, dishes, tables, tableware, and other items for the nearly three dozen guests expected for that day's feast. Concerned more with "flank steaks than flanker backs," Carlson puts his culinary skills on display as he puts the finishing touches on his "Newburg sauce served over homemade pastry shells; plum jelly chicken wings; raw littleneck clams; gherkins wrapped in cream cheese and ham; a Caesar salad; and a spicy bread dip," among other tasty delights.[133]

By the last years of the twentieth century men increasingly conceived of cookery and the culinary spaces adjacent to football stadiums before games as a refuge; a space in which to create community with other men. Former Oakland Raiders football coach and NFL commentator John Madden's rhetoric epitomizes a number of the major shifts in tailgating culture in the 1990s. Madden, one of the sport's premiere personalities, embodied tailgating culture of the late twentieth century with his rugged, plainspoken brand of masculinity often on display. While working as a broadcaster, Madden, who reportedly has a fear of flying, drove from game to game throughout the 1980s and 1990s in a nearly million-dollar recreational vehicle dubbed the "Madden Cruiser." Along the way his love of football and food made him one of the more highly recognizable faces associated with the growing spectacle on the blacktop.

Madden's descriptions of his favorite tailgates underscore the connections we construct between our own gender identity, the food we eat, and football. In 1991 he made clear his tastes when it came to tailgate food and atmosphere, "the worst ones [tailgates] have tablecloths and wine and cheese. Good ones have very little fruits and vegetables. The best ones have big things. Bratwurst and football go together." His favorite tailgaters were those "used to all kinds of weather." To which he adds, "if you're going to tailgate you have to tailgate the whole season. You can't just pick your days."[134]

*John Madden's Ultimate Tailgating*, published in 1998, serves as another key example of the shift to differently gendered representations of tailgating. Madden authored a cookbook containing eighty recipes, most of which feature large cuts of meat and instructions for how to grill them to perfection. Madden celebrates noted male tailgaters and barbecue experts throughout the book, and explains his tailgating philosophy: "Tailgating food is all sinkers. Chili is a sinker. Pork chunk stew is a sinker. Burritos are sinkers. Jalapeno venison meatballs are sinkers . . . It's not the stuff you eat in tiny bites with your little finger in the air."[135]

The title of chapter two denotes "the big cuts of meat" as a food group, while in the opening narrative Madden declares, "you can't have serious tailgating without barbecuing."[136] The recipes themselves are a departure from those of the 1970s and 1980s era cookbooks, as they feature meat-centric dishes like smoked prime rib, salt-cured spit-roasted leg of lamb, and suckling pig. Another, "Garlic-Stuffed Fresh Ham, Roasted on a Spit," deemed "tailgating gold" by Madden, is a "sinker" provided by a Pittsburgh machinist, who roasted his ham on a spit made by the father of another tailgater. The spit is described as a "welded, stainless steel grill with a battery-operated rotisserie . . . a real work of art."[137]

Madden's book helps propel the tailgate away from reliance on prepared-ahead dishes and simple grilling fare and toward the realm of barbecue spectacle. In so doing, the gender dynamics of tailgating shift, too. Men are clearly the intended audience for Madden, as they are both celebrated for and instructed on tailgating properly. The tailgate itself is cast in a decidedly more hegemonic masculine light, replete with heteronormative images and even homophobic undertones. Interestingly, though, Madden does weave the narrative thread back to women when he claims, "like most other things in food, it all goes back to Mom. I think that's true for most people, even the greatest chefs. You don't hear any chefs say, 'Gee, I learned this recipe from my grandfather or my dad.' It's always, 'I learned from my mom or my grandma.'"[138]

Women re-enter the tailgating frame in Madden's world, but firmly within the bounds of appropriate femininity. Such is the case generally for gender arrangements on the blacktop in recent history. Women, while certainly present at tailgates across the land are, for the most part, tangential within a frame where meat and men are the centerpiece.

## Whitewashing the Blacktop: Retelling Tailgating's Past

The gendered histories of tailgating are matched by equally compelling racial dimensions. How we remember that past, retelling it in the present, speaks to lines of power around gender and race. The tailgating exhibit at the College Football Hall of Fame in Atlanta, Georgia provides us with a rare moment when a recounting of the activity's past surfaces in the public sphere. The keenly racialized and politicized process of pulling the past into the present is showcased in the state-of-the-art, highly commercialized celebration of the game sponsored by the National Football Foundation.[139] Visitors can view display after display of tailgating artifacts, photographs, and various other memorabilia, all laid out in museum-like style. The exhibit begins with enlarged photographs of early tailgates, many of which also ran in the mainstream, white press. A 1910 photo of the crowd gathering for the Yale–Princeton matchup at Princeton's University Field shows a sea of well-heeled white men and women waiting to gain entry to the game. A series of images of mid-twentieth-century tailgaters and stadium crowds reveals more of the same—nicely appointed white men and women picnicking behind their cars in grassy lots and cheering on their teams from the stands.[140]

Within the sea of whiteness, there are two photos in the exhibit that include black tailgaters. One, captioned "Cooking with Gas at North Carolina State," features an African American couple with fellow white tailgaters. The photo appears courtesy of the Special Collections Research Center at the NCSU Libraries, where it is simply labeled "Sports Fans" and dated circa 1984–1986.[141] The second, a black-and-white photo of an African American section of fans presumably watching a game at an HBCU, bears no identifying information but for an attribution to Time & Life Pictures/Getty Images. In its failure to identify a contingent of spectators and their location in the one photo of black fans on display, the Hall obscures HBCU football history. Visitors do not see images of the early twentieth-century Thanksgiving Day games that drew large crowds, learn about the student-led halftime "Rabbles," or gain a sense of the cultural events surrounding the rivalry-infused Classics.[142] Instead, a walk through this section of the Hall leaves one with the impression that it is mainly white folks who have shared the football ritual of tailgating, and that Coca-Cola was their product of choice—not unexpected, given that the Atlanta-based soft drink giant is a founding corporate partner of the Hall. The participation of African Americans and other people of color is largely absent from the historical record curated through these displays, as is the rich tradition of football pageantry at HBCUs. Moreover, what remains is a history narrowly defined and constructed as a white past—one that is left unquestioned, thus obscuring critical inquiry into the many ways that race and power operate in retelling tailgating's past. As there are relatively few sites that chronicle the history of tailgating, those commercial entities that attract considerable attention stand out in their failure to present a comprehensive, historically accurate record.

## Conclusion

For well over a century pregame feasting just outside of football stadiums has had a rich and flavorful history. What began as a practical solution to filling empty stomachs before football games has grown and evolved. The transitions offer us insight into cultural shifts around consumption, entertainment, commercialization, and gender. However, the enormous changes do not erase the historical threads woven through-out tailgate history. Once quaint nineteenth-century traditions of pic-nicking on the grass outside the stadium transformed into massive public displays of masculinity where whole pigs are roasted on monster grills affectionately called "grillzillas." While tailgating did not start out as a public spectacle, it has always been a gendered cultural practice, with food at its center.

# 2.

# Cooking Steak with a Hatchet and a Hubcap

## *Spectacle on the Blacktop*

## Introduction

Louisiana State University's November 5, 2016 evening matchup with top-ranked Alabama would bring over 100,000 fans into the stadium, but not before another 150,000 tailgaters filled every conceivable space outside the stadium in the days and hours before the first whistle.[1] Ten hours prior to kickoff, the parking lots, median strips, and grassy areas as far as one could see outside of Louisiana State's Tiger Stadium teemed with those cooking, feasting, drinking, and socializing. It is hard not to be overwhelmed by the myriad sights, sounds, and smells of "Tigah Tailgating," said to be a blend of "*Carnival*, a Louisiana Cajun festival, a music celebration, and a seafood fete."[2] That November day, the acreage outside the stadium was awash in purple and gold, with people as well as tents, canopies, chairs, flags, and giant inflatable Tigers, among other things, proudly displaying LSU colors. Pickup trucks, pulling an assortment of trailers, as well as towable grills and smokers, dotted the landscape. Other tailgaters not satisfied with transporting only a backyard grill to the game brought their homes instead. Motorhomes, many stretching over forty feet in length, were packed in neatly ordered rows in numerous lots near to and far from the stadium. The cost of taking up blacktop space is not cheap for those in homes on wheels; in the premier lots, motorhome parking sets tailgaters back as much as eight thousand dollars, per season, for the opportunity to host a few parties on the blacktop.[3] Large flat-screen televisions and even bigger projector screens were in abundance for those wishing to watch the football action from the parking lot rather than enter the stadium. Generators, small planes flying overhead, live and recorded music, random noisemakers (bullhorns, drums, air horns), as well as the buzz from a crowd populated by a small city's worth of people packed into parking lots, produced a constant cacophony. Grilled and smoked meats created aromas that wafted over the temporary city, rounding out the sensory experience.

On a relatively small sliver of space amid this larger happening, along South Stadium Drive, and a football-throw away from Tiger Stadium, a group of a half-dozen men maneuvered around several grills, coolers, and a forty-gallon pot of gumbo being stirred with a gigantic paddle. They arrived two days early, on Thursday, to stake out the prime real estate under the shade of a large tree very near to the stadium. Mark, who has been tailgating at LSU since 1999 with this group of friends, noted that despite their early arrival they were lucky to secure one of the last two spots in this section. On the menu that day was two thousand dollars-worth of food, which included chicken with jalapeno sausage, deer sausage, duck breast poppers wrapped in bacon, tenderloin, and the pièce de résistance, gumbo. Over seven hours the forty-gallon pot of gumbo would grow to include, among other items, forty pounds of chicken and sausage, five pounds of Andouille sausage, and twenty ducks. The last item's place in the recipe required a coordinated team effort as the birds went in the giant kettle and then had to be pulled out, de-boned, and put back in again. One of the men said of the group that after seventeen years of tailgating together, "we're like a well-oiled machine." When asked why there were no women at this, the food preparation and cooking stage of tailgating, the response was quick: "it's a guy thing" with wives bringing the side dishes or items for the sweet table. Cookery, according to Mark, is often a [central] "part of our socializing."[4]

While the size and elaborateness of the sensory spectacle surrounding Tiger Stadium on the LSU campus prior to home football games is perhaps more pronounced than other venues, the scene is repeated, to varying degrees, at countless other college and professional stadiums during the Fall.

Tailgating is many things, including a space in which gender, and more specifically, dominant notions of masculinity are actively constructed, negotiated, and sometimes resisted. As noted in the book's introduction, we conceive of gender not as a fixed or biologically determined set of characteristics. Rather we understand gender as something that is constructed and enacted in social interactions with others.[5] Thus, dominant understandings of what it means to be a man and to be masculine

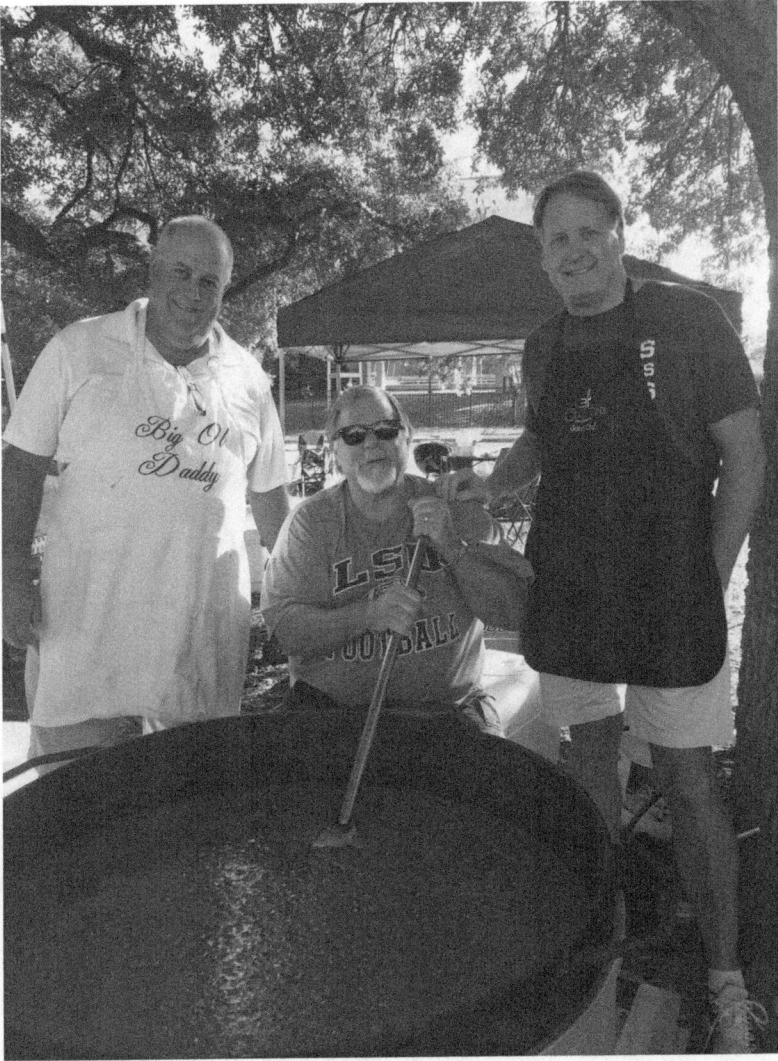

LSU tailgaters in front of their giant vat of gumbo, November 2016.
*Courtesy of Rita Liberti.*

are created and recreated through everyday social activities. These interactions do not occur outside of normative gender arrangements but are imbued with and thus constructed in relation to them, as tailgaters navigate the gendered spaces on the blacktop. Cooking equipment, food and complexity, and vehicles (namely motorhomes or recreational vehicles) all serve to create distinctive spaces in which men "do gender." As we will see, these categories, when taken together, help to distance cookery from its domestic and private, thus feminine, moorings. In this way men are afforded culinary cover by reconstituting cookery as an appropriately masculine endeavor in which to take part.

## "Man Machine": Cooking Equipment and Masculinity

In a television commercial for a Tailgate 360 grill, two police officers come upon the chaotic aftermath of a stadium parking lot tailgate. Beyond the strewn beer bottles and a woman lying on the ground, with little else on except a feather boa around her neck, their sights are set on a futuristic-looking grill off in the distance on the blacktop. They approach and one officer is heard saying, "good golly Miss Molly" as they stand, mesmerized by the grill in front of them. The other officer ponders quizzically, "it looks like some sort of man machine," noting its infrared grill, griddle, warmer, and deep fryer as evidence it is a symbol of manhood. The grill's temperature control dial has eleven rather than ten settings, underscoring the ways in which excess is equated with a specific kind of masculinity.[6] Though absurd, the commercial is a strong representation not only of the grill's central place in tailgating, but of its close association with men and masculinity.

Tools and other pieces of equipment, namely grills and smokers, are central to tailgating and are as gendered as the food cooked on and with them. The grill, and outdoor grilling more specifically, has long been thought of as explicitly masculine. With its "push button ignition, volcanic briquettes, rotating spits, all manner of scented chips, turners, forks, brushes, knives, tongs, aprons, stainless steel marinade injectors . . ." grilling, one observer notes, "is like a shop in the cellar" for men. We are left to ponder if the "BBQ [has] become the garage."[7] Grills are ubiquitous on stadium parking lots before football games. As we discuss in the previous chapter, they are a relatively late addition to the party on the blacktop, but their central place makes up for lost time. Tailgates feature every variety and size of grill, smoker, and stove, from pint-sized Weber gas or charcoal models to gigantic custom contraptions on wheels pulled into stadium lots behind even larger motorized vehicles. One cookbook author cautioned readers, reminding them that "without a grill, a tailgate is merely a picnic."[8] Cold cut sandwiches may have passed tailgate muster in decades past, but in this contemporary moment such is not the case. Tailgate cookbook author Bob Sloan repeats what virtually every blacktop chef knows: "Not every tailgate meal has to be cooked on the grill," he concedes, adding, however, "you can't call yourself a real tailgater until you've proven your quarterbacking skills by taking snaps standing over the hot coals."[9] Sport metaphors serve to link, and add legitimacy to, the connections among cooking equipment, masculinity, and prowess.

The perceived naturalness of the relationship between men and grilling, especially at a football tailgate, is brought sharply into focus across a range of sites in this study. George of the 3rdRail9ers tailgate crew in San Francisco explains the appeal of grilling. It is "just fire and me . . . it's raw and it's primal." Mediated representations of tailgating underscore similar perspectives, including in an episode of *The Simpsons*, "Any Given Sundance." As Homer Simpson pulls into the stadium lot we see a range of images, including a man turning a rack of ribs in the trunk of his vehicle—a converted smoker, two newsmen sitting atop their van grilling steaks in the vehicle's satellite dish, and finally a tailgater who pushes a button on his Hummer, prompting the back of the enormous vehicle to convert into a full professional kitchen, complete with a range hood and sprinkler system. The parody strikes sharply at the perceived place of biological difference in explaining men's preoccupation with tailgating grilling and associated gadgetry. "What childbirth is to women," Simpson declares, "eating trunk meats is to the bewanged [men]."[10] At least according to Homer Simpson, it is in men's nature to act as they do at tailgating events, with the grill at the center of the spectacle.

The tools, pieces of equipment, smokers, and other assorted cooking supplies are key signifiers of masculinity, with the grill (and often its enormous size) forming the focal point of the spectacles on the blacktop. Ray Lampe (also known as Dr. BBQ), author of *The NFL Gameday Cookbook*, like other tailgaters, welcomed the "newfound popularity for large, square charcoal grills" for reasons that underscore the association of grilling and masculinity. The grills, Lampe concludes, are "big and macho and can cook a lot of food."[11] Indeed, size does appear to matter, and keenly so, across the many sites included in our analysis.

The *Tailgate Warriors* series is one such site, as Guy Fieri's attention seemed continually drawn to large, custom grills, including an Oakland fans rig, aptly named "grill-zilla."[12] Its excessive size, with over thirty square feet of grill surface, personifies the blacktop spectacle of masculinity. In other *Tailgate Warriors* examples it was not simply grill size that accentuated the blacktop affair, but rather that the cooking instruments were constructed and customized by tailgaters. For Fieri, building the cooking gadgets on which to prepare food was an archetypal masculine expression, constituting the "big story."[13] In the Chicago Bears vs. Buffalo Bills episode the enormity of the grills, as well as each team's skill at building their own custom equipment, was the attraction and "part of the lore." The host enthusiastically proclaims, "you gotta build some of it, you gotta create some of it." The Chicago club's "spinning grills" (rotisseries) were the clear favorites for Fieri and the others judges of *The Food Network* show, as more questions were asked about the grills than about the food being prepared on them. Built by Chicago team member Bob Bromberek, also known as "the maestro of motors," the grill's system of motors, chains, and sprockets "impressed" all, with Fieri concluding, "these guys are playin' serious culinary ball."[14] It was not just the ability to cook on the grill, but the success of constructing it that created appeal among men.[15]

The teams in *Tailgate Warriors* are not the only participants trying to outdo one another with outlandish cooking gadgets and gargantuan customized grills. Buffalo Bills fan and tailgater Kenny Johnson "stands out" above all others in tailgate circles according to Fieri, not for the presence of any sort of traditional grill, but the absence of one. Kenny, Fieri notes, "doesn't have a grill, [he] has a Pinto [car]."[16] Fieri seems almost in disbelief at the spectacle of masculinity in caricature before him as several men cook on the hood of Kenny's "portable grill." Fieri details the scene: "I've got a guy cooking steak, with a hatchet in a hubcap." Another "dude" cooking chicken wings in "an Army helmet with a sickle." A third man is using a saw as a griddle to cook bacon with a fourth scrambling eggs with a shovel. Finally, Fieri concludes, "Pinto Kenny's" setup includes grilling chicken on top of a toolbox with screwdrivers serving as skewers.[17] The show's preoccupation with "recognizable masculinities" removes the specter of femininity while it confirms tailgate cookery as not only a safe but also seemingly "natural" space in which men prepare and serve food.[18]

On the morning we visited Johnson's tailgate in Buffalo it was difficult to make sense of the sight before us. As we stood atop a small hill overlooking the scene we quickly realized the *Tailgate Warriors* episode did not do this particular tailgate justice. In addition to the hubcaps, helmets, sickles, shovels, and screwdrivers in use on the hood of Kenny's Pinto, we saw bacon frying on a saw and sausage and Italian peppers sizzling on a rake. Next to the car, pulled pork was being cooked in a wheelbarrow, and a member of Kenny's crew was rolling out pizzas on a re-purposed ironing board before sliding them into the top drawer of a filing-cabinet-turned-oven to bake. The front seat of the Pinto served as storage space for rolls, condiments, and other supplies. According to Johnson, "grills just don't look right;" instead he prefers to cook on something a little less "normal."[19] The entire setting is a show to be both performed by Johnson's team and watched by other fans, with expressions of masculinity at tailgate cookery's core.

Car cookery has long been a point of fascination for the creative culinarian. Before Pinto Kenny started grilling merely on the hood of his defunct car, Harriet Riggs experimented with roasting meat inside the motor of a running car. The gendering is thick in Riggs' 1969 *Travel* account of "Cooking on Six Cylinders." "First," she instructs readers, "find the engine manifold." With self-deprecating humor, the author goes on to explain how her teenage son had to help her identify the manifold, chuckling that, "at least I knew I shouldn't look in the trunk." Riggs' attempt to secure a foil-wrapped two-and-a-half-pound cut of beef for roasting during a four-hour drive is cast as a spectacle of curiosity for men presumably familiar with the inner workings of an automobile, rather than as a public performance of skill and ingenuity. In this example, inventive use of the car by a woman is directed toward nurturing one's family and easing the burdens of motherhood, thus bringing it into the feminine realm of domesticity. Underscoring this point, Riggs envisions "the day when cars are made especially for the woman on the go, with a small area enclosed for the lady who wants to heat the baby's bottle or start dinner before she arrives home."[20] As the juxtaposition of these two examples indicates, the gendering of automobiles is different for men and women; even when a woman harnesses automotive possibilities for cooking, the resulting innovation feminizes her and the car. She might be able to feed a family of four with a meal of perfectly roasted beef upon arrival after a long road trip, but her feat remains tied to the domestic. The spectacle makes the man, but not the woman.

As both Harriet Riggs' six-cylinder cooking and Kenny Johnson's tailgate illustrate, it is not simply the grill or grilling that makes the man. Rather it is the activity's occupation in and of the public sphere, in the backyard or on the blacktop, that removes it from the mundane features of daily household cooking and consequently of all things feminine.[21] Grilling is, according to Michael Pollan, a "public ritual" or ceremony in which men can perform masculinity.[22] He adds "there's nothing ceremonial about chopping vegetables on a kitchen counter, slowly sautéing them in a pan, adding a liquid, and tending the covered pot for hours. For one thing, there's nothing to look at."[23] Indeed, that the entire event happens indoors renders it invisible with no performative distinction. Cookery on the blacktop offers a counter to the cloistered spaces of the kitchen. Others seem to agree. "As lord and master of your grill," chef and television personality Mario Batali writes, "you will welcome any opportunity to display your grilling prowess."[24]

For some tailgaters the cooking performances they enact on the blacktop are central to how they understand themselves and their actions. Nick of 3rdRail9ers explains, "one of the reasons why our tailgate has turned into such a spectacle is that we're all used to being on stage and being the center of attention [as band members]." In an oversize space in the parking lot at the new Santa Clara stadium, the culinary skills of the 3rdRail9ers are up for public view as countless folks slowly stroll past or hover around their pop-up kitchen to watch them prepare and cook an array of dishes. Nick and his crew are accustomed to, and enjoy, "putting on a show for everyone." He adds, "it's what we do."[25]

Grilling's place as a public event and (largely) men's station over the coals is not simply a matter of difference in terms of where one cooks. Relationships of power imbue our daily activities, including the cooking and eating on the blacktop before football games. Cooking in the public sphere, beyond the confines of the kitchen, connotes a kind of privilege, freedom, or agency among men, further distancing tailgate cookery from domestic spaces.[26] While Pableaux Johnson, author of the *ESPN Gameday Gourmet* cookbook acknowledges the connection between domestic and tailgate cookery, he is quick to assert the difference. "Even though tailgating is primarily considered . . . an outdoor sport, the fundamentals of cooking start in the kitchen," Johnson opines, adding, "it's the translation of these skills from home to the gameday parking lot that makes a truly great tailgater."[27] The hierarchical distinctions position food preparation in the kitchen as something one moves beyond to gain access to the more advanced and valued sphere of outdoor tailgate cookery.

The gendered divisions between cooking on the blacktop or in the kitchen are made even sharper by constructing the former as leisure and the latter as labor. Whereas women generally cook "to put supper on the table . . . men cook for nobler purposes."[28] The mundanity of cooking chores in the home, usually carried out by women, remains an obligation and burden.[29] On the other hand, tailgate cookery is marked by its extraordinariness and unique departure from the kitchen. Far from a task to simply be completed, food preparation on the blacktop is an *event* and not an everyday one at that.[30] Preparing tailgating feasts, at least according to one observer, provides men "a weekly opportunity for creativity and camaraderie."[31] Amid the pregame festivities, gadgets and grills remain centerpieces of the activity and serve to define the contours of manhood.

Even beyond the grill, the accoutrements utilized in tailgate cookery are conduits through which participants perform gender and bolster traditional conceptualizations of manhood.[32] Mario Batali writes in *Mario Tailgates NASCAR Style* that the desire for "newfangled gadget[s]" for use on the blacktop is what most men seek, because those gadgets, another observer notes, "can be half the fun." Cooking gadgets spark interest among men, as well as a bit of gendered self-reflection. Batali advises that various food preparation instruments may leave you wondering why you asked for "that portable blender for Christmas instead of a new set of wrenches."[33]

Another example of how various cooking instruments on the blacktop are used to bolster constructions of masculinity while simultaneously putting distance between tailgate food preparation and that in the domestic kitchen can be found in an episode of The Food Network's *Tailgate Warriors*, in which even the task of preparing a cake is rescued from its association with femininity and womanhood. Program host Guy Fieri announces that the Oakland Raiders tailgate team is "going to cook a cake on the grill." We then see team member Kirk pull out a large, bright yellow drill (to mix the cake batter). As he is mixing, he says, "here we go, power tools at a barbeque. Mixin' the cake, baby, mixing the cake."[34] As appears to be the case with Oakland's cake-bakers, cooking utensils utilized by men can be cartoonishly different from those implements used by women, which serves to make as remote as possible any association between men's and women's cooking.[35]

Cars, construction skills, and gadgets associated with men and masculinity blend together in providing cover, protecting men from the ambivalence they might feel when they cook. The Food Network's production of *Tailgate Warriors* is far from the only site in which expressions of masculinity are performed and on display in stadium parking lots. Beer brand Bud Light's fictive "Ultimate Tailgate Car" commercial is not very different from the reality of Kenny Johnson's Pinto at the Buffalo Bills tailgate. According to the commercial's narrator, "to make the ultimate tailgate car" involves making a variety of modifications to a vehicle. The car's owner explains that he replaced the gas tank with a keg of Bud

Light (and puts a tap into the tank and pours a beer for his buddy to illus-trate the point). He notes that the heater doubles as a popcorn popper (as we see popcorn coming out of the dashboard). And, he adds, "since we don't have gas, we don't need an engine." At which point the hood opens and exposes a large grill with a variety of meats cooking on it. And as a final touch, the front grill is pulled out to deliver condiments.[36] The com-mercial offers up Bud Light but also sells easily recognizable masculine signifiers in the process.

The extent to which tailgaters will go to customize their grills and other cooking devices underscores, among other things, the uniqueness of the event, as well as efforts to make it a special occasion. At University of Tennessee home games, Herschel's custom-built meat smoker and rotisserie is a popular attraction in Circle Park. His grilling machine features tires from an old Lincoln car he owned, smoke-stacks salvaged from an eighteen-wheeler, and a firebox in the back which he fills with hickory and pecan wood. Herschel did all of the welding on the three-thousand-pound contraption, and doesn't hesitate to put on a show for fans who stop by to marvel at his creation, often lifting the cover of the rotisserie and spritzing the meat with marinade from a spray bottle, treat-ing spectators to wafts of meat-scented smoke.[37] While custom grills do not always equate to oversize assemblages of steel they do speak to a tailgater's investment in the food they cook and the equipment on which that happens. On a considerably smaller scale, Oakland tailgater Sean fashioned his own smoker out of a repurposed twenty-pound drum bar-rel, a piece of rebar, and a stainless steel hook. Before putting it to use on the blacktop to smoke tri-tip and other assorted roasts of meat, he spent considerable time cleaning and seasoning the barrel with oak and walnut firewood. Sean prefers his method of lowering meat hanging on a hook into the smoker so that the meat won't shrink, "like it does on a grill."[38]

Tired of friends knocking over his grill, Jack, a regular at the New England Patriots tailgate in Foxboro, Massachusetts, decided to construct his own on more sturdy footing. In building his grill, Jack welded its base to some steel piping and then fit one end into his truck's hitch. For conve-nience, the grill simply rotates on the pipefitting so that Jack can lower the truck's tailgate, swing the grill from vehicle's bed, and commence cook-ing. Unlike the many other massive assemblies on the blacktop where food is cut or arranged to fit on the cooking surface, Jack constructed his grill to accommodate his signature dish: miniature lamb kebabs. The bite-sized pieces of meat and vegetables on skewers less than a foot long

Oakland tailgater Sean and his custom smoker, December 2015.
*Courtesy of authors.*

fit neatly and perfectly on a grill that isn't much bigger (save for a few spare inches to grill some brats).[39]

Similarly, Mitch, a University of Tennessee tailgater, recounts his efforts to tailor a grill to suit the cuisine, as well as the skillet in which the food is cooked. Initially Mitch and fellow tailgaters modified the lid of a

Weber grill to make room for his beloved twenty-six-inch cast iron skillet, an item he discovered in his parents' attic. Ingredients for their very popular Philly cheesesteak sandwiches were cooked in the large fry pan and it was better to modify the grill, in Mitch's view, than to change out the pan, since "people love a skillet." Not satisfied with the adaptations made to the Weber lid, Mitch special-ordered an oversize grill from the company to house the "monster" cast iron skillet.[40] The language employed to describe the skillet [monster], as well as the item's size, reinforces the notion of excess that feeds the gendered performances in tailgating.

In a good share of these tailgate settings and sites, a gendered spectacle is constructed in a central casting of men and masculinity, but also by positioning women and femininity as the marginalized other. This is evident in *Tailgate Warriors*. With few women on team rosters, serving as judges, or engaged in tailgating banter with Fieri, female participants are relegated to the show's sidelines. When women do enter the *Tailgate Warriors* frame they do so in ways that play on and play up conventional conceptualizations of femininity. In New Orleans, "Jambalaya Girl" (her real name is not asked or given) and her cooking team of "Yum-Yum Girls" illustrate this point. Fieri laments, "I only have the Kulinary Gangsters, she has the Yum-Yum Girls." Interestingly, the squad of "girls" do not cook on the blacktop, rather they serve as tasters who give dishes prepared by others "official approval" through song. In unison they sing out, "YUM YUM! Come get you some!" The camera closes in on Fieri who declares, to the delight of the Yum-Yum squad, "I'm gonna stay here for a little bit." The "girls," in doing gender, provide culinary cover for men as they serve as stereotypical objects of the heterosexual male gaze.[41]

As we have seen, men hold a central place in tailgating, both in the ways the activities are mediated to the public, as well as the lived experiences of those on the blacktop. Women are present, but rarely take up space behind the grill. When they do, we are offered different ways of thinking about gendered performances at the intersection of food and football. For example, Nancy has been leading one of the larger tailgate scenes outside of Stanford Stadium in Palo Alto, California for over a decade. Several canopies, trucks, and trailers comprise this particular tailgate area. She arrives forty-eight hours before game day to drop off trailers and other vehicles, heading back to the spot about seven hours prior to kickoff on Saturday. In that time separate areas for music or DJ setup, a donation table, desserts, drinks, side dishes, and meats pop up, sharing a landscape with lawn chairs, coolers, and trash containers.

Situated in the center of the action is an enormous Weber charcoal grill, with a width measuring over a yard. Nancy, clearly the life of the party, tells us that she invests nearly a thousand dollars each week in food, some of which sits in orderly sections on the massive Weber. As several pieces of tri-tip, vegetable kebabs, a large pot of beans, and other assorted items cook, Nancy seems calm. "She cooks," Nancy's husband chimes in, adding, "I eat and clean up."[42] Nancy is cooking but certainly not in a space defined as the province of women: behind a very large grill at a football tailgate.

The Southern University tailgate in Baton Rouge, Louisiana, where sisters Linda and Glinda take center stage around their lot's enormous grill-smoker- fryer is another location where gender arrangements are

Stanford tailgater Nancy and her mega-Weber grill, September 2016.
*Courtesy of authors.*

negotiated and contested. Linda and other members of their party have tailgated at football games at the historically black institution for three decades. That longevity is reflected in the size and organization of their tailgate. Two RVs about thirty feet apart provide some of the boundary markers for their space with the grill- smoker-fryer offering another. Linda coordinates the week's planning for the event, ensuring that families understand their individual responsibilities. Friday night the six families that make up the party arrive, eat fried chicken and gumbo, and "play the blues and drink booze." Saturday's menu usually includes boiled turkey necks, corn, and potatoes, all stewing in a very large pot with shrimp, red beans, and rice. While clearly women are central to all aspects of tailgate cooking at this location, there remain gendered divisions of labor, as Linda notes that "each lady makes a side dish." Those divisions are far from static, however. Glinda moves to prepare about sixty large chicken wings for the fryer at which point she cautions a male member of the party, "you go sit down, [the] ladies got this. If I need the heat adjusted, I'll call you for that. Now go sit down."[43]

These examples, though rare, push us to consider how gender arrangements in stadium lots prior to football games are far from fixed. On occasion, women do manage to contribute more than side dishes in preparing meat on grills and in fryers. In doing so, they challenge conceptions of food and gender at the football tailgate, in particular the association of men and meat.

## Culinary Complexity on the Blacktop

In a *Men's Life Today* story author Greg Melville was clear in outlining the commitment necessary on the part of serious tailgaters in honing and perfecting their skills on the blacktop. "Sure," the author notes, "the real celebrities are inside the stadium . . . but the parking lot is your place to shine as the Peyton Manning or Tom Brady of tailgating parties. Reaching [an] elite level isn't easy. It takes discipline, practice, the proper equipment and the right coaching."[44] Despite its rather tongue-in-cheek tone, the author's basic contention that committed tailgating is a serious undertaking not suited for amateurs or novices is one we saw plenty of support for across the many sites we explored for this book. One of the ways tailgating constructs spectacle and positions cookery as an appropriately masculine space is through culinary complexity. Given the prerequisite level of sophistication and expertise cookery is believed to require, it is thought to be beyond the capabilities of women and even of some men.

The culinary complexity on display across portions of every tailgate we visited and other sites under review here is in evidence within participant menu creations, preparation work, and ingredient lists, as well as the equipment used on the blacktop. As discussed in this chapter's previous section, spectacle is a unique piece of tailgate culture and here we explore how the notion of complexity informs and accentuates masculine performance in parking lots and other spaces during the pregame. These efforts, embellishments, and technological innovations serve to further separate cooking from the femininely coded domestic space of the kitchen, and distinguish tailgate cooking from backyard barbecuing. As a *Tailgate Warriors* contestant from Green Bay tells Fieri, "we don't just do brats and burgers, we can bring it."[45]

"Bring[ing] it" involves constructing tailgate cookery as a fine and challenging art, so unique it bears no resemblance to any domestic space. This process of complicating male cookery—grilling—is something, according to Michael Pollan, that is actively constructed by men. "Like most American men," Pollan admits, "I do a fine job of mystifying what is at bottom a very simple process, such a fine job, in fact, that my wife [is] by now convinced that grilling a steak over a fire is as daunting a procedure as changing a timing belt on a car."[46]

Both the *Tailgate Warriors* contestants and the fans interviewed on the blacktop display pride in their culinary repertoire and skills, and in many cases, go to great lengths to elevate stereotypical tailgate fare. Fieri and the judges frequently comment on this dynamic during the competitions. Early in the Packers vs. Seahawks episode, Fieri pointedly tells the viewing audience, "it's not all fun and games out here on the blacktop. You think these people are just making hot dogs and cheese dip?" Indeed, the tailgaters go well beyond wieners in their competitive efforts. For example, the Green Bay menu features "BBQ baked beans with a smoky paprika infused slaw . . . elk tenderloin with fresh goat cheese, Door County cherry chutney, and Wisconsin cured pancetta" followed by a dessert of "honey crisp apple fritter with a caramel candy crust and six-year cheddar chaser."[47] Similarly, Kirk from Oakland tells Fieri, "we didn't want to just throw a burger on the grill, anyone can do that." Far from a simple burger, the Oakland team presents "an abalone poke, a pickled-ginger kickin' mango salsa—fresh wild Alaskan salmon with a fresh-made Caribbean jerk sauce," plus "Bad Girl BBQ beans . . . soy sangria marinated tri-tip, arroz con pollo, garnished with some julienne fried potatoes."[48] Scotty from Buffalo tells Fieri, "I'm preparing our spicy corn medley, we've got an onion, a red pepper, an orange pepper, one jalapeno—we may add another. Then we're goin' to add some sweet corn to it and we're gonna finish it off with a little bit of tarragon."[49] In the masculine performance space of tailgating, herbs are not so much feminine signifiers as cool cultural currency.[50]

The preparation required for each contestant's chosen menu is also indicative of complexity. In addition to his grilling duties, BBQ Bob of Oakland, for example, is "in charge of making a marinade for the salmon and it's got nineteen ingredients, seven of 'em chopped by hand." In the Vikings vs. Saints episode, Fieri notes "Reggie's still rollin' the prep table, choppin' never seems to end for this ambitious parking lot menu. Even the pineapple pound cake dessert needs a good deal of prep." In some instances, the prep work for the competition started well before the cameras were rolling. The main ingredient of the abalone poke featured by the Oakland team had to be harvested from the ocean. As Fieri explains, "abalone is a gem of the sea, you can't buy it, you have to have a buddy that goes diving for it and if you don't treat it right it can end up tough and rubbery."[51] Not only is abalone hard to obtain, but it is a high-risk ingredient to cook. Moreover, its procurement is a form of hunting—another archetypal masculine signifier.

The majority of the *Tailgate Warriors* teams have elaborate cooking setups and custom vehicles to transport their mobile kitchens. For example, Oakland's team has a state-of-the-art RV decked out in silver and black Raiders imagery. In addition to the RV's kitchen, the team cooks on a large outdoor grill—the aforementioned "grill-zilla"—and uses the RV to power high-end appliances such as a rice cooker and pressure cooker. The Buffalo tailgaters modified their grill specifically for the *Tailgate Warriors* competition. Scotty explains to Fieri, "we actually took this grill and added a foot to it just for this competition because we wanted to make sure that we had enough space." Fieri appreciates the advantage this modification provides for cooking meat, noting "with twenty-six square feet, that flat surface is big enough for Buffalo's giant pork tenderloin. And the box up on top works like a convection oven." In fact, early in the Chicago Bears vs. Buffalo Bills episode, Fieri surveys the scene and declares, "it looks more like I'm at an *Iron Chef* competition. Check these out, we have scales, really dynamite knives, I mean we've got about every kitchen utensil you can possibly ask for."[52] The Food Network's *Iron Chef*, which features teams of elite professional chefs squaring off against each other in a similar competitive sports format, has been hailed as "a quint-essential spectacle of machismo" and by the Food Network itself as a cross between ultimate fighting and Julia Child.[53] Both *Iron Chef* and *Tailgate Warriors* support hegemonic masculinity and challenge constructions of cooking as nurturing and family-centered labor.[54]

With complexity bordering on professionalization, and references to hunting and the primacy of meat as further cover, *Tailgate Warriors* competitors can focus on presentation without jeopardizing their masculine credentials. After a description of his Louisiana hot sauce reduction, Reggie tells Fieri, "I want it to be up, to plate it. I want it to be pretty."[55] A Buffalo tailgater is similarly preoccupied with the presentation of his sea-food appetizer: "I'm working on a warm bacon vinaigrette that's gonna go over our four straight scallops. The scallops are actually going to be plated on a little bed of baby spinach."[56] These examples indicate the special quality of men's cooking that distinguishes it from the everyday domestic provenance of the kitchen.[57] Tailgating is a prime example of how "the fes-tal pattern of male cooking generates and maintains a celebratory attitude which shows up in the adoption of specialties, the preemption of week-end meals and guest-dinners, or greater inclinations to experiment."[58] This kind of attention to detail is also a function of professional organi-zation. While women are more frequently tasked with cooking for daily sustenance in the home, men typically cook in professional spaces or for special meals or unique social occasions. Fieri, for example, is impressed with Oakland's execution of their menu: "Over on the Raiders side it's economy of motion. You can tell they've been cookin' together for years. These guys are running like a well-oiled machine. I mean, communica-tion, hittin' the mark."[59] Fieri could be describing a restaurant's kitchen staff, or a professional football team's offensive line.

Consumerism linked to equipment is also apparent in the theme of complexity. Food Network shows incorporate elaborate and expensive "food processing, food preparation, and food cooking technology," all of which is on display in *Tailgate Warriors*.[60] Furthermore, the network markets product lines for many of its celebrity chefs and is adept at adver-tising these items during broadcasts of its shows. For example, during *Tailgate Warriors* episodes, pop-up ads for Fieri's line of knives appear numerous times. Indeed, as Adler notes, "liberated male cooks are more likely to spend substantial sums of money on fancy and special-purpose cookware" than female cooks are.[61] Marketing firms, for their part, are quick to capitalize on men's predilection toward purchasing expensive kitchen gadgetry.[62] Not only does grilling over hot flames validate men's cooking as masculine, it also gives men masculine cover when shopping for cookware and other assorted kitchen accessories.

Interestingly for San Francisco 49ers fan and *Tailgate Warriors* competitor Mike, it is the absence of power appliances and gadgets that reaffirms someone's status as a good cook on the blacktop. Where is the skill, Mike asks, in household mixers or rice cookers? Preparing food without the aid of electrical devices "brings up the skill [and] the difficulty." When asked his thoughts on the opposing *Tailgate Warriors* team's use of a powerful rice cooker, he responds tersely, "cheating."[63] While Mike has little use for the technological gadgets employed by other tailgaters, like his culinary colleagues, expertise and technique remain central to how he understands and defines himself as a cookery specialist on the blacktop.

Tailgate cookery performed by men can reinforce particular constructions of masculinity in the ways in which food preparation is discussed. For example, in referencing the "science" of cooking, men perform gender by emphasizing skill and the chemical complexities of preparing meat and other dishes.[64] When asked to name his favorite piece of cooking equipment, 49ers tailgater Nick quickly responds that it is his smoker. To which he adds, "I don't know maybe it's my engineering background. I like all the intricacies that go into smoking and knowing how different cuts of meat react to different heats over time." Far from simple, cookery requires a kind of skill only attainable through lecture and training. "I'm schooling [fellow tailgater] George on different thermometers and all that. The science behind it all."[65]

Like a good scientist, for Nick experimentation forms the core of how best to approach cookery. Nick is proud of himself when "getting outside [his] comfort zone" by testing various rubs and sauces—he also admires the impulse to experiment displayed by others who cook around him. When asked how he honed his cookery expertise, Nick notes that he did a lot of "research and experimented" with different herbs, spices, techniques, and ingredient combinations to perfect his craft. When it comes to his tailgate team he holds the same perspective on experimentation: that it is something to be fostered and admired. Despite what he believes is the high stakes environment of producing great-tasting food at his tailgate, there is little question when a teammate states, "I'm gonna try chicken sliders today."[66] The trust built among comrades in cookery aids in taking risk.[67] Framed as building and honing cookery's technical knowledge, while encouraging discovery, actions such as these are welcomed among tailgaters like Nick. Traditional notions of masculinity are unconsciously performed in these moments, we contend, as the individual tailgater's freedom to experiment connote a kind of agency and independence.

A successful tailgate, given the activity's complexity, requires both skill and strategy, qualities typically assigned to men. Certainly not for amateurs, chef Mario Batali offers direction and perspective to those interested in preparing a pregame feast: "You've got to have a plan. You can't just wake up and decide to put stuff together that morning."[68] Frequent references to football serve as added ways in which cookery, in a tailgate setting, is linked to men and competitive constructions of masculinity. Favorable results on the blacktop necessitate that, "just like an NFL coach, the game-day cook has to have a plan in place if he expects to have a winning result."[69] Creativity and adaptability born out of practice and concentration guarantee that, "the more you cook, the more you'll be able to compensate for the field conditions on any given Saturday."[70] In conflating football and cookery, such narratives close the distance between the two, lending even more credibility to the activity as appropriately masculine.

## "Motorhome: The Ultimate Tailgate Machine"

There has long been a strong relationship between football tailgating (and its precursor—the football picnic) and motoring. Ford's Model A vehicles in the first years of the twentieth century were some of the first motorized carriages to bring picnickers and their assorted culinary delights to the grassy spaces outside of football stadiums. Motorized vehicles continue to be very important in transporting tailgaters to their destinations, though perhaps not always in a form imaginable a hundred years ago. Along with cars and sport utility vehicles, recreational vehicles or motorhomes convey tailgaters in grand (and quite large) twenty-first century style and in doing so become part of the gendered performances within the setting.

The motorhome's relationship to tailgating is one cultivated by those interested in promoting the mammoth homes on wheels, as well as officials from college and professional football. In 2010 the Family Motor Coach Association (FMCA) made its position clear with an article headline, "Motorhome: the Ultimate Tailgating Machine." Beginning in the

1990s a number of chapters of "rolling residences" have formed at various college football locations across the country.[71] The relationship is not just within the college ranks, however. There is no greater clue to the tightly woven connection between the recreational vehicle and professional football than the Recreational Vehicle Industry Association's (RVIA) 2008 multi-million-dollar ad campaign. The group made its first-ever Super Bowl buy of commercial time on television. "Go RVing" was a "featured advertiser" in the game program, and several elements of the recreational vehicle industry had a strong presence at the pregame activities and exhibits in the days leading up to the big game.[72]

Completely altering the fan experience, the (sometimes) enormous homes on wheels brought significant change to tailgating. At lengths stretching up to forty-five feet and costing well over a million dollars, the vehicles glide easily into large parking slots in stadium lots designed with motorhomes in mind. "Consider that the motor home is exactly as big as its name suggests," one observer noted, "it's as though someone put four wheels and a transmission on a standard American two-bedroom ranch dwelling and drove it off the lot."[73] The potential benefits of the supersize rigs to tailgaters are enough to make one giddy. The mobile home's sheer size enhances the "lure of parking lot picnicking [tailgating]" and enables fans to "[stuff] whole kitchens, including refrigerators, grills, smokers, and ovens," among other items, into their vehicles.[74] At some stadiums across the country hundreds of motorhomes "cram together in tight little perpendicular clusters, like bacilli in a petri dish." The tailgate is no longer "confined to three hours—it could last three days," with bathrooms and bedrooms in ample supply.[75] In addition to amending standard tailgating schedules, as well as the size and scope of the tailgate feast, the vehicles also become part of the attraction and spectacle on the blacktop before games, giving men still other ways to express masculinity through the size and extravagance of their RVs.

Kevin's rig, parked on a September day in 2017 at the Raiders tailgate near the Coliseum in Oakland, was one of the larger motorhomes at the stadium and one of the many attractions in that location. He conceded that the recreational vehicle was one of two "big boy toys" he owned, a boat the other. The Raiders fan characterized tailgating before the purchase of his forty-foot Phaeton recreational vehicle as, "slummin' it by bringing the barbecue in the trunk of the car." Those days were clearly a relic of the past as he proudly showed me through a unit that had four televisions, an electric fireplace, and four slide-outs.[76] When Kevin first drove his sizable home on wheels into the Raider lot in 2015, he led other tailgaters eager to see inside on tours through his motorhome. Demand soon exceeded a willingness to supply, however, as Kevin acknowledged his wife put a stop to the tours. Kevin conceded that he was working his way up to a Newell (considered top-of-the-line motor coaches, some with a two-million-dollar price tag), but for the time being the quarter-million-dollar vehicle he owned would suffice.[77]

Parked at the Coliseum, nearby Kevin's motorhome, Jesse's customized van had mural-like Raider Nation images painted across every square inch of its surface. Far from the biggest rig or the most expensive (purchased from its original owner for just twenty-eight hundred dollars in 2016), it had nonetheless become the reason why several tailgaters went out of their way to stroll by, snapping pictures, and giving Jesse a knowing nod of approval as they did. The only foreseeable change in the thirty-year-old van's future would be to update the mural with some current players, but otherwise the plan was to just leave it as he bought it. Its weathered look would be sealed to "leave it looking old, like the Raiders—beat up and hard core," Jesse said. He was eager for the van to carry this vibe to Vegas "to remind folks of who the Raiders are" when the team begins play in their new city in 2019.[78]

A central attraction in the University of Oregon tailgate lots is the original Duck bus, a converted school bus decked out in green and gold Oregon colors and other related football paraphernalia. Mike, the proud owner and custom outfitter of the bus, has it stocked with a microwave, deep freezer, and generator. In addition, there is a deep fryer and a smoker on a metal platform that extends out from the back of the bus, accessible either by ladder or the emergency exit door. Mike and his buddies typically prepare for a crowd of twenty to thirty tailgaters, with the bus serving as the hub around which they revel in "hanging out with friends, enjoying football, good food, and booze."[79] In these examples, a vehicle's excessive size or its unique customization perpetuates long held bonds between masculinity and motoring.

Other outlets are eager to capitalize on the deeply rooted association between motorhomes and football. Dr. Pepper's widely popular advertising campaign and its series of television commercials feature the fictive "Larry Culpepper" as a quirky fan who drives to college football games in his "Tailgate 2000," a classic 1980s motorhome.[80] In the inaugural ad the opening lines are replete with gender symbolism, with the links between man and motorhome (and Dr. Pepper of course) made clear.

Power . . . steering wheel;
Performance . . . shift;
Pigskin . . . seat;
Pepper . . . ice cold.
Perfectly engineered for tailgate, home gate, well any type of gate . . .[81]

Though the commercial is a parody, is it nonetheless instructive as it plays on popular discourses about tailgate culture and the associations commonly assumed about football, masculinity, and motoring.

## Conclusion

Rob Finley, a lifelong University of Arkansas football fan, dreamed of his "extreme tailgate" vehicle for years before it came to fruition. Finley's refurbished fire truck, or as it is affectionately called, "Engine 66 tailgate machine," complete with its flat screen TV, grill, and smoker took well over a year to renovate. Cooking surfaces easily accommodate briskets, racks of ribs, and other culinary treats that can feed more than one hundred people for Razorback home games. Like countless other examples on football stadium parking lots across the country, Finley's "head turning"[82] smoker is the beau of the ball.

It is within these spaces, filled with oversize and creatively engineered grills and other cooking apparatuses, that gender is continually (re)constructed. Masculinities, then, are both displayed and performed via cookery practices on the blacktop before football games and throughout the tailgates. Consequently, the tailgate spectacle is formed in large part by masculine performances, as they are enacted very publicly on the blacktop, where equipment and cookery discourses are fundamental to bolstering gendered expression. This picture is incomplete however, as the spectacle's star is that which is grilled, smoked, or roasted with the gadgets and devices tailgaters use. We turn now to meat and its central place on the grill, as well as its role in the masculine performances on stage at football tailgates.

# 3.

# "We're in the Steel Business, There's Not A Lot of Vegetarians"

*Meat in Tailgate Culture*

## Introduction

If you spend a significant amount of time on the blacktop, there is a good chance that you will come home at the end of the day with your clothes and hair reeking of smoke and barbecued meat. And that you will wake up the next morning still smelling of smoke and barbecued meat, despite showering and shampooing before bed. From Buffalo to Oakland, professional stadiums to college campuses, one overwhelmingly common feature of tailgate culture is meat—pounds and pounds of brats, burgers, hot dogs, carne asada, baby back ribs, tri-tip, pork shoulder, chicken wings, bacon, brisket, hot links, and carnitas prepared in or on a ubiquitous array of Webers, Colemans, deep fryers, rotisseries, and handcrafted smokers of all sizes. In addition, there are the unique-to-place offerings of alligator, lobster, turkey neck, whole roasted pig, duck gumbo, and deer sausage.

In this chapter, we turn our attention to the food that is at the center of the tailgating spectacle, and the myriad ways that food serves as a signifier of gender. The primary focus of our analysis is meat—as both extension of and exclamation point following the various forms of blacktop spectacle noted in the previous chapter. As evidenced in television and film depictions of tailgating, our interactions and observations with those on the blacktop, and throughout the pages of the increasing number of tailgate cookbooks, meat reigns supreme outside stadiums before football games. We consider representations of tailgating and tailgate fare in these forms of popular culture, as well as how gender is performed as tailgaters prepare, serve, and consume food.

Like sports, food is a part of the social construction of gender. Just as physical contact team and individual sports are strongly associated with

Grillmaster George of 3rdRail9ers, October 2015. *Courtesy of authors.*

masculinity, meat has been historically constructed as a masculine food, and eating meat as a male activity.[1] Indeed, "an archetype of gendering food is the relationship between maleness and meat."[2] When we add the positioning of meat as an essential and nutritious food item in many cultures to the discursive connection between meat and masculinity, we see how meat has come to occupy a privileged status as the essence of a meal, to the point that meatless meals are viewed as somehow lacking.[3] In the United States, meat has been culturally established as a necessary component of a complete meal.[4] Alternatively, vegetables and other non-meat foods such as yogurt, fruit, rice, pasta, milk, and chocolate are coded feminine in the gendered construction of food. Thus, these foods, and vegetarianism more generally, are culturally constructed as feminine and associated with women.[5] This discursive connection between vegetarian fare and femininity serves to both symbolically and literally marginalize women and alternate expressions of masculinity that do not hinge on aggressive and dominant behavior.

## Meating on the Blacktop

According to author Michael Pollan, "killing and cooking a large animal has never been anything but an emotionally freighted and spiritually charged endeavor. Then, as now, the mood in fire cooking is heroic, masculine, theatrical, beastly, unironic, and faintly (sometimes not so faintly) ridiculous."[6] Whether it is a few steaks or a whole hog, "cooking meat over a fire," he claims, is "one of the most stirring of those ritual acts" performed by men to mark, among other things, "male power."[7] Grilling or smoking of meat confers a kind of culinary capital on men in which status accrues as a result of conforming to dominant expectations around food and consumptive practices.[8] These ritualistic performances are enjoyed by men and seen as both a leisured choice and as a biological imperative. "Grilling," one observer notes, "taps into the primeval male urge to make and manage fire, and it generally involves two other beloved guy entities: sharp knives and alcohol."[9] Outdoor barbecuing, and its association with meat and tools, provides men a space to affirm their masculine identity at home.[10] As barbecue culture increasingly influenced tailgate culture, men took up the task of devising menus and grilling carnivorous fare for stadium crowds. The domestic male space of the backyard barbecue, aided by the cover of football and meat, transferred seamlessly to the spectacle on the blacktop, thus providing men with another means of affirming masculine identity in public.

Tailgating's carnivorous tendencies, as portrayed in television and film, serve to fortify constructions of rugged masculinity. This is not a surprising dynamic in the mediated space of *Tailgate Warriors*, given the already established brand of Guy Fieri as hypermasculine celebrity chef. It is a brand that depends on the type of male viewers and contest participants who are already invested in the men-and-meat construction of masculinity that Fieri embodies. For example, meat featured prominently in the menus created by the mostly male teams, drove the competitive narrative of the episodes, and through its primacy, relegated vegetables to the periphery of tailgate cooking. The menus and the running commentary of *Tailgate Warriors* provide ample evidence of the primacy of meat to tailgate culture. Each team includes meat as the centerpiece of its entrée, and in some cases, its appetizers and side dishes, too. For example, the team representing the Green Bay Packers submits a menu "built around grilled elk, brat sliders, and chicken."[11] When questions arise regarding the temperature of Green Bay's grill and the time the elk has to cook, Fieri declares, "without the elk, the entry is shot."[12] In the contest between Oakland and San Francisco, the team representing the Raiders indicates how important tri-tips are to their entry when Bob explains, "I've got three tri-tips staggered so we present the best piece of lookin' meat for these judges."[13] In his assessment of his team's performance, Mike from San Francisco reflects, "you know, we pulled it off. We came to the competition—it's about the meat, ribs versus tri-tip, that's it."[14] During the Vikings vs. Saints matchup, the following exchange between Jason (New Orleans) and Fieri displays the competitors' preoccupation with pork:

> Jason: Everything tastes better when it's surrounded by a little bit of pig.
>
> Fieri: I agree with you on that.

In fact, the love of all things pork permeates the blacktop and is encapsulated nicely on camera by an anonymous tailgater during the introduction to the Packers vs. Seahawks episode when he proclaims, "nothing says love like bacon." Banter between Dr. BBQ and Fieri during the 49ers vs. Raiders episode further illustrates the primacy of meat for the judges:

> Dr. BBQ: Arroz con pollo—I'm always happy to see somebody sneak in an extra protein into a side dish."
>
> Fieri: Don't threaten me with extra protein.[15]

Meat's place as a symbol of hegemonic masculinity is, perhaps, nowhere more explicitly seen than in an exchange between Fieri and an Oakland Raiders tailgater. Meat and masculinity merge on the blacktop, elevating the activity to the status of a national ritual. Fieri asserts that tailgating "isn't just a contest, this is an American tradition." With the image of an American flag flying in the background and a pig roasting on a spit in the foreground, Fieri exclaims, "dude, that is fantastic . . . the question is, a whole hog?!" To which the Raider fan declares, "absolutely. She's been goin' since 8:30 last night . . . We slept in the parking lot to keep an eye on her."[16] Male ownership and control of the public sphere is enacted in and through tailgating culture and food, where meat, in particular, forms part of the foundation on which this process occurs.

Preoccupation with meat also drives the broadcast narrative of the *Tailgate Warriors* competitions to create a sense of drama and suspense. In the 49ers vs. Raiders episode, the judges maintain a running dialogue about San Francisco contestant Mike's ribs. Dr. BBQ doubts that Mike can grill perfect ribs in such a short amount of time: "I think the ribs are going to be the real key. That's their signature entrée and one hour's just not long enough to cook ribs properly. Let's see if they can do it."[17] Fieri is incredulous that the San Francisco team is only preparing one rack of ribs for the contest.

> Fieri: You only have one rack of ribs. What if they fall on the
> ground?
> Mike: That's a chance I have to take.[18]

In the Packers vs. Seahawks episode, Fieri's play-by-play throughout much of the competition focuses on Green Bay's elk dish and grill man. Fieri notes that, "Chef Andy is worrying that Chris the grill man is spending too much valuable time on the side dish" and that "Andy's frustrated his grill guy hasn't gotten to the meat." After Chris puts the elk on the grill, Fieri continues to construct drama around meat: "The judges and Chef Andy are also keeping a close eye on the elk tenderloin that finally hit the grill," but "the time spent on the slaw could end up killin' the main course." The judges emphatically reiterate how exalted meat dishes are throughout the competitions, a dramatic device illustrated nicely by Fieri's proclamation: "Perfect slaw isn't going to make up for undercooked elk."[19]

Fictional television and film representations of tailgating further reinforce the primacy of meat in tailgate culture as they simultaneously reproduce gender difference. *The Simpsons* episode "Any Given Sundance," as discussed in the previous chapter, opens with Homer at the wheel of the Simpson family car, en route to the Springfield University football stadium. As the car pulls into the parking lot, we see men grilling meat on all manner of contraptions. Homer proceeds to teach Bart the fine art of tailgate "mooching," and the father and son duo eat their way around the stadium parking lot, consuming steaks, ribs, and hot dogs, thus demonstrating men's affinity for large portions of food that are male-identified.[20] In the meantime, Marge tries to convince a sullen Lisa to enjoy the party—even though she's a girl—by helping her wash discarded foam fingers.[21] In the animated, satirical world of *The Simpsons*, meat is the essential tailgating food, prepared and eaten primarily by men, while girls and women are relegated to the margins of the tailgate ritual.

Similarly, meat serves, in examples from sport film, as the ingredient that reinscribes gender arrangements on the blacktop. Even fleeting tailgating scenes in movies feature meat as the quintessential tailgate food. Early in the film *Big Fan*, we see a tableau of images from tailgate parties in the parking lot of the New York Giants stadium. As Paul, a parking garage attendant who calls himself the "world's biggest New York Giants fan" and his best friend Sal walk through the lot, they pass mostly male tailgaters, grilling sausages and burgers. Here again, meat is presented as the primary tailgate food, and tailgating as a predominantly masculine experience.[22] The classic underdog film *Rudy* is another case in point. The plot revolves around Rudy Reittiger, who despite his small stature, finally gets to fulfill his dream of dressing for a game as a member of the storied University of Notre Dame football team. In a brief scene of tailgaters braving the cold in the South Bend, Indiana stadium parking lot before the pivotal game, we see fans flipping meat on grills and eating hot dogs.[23] There is a good deal of cultural work enacted in these examples, wherein utopian understandings of agency and sport are tightly bound as they help to strengthen the bonds among men, masculinity, and meat.

Gendered discourses underscoring the relationship between athleticism and masculinity are also linked to tailgating's preoccupation with meat in the visual and scripted narratives associated with the activity on the blacktop. In *Tailgate Warriors* Dr. BBQ's appreciation of grilled animal flesh and its links to masculine performativity is on display in the Chicago Bears vs. Buffalo Bills episode. He surveys the blacktop, stating his approval of the tailgate competitors before him: "I see a lot of meat and a lot of fire and that's a good thing." Masculinist understandings of athleticism form the core elements around which Dr. BBQ's admiration flows, but the gendered performances by which he is so intrigued are not only based on skill but also on risk. "Hot pans movin' around, guys with big sharp knives. This is kind of dangerous," he states, "it's exciting. I like it."

Tailgate-themed television commercials, including the following example from Pepsi, borrow heavily from the ritual and rhetoric of an American football broadcast in their depiction of tailgating. Tailgate scenes outside a football stadium are shown as a series of highlights while NFL Films theme music plays in the background and a male voice-over calls the action as if it were game play-by-play. The narrator of the commercial intones: "Every Sunday these bold warriors meet in a quest for glory. Proud gladiators whose game is equal parts preparation and passion. When men become myths and moments become legends. The game is tailgating, the cola is Pepsi." In this commercial, male tailgaters are presented as "bold warriors" and "proud gladiators" as they light a Weber, flip meat with tongs, grill oversize turkey legs, and carefully monitor whole birds spinning on a rotisserie. Despite shots of corn roasting on a segregated grill top—away from the meat—and two men executing a salad bowl handoff as if the bowl was a football, the ad culminates with meat at the center of the action. A male tailgater makes a leaping, one-handed catch of a turkey leg as if it was thrown for the game-winning touchdown—an action that serves as another example of how meat and football are discursively linked in American culture.[24] Tailgaters are transformed from passive spectators to athletic performers in this ad, demonstrating how men's experiences with food are associated with physical strength and action-oriented masculinity.[25]

Similarly, as Bob Sloan writes in *The Tailgating Cookbook*, "a man feels more of a man when he's eating a steak ... When he's eating his steak in the parking lot, in his mind he's down on the field, right there in the huddle, getting his number called for the next play."[26] In this scenario, red meat confers a masculinity that affirms athletic prowess, thereby reinforcing its place at the top of the meat hierarchy and maintaining the cultural idea that meat is needed for masculine performance. Others reiterate the seamlessness of football and meat along with men's natural connection to each. The tailgate is "a time when the grill connects directly to the gridiron,"[27] and the trusty backyard grill is "simple to use and familiar to just about every American male."[28] Debbie Moose underlines this same theme in her note on NASCAR tailgates in *Fan Fare*, claiming that "the food for these speed fans needs to be big: ribs, burgers, and steaks."[29] Appetites among tailgaters, it seems, require sizable amounts of animal proteins to sustain not only performance but one's identity as a man. Thus, the voracious appetites often attributed to football players—and the associated hypermasculine image—are extended to those who celebrate their exploits on the blacktop.[30] Among other culinary functions, the tailgate cookbooks in these examples and others are prescriptive, everyday texts which communicate societal gender norms, thus serving as key artifacts within the social construction of gender.[31]

Importantly, it is not simply the presence of meat but also its size that matters in signifying its gendered position in tailgate culture. Author James Twitchell, almost giddy at the prospect of grilled animal protein in an all-male space, concludes, "you can throw a hunk of meat the size of Sri Lanka" on the heat and by the time you check out the beer supplies for your guests the meat is done.[32] Others, too, make mention of size and the importance of big equipment and meat. No less a football authority than John Madden proclaims, "you can't have serious tailgating without barbe-cuing. There's something about making a fire and gathering around it that brings people together."[33] The heat source and type of grill matter, too. For a thick cut of steak, Madden cautions readers, "you can't do this on a little grill. You need a big grill and you need some way to get the meat about two feet above the fire."[34] His proclamations, along with chapter titles like "The Big Cuts of Meat Food Group" and "Pieces of Meat and Mastering Heat," plus the long litany of meat-based recipes in his book, are further testament to the primacy of meat in excessive form on the blacktop.[35]

References to and associations with small plates and less-than-gigantic food offerings are to be rejected on classed and gendered grounds at the tailgate. Sloan pointedly informs readers that his beef satay is "not the artfully shaped sliver of meat that you might be offered at a gallery opening. Not a miniature swatch of sirloin . . . but an ample, butch piece of tasty grilled beef on a stick."[36] The larger the cut of meat, the more masculine the griller, the eater, and the activity around which they coalesce. Descriptions and value-laden assessments about size are consistently defined by what they are not—small. Johnson, backed by the ESPN brand, reinforces this idea with his proclamation that "fussy little finger foods have no place at an actual college tailgate. . . . What fans crave are dishes that speak to the rough-and-tumble nature of the collegiate gridiron—slabs of meat cooked over an open flame, oversize vats of gut-warming chili."[37] The perceived precious atmosphere of art gallery openings, with their bite-sized portions offered to patrons on silver trays, are no match for tailgate parties in the hypermasculine world of food and football.

Keen attentiveness to meat, given its important place on the menu, extends to the amount of animal flesh cooked as well as the special care given to its preparation. In discussions with tailgaters, it is worth not-ing, the value of special pieces of cooking equipment was almost always linked to the preparation of meat. Brad—a parks and recreation manager during the week and committed tailgater on fall Saturdays at University of Tennessee home games—fills his two smokers with Boston butt, sausage, brisket, burgers, hot dogs, chicken, and almost as an afterthought, baked potatoes. The marinade for his pork butt features apple juice or cider, Gentleman Jack, brown sugar, and agave—and that is after it rests overnight and smokes for three to four hours with a cinnamon-, garlic powder-, and paprika-based dry rub. In another area of the University of Tennessee campus, Herschel and Hank cook one hundred pounds of baby back ribs, chicken wrapped in bacon, and sausage rolls (also featuring bacon) in their custom-built smoker. The night before a tailgate, all of the meat gets a dry rub of chili powder, Mrs. Dash's, pepper, and seasoned salt. Sometimes, there is also a 'whiskey sauce'—Herschel's term for Worcestershire sauce—marinade.[38] On the masculinity scale, carefully concocted, multiple-ingredient rubs and sauce treatments register as highly as big slabs of red meat and gargantuan grills in the tailgating landscape.

Seismic Mike, a Buffalo Bills fan "since they were good," conscientiously attends, like so many other tailgaters, to the care of meat and the instruments on which it is cooked. Several hours before kickoff he

University of Tennessee tailgater Herschel, September, 2015.
*Courtesy of Maria J. Veri.*

works on a huge custom-made combination grill and smoker to feed his employee tailgate parties of thirty to fifty people. When we stopped by during the breakfast hour before an early afternoon game, the flat-top grilling surface featured eggs and two kinds of bacon. The ribs in the smoker, however, were the crown jewel of Mike's tailgate. They had been smoking over Applewood charcoal since seven o'clock the night before.[39] Not to be outdone among a sea of male grill specialists, Stanford University tailgater, Nancy, always has tri-tip on her larger-than-life Weber, regardless of what else is on her menu. The tri-tip meets the charcoal flames only after marinating for two days in a mixture of soy sauce, mustard, garlic powder, salt, and pepper.[40] The high status placed upon meat is reflected in these examples, as is its continued association with gender and power. Even with the forceful presence of female tailgaters like Nancy, meat's totalizing, consuming presence on the blacktop continues to mark the boundaries of manhood and masculinity.

On the University of Oregon campus, Mike of the original Duck bus gives chicken the fancy treatment as the centerpiece of his tailgate. The smoked and brined chicken halves are seasoned with the "holy trinity" of rosemary, thyme, and sage, plus onions, lemon, oil-based salad dressing, salt, brown sugar, and McCormick's Montreal seasoning.[41] Tailgaters aren't as judgmental about poultry as some cookbook authors, but they do often fortify it with an array of flavorful ingredients, or a pork product. As noted in the previous chapter, complex preparations are a common aspect of the tailgate spectacle; this practice is especially evident where meat is concerned.

Not too far away from the Duck bus, Dan's nine-year commitment to his grilling duties at home University of Oregon games and his Traeger smoker represent the embodiment of gendered cookery and food practices. His usually meat-centric menu features brats, hot dogs, burgers, tri-tip, and chicken. The smoker, his most essential and cherished piece of equipment—other than his crew's refurbished bright yellow pickup truck—is the *pièce de résistance* of the tailgate. The large, heavy mass of metal easily carries the pounds of meat cooking on its surface, while also serving as a symbolic artifact in fortifying a masculine identity—tied as it is to food. Referencing his occupation, Dan shares, "we're in the steel business," adding, "there's not a lot of vegetarians." Among other cultural and culinary functions, the smoker yields "the best bacon on this earth."[42] On a slightly smaller scale, the deep fryer is the most essential piece of cooking equipment in the tricked-out kitchen of Mike's converted duck bus. If the

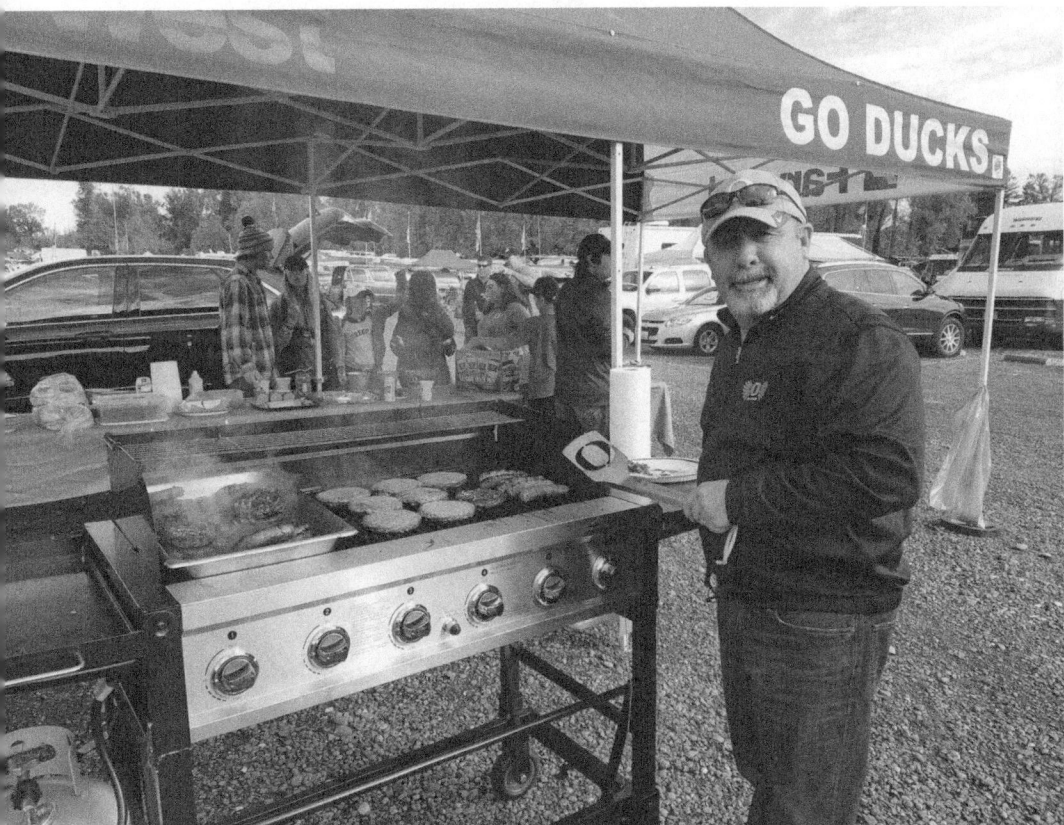

University of Oregon tailgater Dan, October 2016. *Courtesy of Maria J. Veri.*

deep fryer isn't there, he says, "people want to know where it is."[43] Mike and his buddy Mark use it for french fries, onion rings, jalapeno mozzarella sticks, and corn dogs, but the one item that's a must is chicken wings. Tailgaters, as this example illustrates, often accessorize meat with other items that are seen as masculinizing—fried fare, spicy foods, but not, say, asparagus or tofu.[44] Sometimes tailgaters prize simple tools for the preparation of meat. Nick of the 3rdRail9ers stressed the importance of having good tongs on the blacktop—"there's no fork in my tailgate, because I'm not piercing anything"—and his meat thermometer is always at hand, typically in a pocket of his shorts, for precisely measuring the temperature of the meats he smokes. For serious blacktop specialists like Nick, the piercing of the meat is a negligible sacrifice for the sake of the specific scientific value the thermometer provides. Throughout these examples, the thorough attention to detail, intense preparation, specialized equipment and care help to secure meat's place at the top of the tailgate food chain and as the foremost marker of masculinity.

All meat is not created equal, however, as there is a clear and established hierarchy that exists in the construction and reification of masculine identity on the blacktop as reflected through discourses about various food

Nick of the 3rdRail9ers at work in front of his smoker, October 2015.
*Courtesy of authors.*

items. The ordered rankings represent more than personal taste and are linked to understandings of gender and man- or womanhood. Red meat is king, followed by pork products, with poultry trailing further behind. Fish and seafood are barely able to hold a place on the tailgater's grill and table. Recall, for example, that in the 49ers vs. Raiders *Tailgate Warriors* episode, abalone is acknowledged as one of the team's appetizers, but host Guy Fieri is quick to note its exceptionalism. While abalone is the "gem of the sea," you cannot just run to the grocery store to get it, you instead must "have a buddy [go] diving for it."[45] The skill and risk in acquiring it afford the marine snails masculine credibility and thus a place at the table.

Generally, however, distinctions are made to distinguish red meat and pork from poultry and fish. Tellingly, in chef Mario Batali's conception of tailgate fare, chicken and fish are presented in a chapter separate from red meat. In the notes to his Salmon Hobo Packs recipe, Batali explains, "since the fish are cooked wrapped in foil, you won't consternate a steak or burger that might happen to be sizzling on the other side of the grill."[46] Sloan voices a similar concern in his red snapper recipe, reassuring readers that "since the fish is entirely wrapped in foil, the steaks and burgers don't even have to look at it while they are sizzling blissfully on the grill."[47] Red meat here is so prized that it needs to be protected from the influence of those lesser items. The gender symbolism apparent in these examples of food writing is articulated by a character in MTV's *Guy Code* segment on tailgating, who intimates that the influence of women is so troubling to men that, "only a married man would want to turn a three-hour excursion into a ten-hour excursion."[48] Men are not just distancing themselves from foods perceived to represent femininity, but from women themselves. Here, meat-eating, as well as tailgating in general, are framed as masculine activities and presented as a rejection of feminine influence.[49]

While rare, female contributors sometimes aid in the perpetuation of narrow conceptualizations of gender that privilege particular identities within food discourse. Debbie Moose furthers the gender stratification of food in *Fan Fare*. She privileges pork—and links it to a homophobic version of masculinity—in her description of the scene at a Green Bay Packers tailgate: "The smoke rising from dozens of grills surrounding the legendary Lambeau Field carries not the aroma of namby-pamby boneless chicken, but the manly pungent whiff of meaty pork links."[50] Chicken is a decidedly nonmasculine signifier in tailgate culture, unless maybe the bird, fully boned, has a beer can inserted in it while roasting over a grill. This notion that chicken is not afforded the same privileged status as pork and red meat is continued, quite explicitly, in *ESPN Gameday Gourmet*, whose author instructs readers that, "in the world of tailgate grilling, chicken is a necessary evil."[51] In a nod to the misogyny that is peppered throughout tailgate discourse, the author adds, "often, *all* of these poultry-pickers will be women."[52]

Culinary discourses not only describe meat in particular ways to establish the boundaries of masculine identity, they also use food to play up sexual innuendo grounded in heterosexism and homophobia. The editors of *Southern Living: The Official SEC Tailgating Cookbook* note of the University of South Carolina mascot, "regardless of size or ability, true gamecocks are aggressive, territorial, and ready to fight." Sexual innuendo is perhaps unavoidable when the mascot of a university's football team is a gamecock; South Carolina's Williams-Brice stadium is nicknamed "The Cockpit," and of its tendency to shake when the team takes the field in front of some eighty thousand fans, a former coach was inspired to proclaim, "if it ain't swayin', we ain't playin'!"[53] The propensity to resort to sexual allusion isn't limited to the football culture of Columbia, South Carolina. In a number of recent tailgate cookbooks, especially those authored by men, as well as the advertising industry's portrayals of tailgate culture, the primacy of meat is linked to retrograde masculinity through (hetero)sexually suggestive commentary, both overt and covert.[54]

*Southern Living's* tailgate cookbook, and others of the early twenty-first century, share characteristics with men's food writing of the 1950s and 1960s—decades that saw a rise in the by-men-for-men genre. Most publications instructed men on the finer points of grilling meat—by that point already well established as a symbol of masculinity and power—over an open flame.[55] In addition to the multitude of references to meat and fire, such cookbooks and magazine columns also relied on aggressive adjectives, minimal instructions, additions of alcohol, and sexist language in recipes and narratives to reinforce the masculinity of male cooks.[56] Even dishes and ingredients were sexualized, with names like "Spanked Baby Dressing" and "Sweater Girl Salad," which was comprised of "chilled peach halves filled with cottage cheese, placed upside down on lettuce leaves and topped with a maraschino cherry."[57] Moreover, cooking columns in men's periodicals like *Esquire* and *Playboy* attempted to "masculinize cooking and food . . . [as] integral to a masculinized and urban domestic culture" so as to further distinguish men's cooking from what had long been understood as the feminine realm of food preparation and the domestic kitchen.[58] *Playboy* food and drink editor Thomas Mario accomplished this cultural feat by championing the playboy lifestyle and making explicit connections between food, cooking, and sex in his columns.[59] Notably, the cultivation of a successful masculine cooking practice was positioned as a useful skill for seducing women. Through this fusion of masculinity, heterosexuality, and financial success around cooking, food writers were able to draw a sharper contrast between the leisure of men's culinary efforts and the construction of cooking practice as feminine domestic labor intended to sustain the family.[60] And, by resorting to blatant sexual references, writers were also able to allay fears of the effeminizing effects of cooking on straight men.[61] Thus, with its emphasis on meat, fire, fun, and the seduction of women, men's food writing did much to buttress hegemonic masculine ideals.

More recent tailgate cookbooks of the early 2000s tend to reinforce the (hetero)masculine performativity of men's cooking, thereby reverting to mid-twentieth-century gender tropes. The trend is particularly evident in recipe names, chapter titles, and author commentaries. Chapter titles such as "The Equipment Room," "Crunch Time," "Hot Prospects," and "Between the Hash Marks" use sports references and sexual allusions to signal the masculine nature of the recipes included in them, while recipe names like "Keg of Nails Beer Batter Bread" and "Mashed Steeler Hash" leave no doubt regarding the macho qualities of the resulting dishes—or the man who makes them.[62] Sexually suggestive language with more than a hint of misogyny features prominently in the narratives of these publications as well. In a note about grilling brats in *The Tailgating Cookbook*, Sloan tells readers to "keep in mind that standard packaged hot dog rolls will not accommodate a brat's girth, so you need special buns."[63] Not to be outdone, Johnson infuses the directions to his presumably male readership on how to properly season hamburgers with a caution to "just be careful not to overwork your meat (insert your own suggestive frat house joke here). . . . If the mixture starts to blend smooth, the patties won't be as juicy when they hit the buns. (Insert second joke here.)"[64]

Mario Batali alludes to sexual performance anxiety in a note to readers about the importance of maintaining a hot grill while tailgating: "Nothing is more humiliating than watching your flame sputter out just as the steaks hit the grill. (And no one makes a little blue pill to solve this particular problem.)"[65] These double-entendres invoke sex to reify cooking as masculine practice and signal the manly prowess of the men doing the cooking, but that is not their only function. They also contribute to the marginalization and objectification of women in tailgate culture. And, read in light of the #MeToo movement, they are messages that reinforce and perpetuate the deeply entrenched culture of sexual harassment in the culinary world inhabited by chefs like Batali—a culture that is then transferred to the tailgating blacktop.[66]

Tailgate-themed television commercials, often with meat at their core, perpetuate this culture by sexually objectifying women through visual imagery and scripted content. A prime example is the "Tailgate Doctor" television spot for the fast-food burger chain Jack's. The plot of the commercial revolves around the antics of a male tailgater who is attempting to pick up women in the gameday parking lot of a football stadium. In this tailgate-bro fantasy, he uses the large-screen image of a juicy hamburger to lure women to his tailgate area. The lead character watches intently, as if a hunter waiting for game to enter his trap, and then springs into action when his quarry, a beautiful brunette clad in a halter top, short shorts, and wedge sandals, falls for the ruse, hits her head on the screen, and crumples to the pavement. Posing as a doctor, complete with scrubs and stethoscope, he then pretends to treat the woman as she comes out of her burger-induced trance.[67] This depiction is problematic for a number of reasons; namely because the ruse allows a male tailgater to forcibly manipulate the object of his sexual fantasy.

Honda uses a similar, though more subdued, tactic to sell its generators to tailgaters. The action in the company's "Tailgate" television commercial begins when one male tailgater walks over to admire the elaborate setup of another, who stands proudly in the midst of his tent area, including a blender, plasma television, Weber grill, and a beautiful woman draped over each of his shoulders. Neither woman speaks, appearing more as decoration than fan, while the generator that powers their tailgate fun is featured in the foreground.[68] This scene presents what is perhaps a modern-day blacktop version of the swinging *Playboy* bachelor, who charms women with his entertaining skills, state-of-the-art gadgetry, and culinary prowess.

A different facet of retrograde masculinity can be found in the pages of recent tailgate cookbooks, as some texts emphasize the heteronormative aspects of dating and family tailgating rituals in the narratives that accompany recipes. The *Southern Living* cookbook editors sprinkle stories that underscore compulsory heterosexuality in the descriptions of tailgating spaces around the Southeastern Conference. At the University of

Mississippi, a male tailgater who proposed to his wife at a football game is quoted as saying, "every good Ole Miss girl wants to get engaged in the Grove at a tailgate."[69] Of the Texas A&M tradition for men to kiss their female dates every time the Aggies score, a male alum explains, "I still remember seeing my mom and dad kiss after every score. Now kissing my wife is my favorite part of game day in College Station."[70] In 2012's *Game-Day Fan Fare*, the recipe contributors often note for whom they cook—usually male family members. Statements like, "my two sons and husband devour them," "I often make this for my husband," "these are a hit with my son and husband," and "we have one daughter and five hungry sons" illustrate how male appetite is often socially integrated into a network of heterosexual family relationships.[71] Furthermore, these examples demonstrate similarities between contemporary tailgate cookbooks and their more traditional precursors. Historically, cookbooks have promoted heteronormative family structures, and dominant cooking discourses have normalized "the idea that cooking is a woman's way to express love for her husband and children."[72] In the absence of other perspectives (single parents, men cooking for women, gay couples, etc.) tailgate cookbooks signal a traditionally narrow representation of masculinity, femininity, tailgate culture, and the family.

Occasionally a site within popular culture will offer up a resistive reading of traditional meat-infused tailgate spectacles. In an episode of the television show, *Portlandia*, the writers disrupt several aspects of traditional tailgate culture, including showcasing soup rather than steak as the food around which the party centers. In the show's "Pull-Out King" episode, comedic effect is established with the absence rather than the presence of meat. The tailgate has shifted from the typical football stadium scene to the parking lot before a live performance of the radio show *Prairie Home Companion*. White, middle-aged couple Malcolm and Kris serve as the hosts of a party that is the antithesis of most tailgate gatherings. The set up includes blankets, fold-up chairs, a table, potted green plant, and a turf rug complete with a welcome mat. The hosts regale their rather small, sedate group of fellow "partiers" with stories about previous *Prairie Home* concerts (including one where *Fresh Air's* Terri Gross made a surprise guest appearance) and serve them yerba mate, which Malcolm claims they snuck through customs and Kris warns has a "bite." The centerpiece of the tailgate is soup, which Malcolm tells their guests, you want to "warm it up . . . you want a really low flame, you want it so . . . you want it off." To complete the alternate universe setting, the tailgaters raptly listen to an NPR news report before dancing (badly) to bluegrass music from a car radio.[73] In this sketch, *Portlandia* pokes fun at NPR listeners to upend the hard-drinking, meat-eating, flame-grilling stereotype of the macho tailgater. One certainly would be hard-pressed to find a tailgate in which a low-simmering soup holds forth as the focal point of the spectacle on the blacktop. Given the social construction of carnivorous fare as a source of entertainment, the absence of meat and flame would be disconcerting, to say the least.[74]

Meat is so central to tailgating that when its primacy is challenged or erased, such as in the *Portlandia* example, even in small ways, people notice. In a relatively small corner of the San Francisco 49ers tailgate area in Santa Clara, buddies Raul, Mike, and Nick gather together to fire up their red Coleman gas grill for most home games. Of their typical spread, Nick explained, "it's a lot of meat, obviously." One week he suffered the consequences of trying to innovate by putting carrots in the turkey burgers: "[they] got mad at me because I snuck vegetables in . . . they were about to kick me out of the tailgate."

## The Vassal Vegetable

Nick's carrot faux pas, in an already questionable inclusion of turkey, leads us to the marginalization of vegetarian fare, and by extension, those who prepare and eat it. In the recipes, notes, and images of tailgate cookbooks, vegetables are often relegated to the margins of the plate or grill. Most texts include a chapter on vegetables and sides, but with qualifications. Batali sets the following tone at the outset of his chapter on vegetables: "During race weekend, green vegetables tend to take a backseat to every other known food group. And, as race cars have no back seat, they tend not to appear, even in spirit."[75] Vegetables and nonmeat sides are something to grudgingly accommodate, not feature. "An experienced griller," Batali notes, "can find a little empty space on the grill for some corn," while potato packets fit "in the empty spaces on the grill where you're not cooking anything else."[76] Sloan echoes this theme with a football analogy in *The Tailgating Cookbook*: "Great quarterbacks find a way to get the ball to a receiver even when there seems to be no apparent opening . . . one of the skills of a great tailgate grill man is finding a way to get the ears of corn on the grill under similar conditions."[77]

Using retrograde masculine rhetoric, some tailgate cookbook authors not only relegate vegetables to the margins of tailgate culture, but demean and objectify those who prepare and insist on eating them. This rhetorical tactic serves as a defense against the potentially emasculating effects of women's cooking.[78] We see evidence of this pattern throughout the pages of *Gameday Gourmet*. It starts in the introduction, with Johnson's description of "the ranch hand" tailgater: "A picky eater who tends toward the vegetarian side (often the really hot girlfriend of your most annoying college buddy). Favorite fare: celery sticks and sandblasted baby carrots."[79] Similarly, Johnson manages to put down both casseroles and women in the opening note to the chapter "Hot Prospects." Readers are cautioned "not [to] freak out at the sight of the word 'casserole'" or be consumed by "visions of bored housewives in frilly aprons trying to be 'creative' with their leftovers."[80] He begins the chapter "It Isn't Easy Being Green" by reasserting the primacy of meat, as if readers were likely to forget: "When it comes to traditional football foods, seared meat reigns supreme and gooey cheese products come in a close second, but vegetables? Unless you invited your mom to whip up a batch of her Peanut Butter Broccoli Surprise, vegetables and salads are probably way down the priority list for the average tailgate." Johnson continues, "but the sad reality is that there will always be someone . . . who wants to see some kind of vegetable matter on the table."[81] To assuage those misguided guests, he recommends vegetable dishes that are hearty and durable enough to stand up to meat and withstand the outdoor buffet table conditions of most tailgates. Though Johnson grudgingly instructs readers to acquiesce to requests for vegetables in one's tailgate, meat rather pointedly remains the ideal masculine food, and thus retains its status as the epitome of masculine consumption.[82] Sloan employs similar rhetoric in the introductory note to his recipe for tuna with sweet and spicy sauce. Per his explanation, the dish, although special, is unexpected at a tailgate. "It's probably not what the offensive linemen are eating after the game. Maybe the place kicker. Actually, maybe the place kicker's wife."[83] This not-so-implicit chauvinism extends beyond symbolic marginalization to a heterosexist denigration of women (and some men). A little later in the book, Sloan concedes that "the tailgate world is changing," albeit grudgingly. "It is no longer solely the domain of the meat eater. Eventually you'll find yourself tailgating with someone (most likely a woman) who might want some fish or grilled vegetables."[84] Here, both women and nonmeat fare—and, by implication, men who would prefer a respite from the tyranny of meat—are othered as they encroach on the masculine territory of the blacktop.

In some instances, cookbook authors relegate vegetarian fare to the margins by qualifying meatless dishes. Of her Very Veggie Lentil Chili, *Fan Fare* author Moose—she of the "namby-pamby" chicken—writes, "even meat-eating fans will be satisfied with this thick, rich chili. The flavors are bold enough to transform this lowly legume into a tailgate feast."[85] Food and sport remain at the center of the social construction of a traditional gender binary in Moose's recipe for Shelley's Girly Breakfast Casserole, with its title and introductory note: "this brunch favorite appeals to women because it contains vegetables and chicken instead of the customary bacon and sausage. But sports-loving men like it, too."[86] Moose's conception apparently doesn't allow for women who like bacon and sausage, or account for men who would welcome a departure from those brunch staples. Similarly, gender difference is the primary distinction around which Ray Lampe advises selection of appetizers in the *NFL Gameday Cookbook*. In his chapter on tailgate starters, Lampe relies on the masculine construction of spicy foods. Dr. BBQ instructs his presumed-male readership, "if it's a bunch of your beer-drinking buddies, you can get hot and spicy and probably skip the veggie dip," but, he cautions, "if the girls are coming, they might like the veggie dip and cheese fondue."[87] While the 3rdRail9ers tailgate crew operates by the motto "everything is better when it's wrapped in bacon," they are also committed to experimenting with new dishes. On their list for the near future: casseroles, a dish not often associated with men, meat, or tailgating.

In the 49ers vs. Raiders episode of *Tailgate Warriors*, Fieri's play-by-play of Oakland's baked beans dish indicates that vegetables are insufficient on their own: "Beth is slicing bacon to fortify her baked beans." In the Packers vs. Seahawks episode, Dr. BBQ expresses mild approval for an appetizer he expected to be lacking: "I'm not a big vegetable eater, I'm Dr. BBQ, so I kind of liked it that they put noodles inside and enough chicken." Lampe provides a recipe for bean and barley vegetarian chili in *The NFL Gameday Cookbook*, with the proviso that "You won't miss the meat at all in this hearty chili."[88] In print, Dr. BBQ himself displays a growing acceptance of vegetarian fare. Lampe instructs readers, "if you're serving a lot of meat, you should consider a salad of some sort and possibly a fruit or veggie side . . . the sides are the critical course to bring it all together."[89] This is a different take on vegetables; in their marginalization, they are credited with completing a meal rather than contaminating it. The credit, however, is still prefaced by an abundance of meat. Finally, Sloan takes a softer tone in his recipes for grilled vegetable sandwiches and salmon burgers. Of the former, he writes, "every once in a while you come across a vegetarian in our tailgating crowd. Rather than relegate him or her to a meal of cotton candy and pretzels . . . you can throw this sandwich together without too much fuss."[90] Here, at least, the author recognizes that vegetarians can be either male or female and indicates a desire to provide tasty tailgate food for them—as long as it doesn't take too much effort. Sloan displays a similar desire in his wish to accommodate "non-beef-eaters who still want to have a burger experience" with a salmon substitution. He does, however, go on to describe those tailgaters as "the ones who, while they are watching the game, are heard to exclaim, 'did they have to tackle him so hard—he didn't even have the ball?'" Exclamations like that earn "a discreet sigh" from Sloan; even as they are accommodated, those who lack a taste for meat are ostracized within the masculine realm of football, thus demonstrating that in the midst of cultural change, men grilling meat endures as the primary definition of a tailgate.[91] Even outside the context of football, those who follow a nonmeat diet are likely to be marginalized, mocked, and maligned for their alternative dietary practices.[92] It is worth noting that players themselves are not exempt from ridicule, despite the privilege afforded them by their status as professional athletes—the ultimate masculine cover.[93]

In tailgate-themed commercials, vegetarian fare like quinoa is often played for laughs. In a Bud Light ad, the centrality of meat in tailgate culture is reinforced by consternation over its absence. A male fan is troubled by the quinoa 'burger' his wife packed for him to grill, pronouncing it "queen-o" for comic effect. His buddy spots the foreign object and asks, "is that a loofah?", making the foreign 'othering' and feminization of a nonmeat product part of the punch line. The griller has to rationalize the inclusion of quinoa in his tailgate, ultimately deciding it's okay because his team won the last time he ate it. The commercial ends with the Bud Light tag line, "for the fans who do whatever it takes," the "whatever" here being the brave act of eating a meatless burger in plain sight of one's fellow tailgaters. Vegetarian products like quinoa present a challenge to hegemonic masculinity, but the threat is diffused under the culinary cover of the football environment. Beer is central to mediated and lived football culture, and as the main product in this ad, it functions similarly to red meat as a masculine signifier. The Bud Light grilling setup illustrates another way that meat and football are discursively linked in American popular consciousness and the promotional culture of the NFL. The quinoa narrative of this beer commercial ends up perpetuating the centrality of meat.

Vegetarian fare is also trivialized in the *Tailgate Warriors* series. Vegetables are relegated to the sidelines of the menus, and even then, the judges cast doubt on those dishes and the time devoted to their preparation by the contestants. For example, in the Vikings vs. Saints episode, Fieri chastises the Vikings team for spending too much time on fava beans: "It's a lot of work, a lot of time, and a lot of tension for just one side dish." Fava beans do seem a poor choice for a timed cooking competition, yet one wonders if the judges would have been just as critical of a labor-intensive meat side dish. And in the Packers vs. Seahawks episode, Dr. BBQ patronizingly compliments a meatless side dish, saying, "and the sweet potato salad . . . I thought that was a nice little side dish." Not only is meat the featured component of meal events, but meatless dishes are often found lacking in taste and fulfillment.[94] Even Dr. BBQ's understanding of his moniker indicates that grilling and vegetables are mutually exclusive concepts to him—an underlying assumption of many twentieth and twenty-first century barbecue cookbooks, including his. The place of vegetables on the menu is analogous to the place of women in a patriarchal society, and more specifically, (hetero)masculine cultural spaces such as the football stadium blacktop. In *Tailgate Warriors*, women account for only a handful of the thirty-two contestants, and when we do see a female contestant, she is usually charged with the preparation of side dishes, dessert, and vegetarian fare. Even with current food trends toward healthier eating, vegetarian fare and women both remain marginalized in this context.[95] In tailgate culture, it seems, "the vassal vegetable should content itself with its assigned place and not attempt to dethrone king meat."[96]

Though few and far between, there are departures from meat-centricity in the use of smokers, grills, fryers, and flames on the blacktop. For example, Buffalo tailgaters Drew and Tina use their deep fryer for homemade French fries, cut from homegrown potatoes. Tina explained, we "gotta have it every week." The couple grow their own vegetable garden each year, which features everything from okra to eggplant. When it is in season, they get fresh corn from a neighbor's farm. At their tailgate, Drew and Tina prepare the corn on the cob in a custom-made steamer—a retrofitted metal garbage can with a grate and steam holes, painted in the red and blue colors of the Bills. Although meat reigns supreme among tailgaters, using specialized equipment to cook nonmeat fare, just like planning new casserole ideas, indicates an increasing creativity within the carnivorous culture. Under the protection afforded by culinary cover, this creativity bolsters masculinity on the blacktop, rather than mitigating it.

## Conclusion

The larger culture's preoccupation with meat manifests in many different ways in representations and lived experiences of tailgating. In an illustrative example from a *Tailgate Warriors* episode, the team from Chicago has a signature, custom-made brand that they wield to mark their grilled meat. One of the judges observed, "you really have to live up to the expectations when you put your name on it."[97] Notably, the Chicagoans do not use their brand on side dishes or nonmeat items, but reserve it for their meat entrée, indicating the singular quality of meat as the centerpiece of the tailgate. This example not only marks the meat as special, but also conveys ownership and power over it, thus linking the performative aspects of tailgating to masculine dominance.[98]

Food practices such as the ones on display in *Tailgate Warriors* and in other media depictions, as well as those demonstrated by tailgaters across the country, help confirm the traditional tastes of manhood and allow for the construction of strong male identities and relationships.[99] Those who subscribe to hegemonic ideals for masculine behavior enjoy a sort of culinary capital. Yet, as we have seen, tailgating also contains space for resistive practices, and the customs of some tailgaters in particular show us that gender is never a static construct. While gender figures prominently in understandings of the food and the performances at the heart of tailgate culture, the analysis is far from complete without a consideration of the ways race and ethnicity intersect throughout this setting.

# 4.

# 'Ethnic Edibles' and 'Hindu' Spices

## Racial and Ethnic Representation in Tailgate Cookbooks

## Introduction

Food is a cultural product through which ethnic and racial identities are constructed, reproduced, negotiated, and realized.[1] As our main purveyor of information about food, cookbooks—and food writing more generally—have wielded enormous cultural influence throughout history. Despite the potential of cookbooks as valuable sites in exploring negotiations of power, for much of the twentieth century, cookery tomes were relegated to the margins of scholarly inquiry.[2] Dismissed as "trivial" given their association with women and domesticity, according to Inness, cookbooks historically rested at the margins of serious study.[3] In the early twenty-first century, scholarship devoted to examining the cultural significance of cookbooks has increased greatly. Academic and lay authors have considered cookbooks as rhetorical documents that shed light on the lived experiences of their authors, analyzed recipe collections for articulations of communal identity, and constructed cultural histories of cookbooks as signposts of their times.[4] We seek to build on this growing body of literature, recognizing that cookbooks do indeed matter, and while they are key sources of information about food and its preparation, these texts are also more than merely prescriptive or aspirational. Among other functions, cookbooks have the power to shape attitudes about different foods and the groups associated with them, to celebrate forgotten or obscured culinary heritages, and to challenge stereotypical renderings of food.[5] As such, cookbooks stand as important texts for the study of history and culture; thus, they are the primary point of analysis in this chapter. In particular, we explore how race and ethnicity are represented in tailgating cookbooks, as well as how this genre has both shaped and revealed American perceptions of ethnic foods and the cultural groups associated with them. Moreover, it is equally important to situate this influence in a broader historical context. Cookbooks do not exist in a cultural vacuum; accordingly, at times in this chapter, our analysis expands to link these texts to constructions of race and ethnicity throughout history and in representations of tailgating across other forms of popular culture.

As social texts in which "narratives of culinary knowledge intertwine with narratives on ethnicity," cookbooks do much to influence ethnic culinary knowledge and how it is integrated into American cooking.[6] Moreover, racialized relationships of power are also evident across the pages of cookbooks, with whiteness operating as the normative center around which narratives are constructed in these texts. When we view cookbooks from this perspective, we see their significance not just in the reproducibility of the recipes included therein, but as cultural tools which shape attitudes and inform everyday practices.[7] In tailgate culture, cookbooks provide numerous examples of how racial and ethnic ideologies are constructed and sustained. By considering tailgate cookbooks in light of the broader history of American cookbook literature, we can see how these texts follow a pattern similar to that of general cookbooks when it comes to representations of racial and ethnic identity.

Cookbooks reproduce constructs of race and ethnicity through their narrative content, as well as the organization and names of recipes, descriptions of ingredients, and accompanying notes, photographs, captions, and illustrations. As Vester argues, food writing can contribute to cultural appropriation, exoticization of cuisines, and the othering of immigrant foods.[8] In American cookbooks throughout the twentieth and into the twenty-first century, nonwhite groups are often exoticized, the culinary histories of marginalized groups ignored, appropriated, and/or maligned, and both subtle and not-so-subtle forms of culinary racism are evident.[9] As we will demonstrate throughout this chapter, the textual content of tailgate cookbooks mirrors these patterns and themes and intersects with constructions of gender around food.

## General Cookbook History

A consideration of ethnic and racial representation in general cookbooks throughout American history provides a lens through which to view contemporary tailgate cookbooks. Early American white-authored cookbooks are noted for mostly excluding what was considered "foreign," "ethnic," or "immigrant" food, and for outright ignoring African American contributions to culinary culture. Culinary knowledge about immigrant foodways was largely absent from the narratives of late nineteenth and early twentieth-century cookbooks. When writers did include recipes for foreign dishes, mainly those that did not originate from northern and western Europe, it was with little, if any, explanation of their origins. Similarly, white cookbook writers rarely even mentioned African American cooks, dishes, or preparation styles, despite the considerable number of black women who did the majority of cooking, especially in the kitchens of the antebellum and postwar South.[10] Moreover, dishes that mixed African technique with American ingredients and European recipes disappeared in publications written for white audiences.[11]

As the twentieth century progressed, foreign dishes were more likely to be included in cookbooks if they were simple, easy to modify, and conformed to already established American tastes. By the 1940s, as white European ethnic groups were increasingly accepted in American society, cookbook writers shifted their approach to ethnic fare, presenting recipes in one of three ways: standardization (obscuring the distinctive features of a dish), Americanization (emphasizing the similarity of dishes to American ones), or ghettoization (grouping foreign recipes together).[12] In many ways, these categories of representation reflect the main ways first- and second-generation European immigrants assimilated into United States culture. Overall, ethnic dishes like goulash, pasta, and chili con carne were modified to conform with American values and principles of cooking during this era.[13] The African and African American origins of black ethnic dishes, however, continued to be obscured.

For African Americans whose foodways were not acknowledged to the same degree as those of European immigrants, representation in white cookbooks of the early- to mid-twentieth century remained marginal at best and offensive at worst. The racist attitudes underlying slavery that remained entrenched in Jim Crow America played out on the pages of cookbooks of this era. When white authors did present African American cooks and their dishes, it was often with condescending commentary and stereotypical images, essentially freezing "black food workers in trophy-like portraits of antebellum characters."[14] The most pervasive of these racist caricatures was embodied in the ubiquitous mammy figure of the Aunt Jemima character—a fabrication intended to discredit the skill, knowledge, talent, autonomy, and ingenuity of black female cooks by presenting their culinary abilities as nothing more than instinctual habits.

By framing African Americans as naturally gifted cooks, white authors belittled their community heritage and willfully ignored the intense training, hard work, and creative expression fundamental to black culinary expertise. Aunt Jemima (and other racist images in food advertising), together with the marginal representation of African Americans, obscured black culinary traditions in food writing, thereby maintaining the fiction of white expertise and superiority in all things food-related.[15]

Culinary boundaries were more relaxed in cookbooks published in the second half of the twentieth century, especially in relation to European fare. Writers emphasized the similarities between American and ethnic dishes, leading to an increase in the variety of recipes offered and the production of more multiethnic cuisines. In this way, ethnically identified foods became a resource for diversifying American taste, thus promoting a wider range of food choices.[16] At the same time, "ethnic dishes were detached from the ethnics and redefined in articulation with the mainstream culture," while Latino, Native American, and African American foodways continued to be ignored or co-opted.[17] Similarly, tailgate cookbooks failed to recognize the black labor or the black southern origins of barbecue and other traditions that have become so central to contemporary tailgating.

Cookbooks, as well as restaurant menus of the 1960s and 1970s, often signaled ethnic integration by presenting dishes with ingredients believed to be symbolic of an entire foreign cuisine—a reductive, stereotypical practice that dates to the late nineteenth century—rarely noting the ethnic culture or the people behind the food.[18] Common ethnic signifiers included curry powder, pineapple, soy sauce, and garlic, which were used to represent, respectively, anything remotely Indian, Hawaiian, Asian, or Italian. African American dishes were co-opted without credit. As Vertamae Smart-Grosvenor notes in the introduction to *Vibration Cooking*, ethnic modifiers such as those for Spanish rice, Italian spaghetti, and Chinese cabbage commonly preface ingredients or dishes in the pages of white-authored cookbooks, yet black ethnic culinary contributions go unheralded.[19] This lack of distinction serves to erase the origins of African American cooking, even as they escape stereotypical ethnic marking.

The number of black-owned presses increased sharply following the gains of the Civil Rights Movement—a shift in the publishing industry that led to a notable increase in the publication of African American cookbooks beginning in the 1960s.[20] Many authors of these volumes sought to establish African American culinary authority as they challenged prevailing racist stereotypes. Cookbook writers also endeavored to recover and celebrate the origins and historical development of African American cuisine, with explicit acknowledgement of its African, Caribbean, Creole, and black southern US roots.[21] Soul food cookbooks, in which black authors challenged white co-optation of African American foodways and reclaimed traditional dishes like fried chicken and collard greens from stereotypical representations, cast them instead as expressions of black dignity and pride.[22] In the 1970s, some authors, like the renowned chef Edna Lewis, made it a point to position African American cooking as American cooking, with less focus on political expression.[23] These trends, however, are absent from tailgating cookbooks, which were largely authored or edited by white women during this time period. Some publications include recipe contributions from male coaches or players, most of whom are white, which lend a greater air of masculine sporting authenticity to the texts, yet reify the whiteness of tailgate culture.

By the 1980s, there was a greater willingness among Americans to try ethnically identified foods; as a result, a more multicultural trend emerged in cookbooks.[24] This trend, along with fusion cooking, continued through the 1990s and into the twenty-first century, with the publication of more ethnic cookbooks and more informed integration of ethnic fare. Additionally, the number of cookbooks devoted to single ethnic cuisines dramatically increased during this time period.[25] African American cookbooks of the era followed a similar pattern. Authors promoted expressions of black ethnic identity through food by continuing to feature soul food while highlighting inspirations from Africa, the Caribbean, and Creole Carolina and Louisiana.[26] We see many parallels between these trends in cookbooks and those more narrowly focused on tailgate fare, with the exception of greater African American representation or acknowledgment of African American foodways.

Cookbook sections devoted to tailgating, along with cookbooks solely dedicated to tailgate food, first began to appear in the late 1960s. This historical moment provides us with a useful frame of reference for analyzing how these books "narrate ethnicity."[27] The first wave of tailgate cookbooks, published from the late 1960s to the early 1980s, emerged during the "ethnic revival" which marked that period, and reflect many of the general cookbook trends noted above.[28] We see evidence not only of ethnic revival in these publications, but also of racial and ethnic exclusion, ghettoization, adaptation to American tastes, and the use of signifying ingredients. The second wave of tailgate cookbooks, published from roughly the mid-1980s to the early twenty-first century, contain numerous examples of the celebration of ethnic identity through food, and of the eventual integration and acceptance of ethnic fare into American culinary traditions, thus reflecting the societal changes of that time period. As we will see, however, despite greater positive imagery and more diverse ethnic representations in tailgate cookbooks in more recent decades, the majority of texts are still written by white authors for (seemingly) white audiences. Moreover, as contemporary general cookbooks have moved toward more credible, less condescending, and wider inclusion of African American foodways and culinary contributions, tailgate cookbooks notably have not.

## Tailgate Cookbooks, First Wave: 1960s–1980s

### ETHNIC REVIVAL

The ethnic revival, which began in the late 1960s, was in many ways a response to the assimilationist tendencies of the prior era. African Americans, ethnic whites, and others proudly stood to distinguish their uniqueness—laying claims to difference as opposed to sameness. Cultural pluralism reigned and cuisine was one among many artifacts that delineated the boundaries of *us* and *them*. Yet, food simultaneously provided spaces where divisions between and among cultural groups could be breached in ways seen as nonthreatening. For example, tailgate cookbooks accomplished what occurred in ethnic restaurants of this time period: they allowed (white) patrons to believe they had an 'exotic encounter' while remaining safely situated within the boundaries of their own cultural expectations.[29] Recipes for Americanized versions of 'authentic' ethnic dishes relied on stereotypical ingredients as symbolic ethnic signifiers in the first wave of tailgate cookbooks, allowing users to feel like they were having a unique cultural experience, all the while maintaining their American identity. Within this framework, culinary gatekeepers made the most concessions for European food traditions.

Hyla O'Connor's 1981 *The Complete NFL Cookbook*, a compilation of recipes from NFL notables, provides at least two explicit illustrations of the ways in which the ethnic revival took place on the pages of first-wave tailgate cookbooks.[30] This trend is seen both in the contributions from ethnically identified individuals and in the ways ethnic groups and foods are written about by white American authors of nondistinct ethnic heritage. Los Angeles Rams coach Ray Malavasi offered that the inspiration for his recipes, "particularly the Italian ones," originated with his mother. Malavasi explained his desire to make dishes he remembered enjoying as a child, namely polenta and baccalà. For readers unfamiliar with these items, Malavasi clarified that polenta is corn meal and baccalà is dried, salted codfish that looks "something like baseball bats."[31] Baccalà is one of those smelly, exotic signifiers of Italian otherness that cookbook editors often felt compelled to explain for readers. In fact, the story Malavasi shares about his difficulty preparing it correctly is indicative of his assimilation into American culture and distance from the culinary traditions of his mother.

The relationship between and significance of food and a male athlete's ethnic identity is made even clearer in the description provided of NFL quarterback Ron Jaworski's move to the Philadelphia Eagles in 1977. Author O'Connor notes that the Eagles threw a party for the press and other interested observers at the time of the trade. The featured item at the affair, according to O'Connor, "besides Jaworski, of course—was stuffed cabbage." O'Connor continues, "thus a fitting ethnic food heralded a new chapter in the career of the player known as the 'Polish Rifle.'" Athleticism, ethnicity, and cuisine remained closely aligned, as the author reassures readers that while the on-the-field triumphs for the quarterback cannot be attributed to stuffed cabbage, Jaworski continues to be a "connoisseur of Polish food."[32] This example grounds Jaworski in ethnic otherness while at the same time celebrating it—with the not-so-implicit comparison to a stuffed cabbage. Notably, the inclusion of recipe contributions from male NFL players and coaches signals authenticity in tailgate cookbooks and grounds food alongside masculinity in football culture. Far from something to be hidden, white ethnic identity became, in the 1970s, a "badge of pride," with food and football the cultural locations around which such constructions and negotiations occurred.[33] However, interest in ethnic fare extended beyond the preoccupation of Italian and Polish folks with their own foodways. The ethnic revival spurred a more general enthusiasm for ethnic cuisine during the period, making "salsa more popular than ketchup" by the early 1990s.[34] It also demonstrated the eventual access to whiteness gained by many European American immigrant groups. Additional examples of ethnic cuisine can be found in *The Complete NFL Cookbook* and other publications in this collection, including empanadas, moussaka, paella, cioppino, Polish pickles, and lamb curry.[35] As this list suggests, a more diverse spread of culinary treats found their way onto the tailgate table in this period—one that featured an array of meat, seafood, and vegetarian dishes consistent with the era's trend of mostly prepared-ahead fare.

## WHITEWASHING HISTORY AND HERITAGE

Across the balance of first-wave books examined, the attention paid to ethnic cuisine as tailgate fare did little to advance cross-cultural under-standings of "the other," much like in general cookbooks of the era. Rather, dominant (largely white) constructions of ethnic food seemed securely lodged in stereotypical renderings of cultures and peoples. As Reddinger contends, cookbooks tend to "evacuate detail and historical specificity" when discussing the ethnic other, presenting people and food as "simple and exotic."[36] The narratives of some tailgate cookbooks further this prejudice by whitewashing history in subtle ways. In *Pigskin Picnics*, Candy Coleman offers menus representative of the regions of the coun-try where "fourteen Super Bowl spectaculars have been played."[37] Each section of the book is framed with a narrative about the geographical location of the Super Bowls featured. The title of a New Orleans section, "A Picnic with Scarlett," evokes an Old South of plantations, slavery, and privileged whiteness. The story about fans extending their Super Bowl stay to tour antebellum plantations restored to their original beauty, where "they could envision life along the Mississippi River and hoist a mint julep in commemoration of days past" conjures an idealized white past untroubled by the racism that marked much of the South in very real and painful ways.[38] In a description of New Orleans early settlers and cultural history, Coleman refers to enslaved persons as "Negro slaves," a description that might have been deemed appropriate language in the 1940s, but certainly not by the 1980 publication date of her book.[39] These attitudes, and the symbols of the Old South that pervade southern foot-ball culture, including tailgate cookery as one of the rituals surrounding the game, maintain an exclusionary form of whiteness.

In the West Coast section of *Pigskin Picnics*, Coleman manages to whitewash Native history, too. In her description of the Golden State, she writes, "before 1769, California had only Spanish inhabitants who later taught settlers how to plant vineyards and citrus orchards as well as how to use avocados and spicy peppers for chili."[40] The categorically false first segment of this statement effectively removes Indian tribes, colonial oppression, and cultural genocide from the historical record. The fruit, avocado, and chili origin stories paint a rosy, mythic Thanksgiving-like picture of California's cultural past. Although ostensibly focused on food and the people who prepare and consume it, tailgate cookbooks like Coleman's promote a kind of historical ignorance that creates a cultural illiteracy among Americans, which enables the continued use of the Confederate flag in college football and deems the use of Indian mascots for entertainment purposes an acceptable practice (both issues we address later in this chapter). These narratives, and others like them, do so much more than communicate information about cooking on the blacktop. They perpetuate ideas about race and privilege that maintain relationships of power.

## 'ETHNIC EDIBLES': GHETTOIZATION AND OTHERING

Ethnic difference, or the construction of the "culinary other" in tail-gate cookbooks, is apparent in a variety of ways, sometimes explicitly marked in the texts, as is the case with 1972's *Tailgate Cooking and Other Gastronomical Horrors*, a recipe book sponsored by The Minneapolis Twin City Federal Bank. Fare labeled "Ethnic Edibles" (complete with drawn images that symbolize the concept of the "ethnic," which we will address shortly) is relegated to a two-page section that features recipes for a Belgian casserole, eggplant parmigiano Americano, gazpacho, and speidis. With this ghettoization of foods deemed "ethnic," the book's authors do not simply instruct readers on food preparation; rather, they actively define ethnic distinction and categories of difference—and ulti-mately the boundaries of self and other.[41]

In still other ways, the images in first-wave cookbooks underscore the broad generalizations and stereotypes at work in identity construc-tion of ethnic others by members of the dominant group. Several of the illustrations in the cookbooks reflect this point, including in *Sagehen's Retriever Club Tailgate Cookbook* from 1967. For example, a tropical seafood salad is accompanied by an image of a male figure in a banana boat, while a chicken and Spanish rice dish is joined with a drawing of a burro and young man wearing a sombrero. A snake charmer illustration is linked with a curry Madras recipe, and a sketch of a football player in a sombrero—that all-too-ubiquitous signifier of Mexican identity—is featured beside guacamole, chalupa, and chile con queso recipes.[42] The ethnic caricatures in these images become stereotypical signifiers of specific cultures, each told to us by the book's creators. The banana boat, a term that originally referred to the fast ships used to carry highly perishable bananas from Central American countries to US markets, later became part of a derogatory phrase used to describe recently arrived Afro-Caribbean immigrants in Great Britain.[43] The sombrero, snake charmer, banana boat "enact this signification by calling on a vague sense of the primitive and the unusual."[44] In doing so, mainstream culinary texts, through images found within their pages, define and further distance readers from the exotic other, whose cultural and culinary traditions remain foreign.

Paralleling the larger genre of mainstream cookbooks, tailgate cookbooks during this period devote little attention to providing a cultural context for the specific ethnic foods featured. When tailgate cookbooks did offer up comments about food in association with a place or people not generally considered in the mainstream, they did so from an uninformed perspective and with a disregard for even a cursory understanding of culture. For example, Fleishmann's 1967 volume lists the ingredients of curry Madras to include applesauce, curry powder, "Hindu-style" spices to taste, bacon, and sirloin steaks. Of course, for many observant Hindus, who are largely vegetarian, the last two items would most likely not make their way into a dish, let alone onto a table.[45] One is also left to wonder about the religious qualities of seasonings—what, for example, might be Christian-style spices?

Similarly, in Sunset's 1982, *Picnics & Tailgate Parties*, the authors take no account of cultural context as they offer comments about picnicking as a "Nomads' Feast." The "nomadic Bedouins of the Middle East," are, according to the book, "experts in picnicking," and thus worthy of note.[46] A recipe for a lamb and rice dish is provided with further explanation that it is just "one example of the portable meals enjoyed by those nomadic people who picnic on the sand every night of the week."[47] It is easy enough to conclude that Bedouin life is filled with frivolity as the realities of their lives that give rise to a nomadic existence in the desert are left unattended. Moreover, *Sunset*'s narrative advances the erroneous notion that all Middle Easterners are nomadic. Rather than using the opportunity to better explore this cuisine and culture, we are instead provided tips about the need for picnics to include "clusters of cushions to help create a Middle Eastern mood."[48]

The Luau craze that swept mainstream cookbooks and society in the 1960s made an appearance in first-wave tailgate cookbooks, and the examples serve as ways in which cultural and social histories are, "rendered invisible by over-simplified mainland representations" of a people and place.[49] The complexities of Hawaiian culture are obscured in Dottie Dekko's 1978 book, *Cooking for Kicks*, in which the ubiquitous pig on a spit is the stand-in to symbolize all of Hawaiian cuisine. Moreover, the preparation of the dish (on a spit) is more a product of the dominant culture's imagination of authentic island cuisine than anything connected to Hawaii or its culinary traditions. The customary underground oven, an *Imu*, is replaced with the visually striking swine spinning on a stick.[50] The dominant group's interest in ethnic foodways, at least in this case, did not translate to any understanding of the invoked culture or its people. In a final example from Dekko's text, the author's misspelling of the word 'Hawaiian' (the second 'a' is left out) throughout the section is symbolic, not only of a profound lack of knowledge, but the politics imbued in "eating the other."[51] In another classic instance of stereotypical representation of Hawaiian identity, *The Tailgate Cookbook's* Hawaiian beefballs recipe presents pineapple as the distinguishing ingredient of Hawaiianness, and in so doing provides readers with the "illusion of authenticity."[52] While pineapples are abundant in Hawaii, it is reductive to present them as representative of Hawaiian ethnic identity. Doing so obscures Hawaii's colonial past, the complex cultural heritage of Hawaiians, and the rich food culture of the state.[53] It stands as one more illustration of how cultural history is whitewashed through the representation of food in tailgate culture. Taken collectively, these examples demonstrate some of the ways "food writers have detached culinary knowledge from its owners, modified it, and reassigned new versions of dishes associated with American food culture."[54]

Food writers have not only co-opted and misrepresented the food traditions of various ethnic groups, but have further reified the whiteness of tailgate culture by excluding, simplifying, or obscuring the culinary practices of black ethnic groups. O'Connor presents a recipe for Senegalese chicken in *The Complete NFL Cookbook*, but without an explanation of the entree's title or origins, readers are left to wonder what it is about the combination of poultry, lemon or lime juice, cider vinegar, black peppercorns, salad oil, onions, and crushed red pepper that makes the dish Senegalese.[55] In *Cooking for Kicks*, Dekko labels recipes for steamed cabbage stew and joloff rice as Guyanese and Nigerian, respectively, but provides no distinguishing information about the origins of each dish beyond noting that the couple who provided the recipes (a Nigerian male soccer player and his Guyanese wife) "rarely eat English food and do no measuring when cooking."[56] Dekko others the couple with her note about their non-English eating habits, and by commenting on their measurement-free cooking, perpetuates patterns from early- and mid-twentieth-century general cookbooks that presented black cooks as instinctual and lacking scientific precision.[57]

As barbecue culture flourished in postwar suburban America, African, Afro-Caribbean, and African American barbecue traditions were ignored in books and articles about grilling.[58] Thus, sources for food preparation techniques that eventually influenced changes in tailgating fare offered tailgaters a limited perspective from which to draw on for crafting menus on the blacktop. Moreover, like general food writing, tailgate cookbooks failed to acknowledge African American foodways and the culinary traditions of black Southerners.[59]

## SIGNIFYING INGREDIENTS

In the first wave of tailgate cookbooks, recipes often include one or two signifying ingredients, such as the pineapple, that are intended to signal the ethnic authenticity of a dish. Authentic food "implies that products are prepared using the same ingredients and processes as found in the homeland of the ethnic, national, or regional group" being represented.[60] In many tailgate cookbooks of this era, just like general cookbooks, there is an emphasis on authenticity that is "unfaithful to the culinary traditions" of the country of origin of a dish.[61] This departure from authentic traditions is seen in methods of preparation, ingredients used, and presentation of food.[62] A case in point here is the addition of applesauce, arguably an American signifier, to curry Madras (not to mention bacon and sirloin), an ingredient no doubt intended to render Indian food 'safe' for Americans unfamiliar with the cuisine. In Americanized ethnic food of much of the twentieth century, the traditional characteristics of dishes were modified to suit already-established dominant American tastes.[63]

Likewise, tailgate cookbook authors of the 1970s demonstrate a heavy reliance on signifying ingredients. For example, Herbert devotes an entire section in her barbecue chapter to "United Nations Burgers," noting that "from the All-American standby to these international flavors is just a matter of seasoning. I like to serve at least two different 'nations' (mix the egg and beef and season half, say, Oriental, and the other half, Mexican)." There is a lot going on in this narrative—"American" is presented as the standard by which other burger variations are compared, and a smattering of ingredients are reductively employed to represent entire countries of people. Her Oriental burgers add water chestnuts, soy sauce, and scallions to the base recipe, while her Mexican burgers rely on chili sauce, parmesan cheese, shredded lettuce, and tortillas to distinguish them. The parmesan cheese is a curious choice here, as it is a noted product of Italian cuisine (whose burgers are differentiated by mozzarella cheese, salami, and oregano—common Italian signifiers).[64] Similarly, Fleischmann's East Indian sandwich recipe calls for mayonnaise, chutney, turkey, and spinach, with chutney being the only ingredient that seems remotely Indian.[65] A recipe for "Original Beef Stroganoff" in the same book begs the question, "original to whom?" With ingredients that feature canned mushrooms, cans of mushroom sauce, and filet mignon, this stroganoff seems original only to American casserole cooking of the 1960s.[66]

In their quest to adapt ethnic dishes to American tastes, general and tailgate cookbook authors of this era also felt compelled to warn their presumed female readers of "unusual" or "spicy" ethnic ingredients. In *Souper Bowl of Recipes*, readers are cautioned that Chicken Kiev has an "unusual flavor because of the tarragon spice."[67] In another recipe instruction in Herbert's *The Tailgate Cookbook*, this one for Armenian meat pie, the author explains, "the unusual flavors in this recipe are enhanced when the pie is served at room temperature." The unusual ingredients in question are nutmeg, cinnamon, and pine nuts. Those flavors may very well be more pronounced at room temperature, but framing them as "unusual" renders them exotic and others Armenian cuisine and by extension, Armenians.[68] Miami quarterback Bob Griese tells readers that the Cuban pork in his sandwich "is very spicey [*sic*] and should be used in small quantities," while the Eagles' Wade Key instructs those who attempt his Chili Con Queso to "add pepper *only* if you desire spiced foods"— the pepper in question being a jalapeño. He also notes that his chili is "good with Doritos."[69] The recipe for Redmond Red Chili, featured in *The Complete NFL Cookbook*, comes with this cautionary note: "Those who prefer hotter chili may add chili powder and jalapeños to taste. But it is best to begin mild and work up to hot, particularly if you are serving guests with unfamiliar tastes."[70] In Herbert's curried shrimp recipe, she informs readers, "in India, the hotter the weather, the hotter the curry, but I recommend adding this spice judiciously."[71] American palates, it seems, were considered too sensitive for curries and chiles by these authors. However, from the mid-twentieth century on, general cookbooks and magazines perpetuated the notion that foods most suited for men should be hearty and substantial as well as spicy, leading many to assume that men who don't enjoy such culinary delights are somehow less masculine.[72] This cultural construct presents a contradictory juxtaposition of ethnic identity and masculinity. On the one hand, spicy ingredients indicate ethnic otherness, but on the other, they stand as a masculine signifier, especially when included in hearty dishes like chili.

In some cases, cookbook contributors demonstrate cultural illiteracy as they reduce ethnic cuisines to a few basic signifying ingredients. *Sunset* editors provide their own simplification of Bedouin culture with the recipe for mansaf, a "one-dish meal of lamb, rice, and pine nuts" that can be "adapted for picnic use during your own nomadic wanderings."[73] The adapted recipe includes butter and cream cheese—perishable ingredients that would be quite a significant departure for a nomadic-based cuisine.

Later first-wave tailgate books integrate more ethnic fare, and in some cases provide more informed recipe narratives. In *Tailgate Parties*, Wyler presents both individual recipes and themed menus for football party gatherings. The author tells of a picnic she attended in Cuernavaca, Mexico in the backstory for the menu titled "A Country Outing," noting that she had firsthand experience enjoying the dishes included "many years ago under a grove of tall mango trees."[74] The recipes in Wyler's book also include less modification, as illustrated in her menu titled "Superbowl Party." Of the Tex-Mex inspired theme, she tells readers, "whether it is the tequila in the margaritas or the glowing warmth engendered by the spiciness of the food, good cheer and high spirits always seem to go hand in hand with Mexican food with an American accent." Here she equates spiciness with warmth, and goes on to explain that "the chili is made with two kinds of chili powder—one for deeper flavor and the other for heat," a significant contrast to the warnings of other cookbook authors.[75]

## Tailgate Cookbooks, Second Wave: 1990s–Present

Second-wave tailgate cookbooks continue the aforementioned trend of greater ethnic integration and inclusion, thus "mirroring the incorporation of ethnic cultures into the culinary mainstream."[76] The number of cookbooks devoted to tailgating dramatically increased during this time period, especially in the late 1990s and 2000s, following the explosion of cultural interest in cooking and the proliferation of food television of the era.[77] Along with more diverse representation of food, the majority of these cookbooks were written by men for a presumed male audience. The ethnic representation in them is more inclusive and less stereotypical than in first-wave tailgate cookbooks, though some cultural exclusivity and insensitivity does remain. Indeed, the introductory narrative to *The Browns Fan's Tailgating Guide* claims, "all of the things that divide us as citizens—race, ethnicity, gender, creed, age, social status—get put on hold for awhile when people come together as tailgating fans."[78] A romanticization of the blacktop, perhaps, but also a distinct shift from the narrative discourse of first-wave books like Candy Coleman's.

Recipes in Mario Batali's NASCAR tailgate cookbook signal this shift.[79] A case in point is Batali's recipe for Cocido Bogotano, "a classic stew from Columbia [*sic*]" (note, though, the misspelling in Batali's rendering). Here, the author, a renowned chef noted for his knowledgeable approach to food, presumably hews closely to the original ingredients. Of the stew, Batali explains, "it has nothing to do with NASCAR, but if you show up with it at a tailgate—maybe the Telcel Motorola 200 in Mexico City—everyone will be very, very happy."[80] The inclusion of Cocido Bogotano normalizes Latinx cuisine in tailgate culture, and given the 2006 publication date of the NASCAR-branded cookbook—one year after the Telcel Motorola 200's Mexico City debut—is possibly related to the racing league's attempts to expand its Latinx fan base.[81] Moreover, by positioning the cocido as most appropriate at a race in Mexico, the dish functions as an ethnic signifier, even as it expands the range of tailgate food.

Batali's take on a ham and cheese biscuit in the breakfast section of the book is also indicative of a shift in tailgate culture. Batali suggests a substitution of prosciutto and sweet Gorgonzola, a variation we can read as Italianization—the adaptation of an American food item to Italian tastes—and one that flips the ethnic script of earlier cookbooks. By extension, Batali equates Italian ethnic identity with masculinity with his quip, "you know you're a man if you have Gorgonzola in the morning."[82] This isn't a surprising equation from a proudly Italian American male chef, yet it is one that is also found among other non-Italian Food Network hosts. In *The Naked Chef*, for example, British food celebrity Jamie Oliver often invokes what Hollows refers to as 'Italianicity' to construct a dominant culinary masculinity. In Hollows' analysis, Italian food is associated with rustic, hearty qualities and working-class identity, which are set in opposition to the posh, refined attributes of French cuisine. Italian identity thus becomes a "fetishized object of consumption" and a signifier of masculinity. [83] Here, it is another example of how gender and ethnicity intersect through food to lend culinary cover to men.

This fetishization stands in contrast to how some tailgaters celebrate their ethnic Italian identity. For brothers Tony and Charlie and their nephews Taylor and Sam of Knoxville, TN, inclusion of Italian fare in their tailgate menus is a matter of family history. Their grandfather, a first-generation Italian immigrant who settled in Philadelphia, passed down recipes to his kids and grandkids. The family makes those dishes, like Italian sausages and gravy (colloquial for tomato sauce in some areas of the American Northeast) and a crab-and-shrimp boil, for special University of Tennessee games each season. As they celebrate their cultural heritage, Tony and Charlie are also reinforcing the dynamic of men cooking for special occasions—another intersection of ethnicity and masculinity.

We see examples of the normalization of ethnic fare in other second-wave tailgate cookbooks as well. Sloan's *The Tailgating Cookbook* includes recipes for a range of dishes, including Wasabi peas, ceviche, empanadas, Korean-style spareribs, Cuban sandwiches, and beef satay. Quesadillas are described as "a natural for tailgating."[84] In the *NFL Gameday Cookbook*, Ray Lampe describes a recipe for "Gringo Huevos Rancheros" as "my version of the classic."[85] With the acknowledgment of his dish as a gringo variation of the Mexican breakfast staple, Lampe doesn't pretend to pass off his *huevos*—or himself—as authentic.

In *John Madden's Ultimate Tailgating*, the former Oakland Raiders coach seems to accomplish both a normalization of ethnic food and a stereotypical presentation of it. His book includes recipes for marinated steak chipotle, Cajun spice mix, homemade Italian sausage, haluski, and chimichurri sauce, plus a section titled "Mostly Mexican." That section features fajitas, rice and beans, tamales, and a few different versions of chili. Madden often cites the sources and inspirations for recipes, lending a somewhat authentic air to the dishes with his stories about restaurant owners, former players, and relatives of colleagues from distinct ethnic groups in the US.[86] However, Madden also casts his collection of recipes in a stereotypical light in his introduction to the book. In making a case for the everyman nature of the recipes, Madden writes, "it's about good food. But it's not fancy food. I don't go in much for fancy food and never have. . . . There can't be a fancy Mexican restaurant. If it is fancy it is not a Mexican restaurant because a Mexican restaurant is not fancy. And if it is catfish you can't make a French thing out of it. So this is not a fancy cookbook."[87] It is, however, a cookbook with recipes tested and refined by professional chefs, with some out-of-the-ordinary ingredients and labor-intensive dishes. In his failure to recognize that there could be such a thing as upscale Mexican food, Madden presents a narrow version of Mexican cuisine as representative of the entire country, based on an underlying class assumption that real tailgate food is unpretentious, blue-collar fare.

*The Gameday Gourmet*, an official ESPN publication, presents another interesting intersection of class and ethnicity. In his introductory comments on tailgating, author Pableaux Johnson explains, "tailgating . . . is not the place to get fussy . . . A tailgate shouldn't involve high-dollar menus, sushi rolls of any sort, or mango chutney slathered on anything . . . [it] is the pregame feast that demands a certain amount of blue-collar respect."[88] This statement equates ethnic tailgate fare with an upper-class snobbery, yet a number of the recipes in this book draw inspiration from ethnic food traditions and feature fairly expensive ingredients and complex cooking methods. In a note to his recipe for margaritas ("cold Mexican treats"), Johnson admonishes readers not to skimp on tequila, instructing them to "avoid cheaper brands named after random Mexican icons (Sombrero, El Boracho, or La Bamba)" and instead "invest the extra two bucks in a mid-grade silver tequila from one of the familiar distilleries."[89] Notably, the labels mentioned seem more like stereotypes than icons.

Authors play up and on stereotyped constructions of Mexican iconography and food elsewhere in second-wave cookbooks. Johnson describes his Seven-Count Layered Mexican Dip recipe as a "suburbanized take on Tex-Mex cuisine that has been around as long as Fritos."[90] In other words, a white, middle-class version of an already hybridized dish. Fritos is a curious reference here. The commercially mass-produced corn chips have been around since 1932, when confectioner C. E. Doolin began searching for the perfect corn snack. After spotting a Mexican man named Gustavo Olguin making fried corn chips out of masa at a gas station cafe in San Antonio, Texas, Doolin bought Olguin's recipe and equipment for making *fritas* for $100. With the help of his mother, he perfected what became the Fritos recipe at home, and then went into mass production, eventually hybridizing his own variety of corn and applying assembly line techniques to the manufacture of his corn chips. This act of cultural appropriation of Mexican borderlands foods led to the development of one of the most successful snack chips in American history, as well as restaurant franchises, recipe collections, and eventual global distribution under the Frito-Lay brand. In 1967, eight years after Doolin's death, the snack food company moved from appropriation to offensive stereotyping. A new mascot was introduced to market Fritos— the Frito Bandito, a cartoon caricature based on the sinister "Mexican bandit" stereotype of American Westerns. The Frito Bandito character spoke broken English and sported a sombrero, long, skinny mustache, and crisscrossed bandoliers around his torso. In a circa-1968 ad, the Frito Bandito is pictured on a wanted poster holding a bag of Fritos in one hand and a pistol in the other above the copy "He loves cronchy [sic] Fritos corn chips so much he'll stop at nothing to get yours. What's more, he's cunning, clever—and sneaky!" The mascot's combination of machismo and stereotypes of Mexican culture was Frito-Lay's attempt to position Fritos as a unique snack choice for consumers by creating an aura of danger and exoticism.[91] The mascot, with its blatant ethnic stereotyping, was discontinued in 1971 due to complaints and organized protest from the Chicano movement.[92] It stands, along with Aunt Jemima, as an example of commodity racism—the perpetuation and exploitation of a racial or ethnic stereotype to sell food products—and can be read as a more sinister version of the ethnic caricatures in illustrations of first-wave tailgate cookbooks.[93]

Cookbooks, as Psyche Williams-Forson reminds us, "represent cultural sites where food and memory intersect."[94] Although the Frito Bandito was retired in 1971, its image endures, and negative stereotypes of Mexicans and Mexican Americans proliferate, even as southwestern cuisine and other appropriations of Mexican foods enjoy great popularity in the United States. The juxtaposition between this popularity and hostility towards Mexico, Mexicans, and Mexican Americans is indicative of a cultural amnesia. According to food scholar Amy Bentley, "Americans embrace, enjoy, and explore literally the fruits of this region [Mexico], but seem to sever easily the food from the people and region whence it came."[95] This affliction is shared by a number of both first and second-wave tailgate cookbook authors.[96]

A pattern of retrograde ethnic representation emerges in Loran Smith's *Spread Formation*, a 2014 collection of "tailgating and home recipes from college football greats."[97] Among the wide range of recipes presented, there are a few which would not be out of place in first-wave cookbooks. For example, the recipe for Italian meatballs from former Boston College athletic director Gene DeFilippo and his wife Anne calls for one pound of ground beef and an optional quarter teaspoon of basil. This heavily Americanized recipe makes the only seasoning, apart from salt and 'Italian-style' breadcrumbs, an option—and in a miniscule amount, at that.[98] Similarly, former Auburn kicker Al Del Greco and his wife Lisa contribute their recipe for Extra-Point Italian Chicken—a pasta dish featuring tomato sauce from a jar and vague "Italian seasonings."[99] We offer these examples not as a criticism of the food practices or assimilation patterns of recipe contributors, but to demonstrate the ways second-wave tailgate cookbooks replicate the narrative features of earlier publications.

In other sections of the book, however, ethnic identity is celebrated and more authentic dishes are presented. Smith describes tailgating at the University of Cincinnati as "a German heritage thing" that "might make you think you have happened upon a beer hall somewhere in Germany." A Bearcat alum notes that tailgates are "steeped in German heritage," and explains that "on game day, there are copious amounts of beer and plenty of brats."[100] Tailgate culture thus forges a connection between the university and the city's ethnic heritage, albeit with a slightly reductive nod to German fare. As a former All-American quarterback at Purdue University, Bob Griese gets page-time in *Spread Formation*, too. As in the earlier *Souper Bowl of Recipes*, his Cuban Pork Sandwich recipe is featured, but this time without the caution about the spicy pork. Elsewhere in the book, Mary Kuligowski, the wife of Missouri's defensive line coach, shares three recipes—Baklava, Dolmades, and Galatoboureko—she learned from her Greek mother. As Kuligowski explains, "most were unwritten, measured by handfuls and what looked right to her. I had to put them to paper so that I could reproduce them for myself. I did a pretty good job and they soon became requested at tailgates."[101] Her story is a common one for those second- and third-generation immigrants who learned to cook at the sides of mothers and grandmothers who did their measuring by sight and feel. Notably, her story is presented more respectfully than those of African American cooks in general cookbooks of the early- to mid- twentieth-century.

Perhaps more striking than the integration of ethnic food in the book's narratives, though, is the absence of people of color in the images scattered throughout the second-generation tailgate cookbooks. In *Spread Formation*, a 192-page book that includes fifty-six universities situated across all regions of the United States, only five out of over eighty photographs include people of color. And, in this disproportionately small number of photographs, only two feature a person of color as the center of attention or action—one of an Asian man setting up a Chinese buffet at the University of Michigan, and the other of a black man dropping a piece of meat as he tries to remove it from a flaming grill at an Ohio State tailgate. This lone action shot of a black tailgater in a dark hoodie with something going wrong is problematic given the book's overall lack of African American representation, and the fact that the only other image that includes an individual black man is of a repurposed bus in University of Arkansas colors. A black man scalping tickets appears incidentally in the frame, walking through the University of Arkansas tailgating section where the bus was parked.[102]

Furthermore, of the fifty-six universities Smith included none is an HBCU, nor do any have a sizeable African American population—a content choice that excludes African American food culture and presents college football tailgating as a white cultural space. This troubling pattern is found in both first- and second-wave cookbooks and is remarkable given the disproportionately high percentage of African Americans on college football rosters at the majority of the universities included. That this publication is supported by the National Football Federation and for sale in the College Football Hall of Fame serves to further perpetuate the racial exclusion that marks cultural and historical representations of college football and tailgating.

While second-wave tailgate cookbooks distance themselves in some ways from the earlier generation of texts with regard to explicit ethnic stereotypes, the newer books nonetheless remain largely written by white authors for seemingly white audiences. *Southern Living*, in their *Official SEC Tailgating Cookbook*, offers up a blend of contemporary recipes and Old South tradition. The book, divided into sections based on university towns and football teams in the Southeastern Conference, includes a wide range of dishes, many of which demonstrate how integrated ethnic ingredients have become in American cuisine. There are recipes for avocado-mango salsa, poblano fish tacos, southern tortellini minestrone, pancetta-arugula-turkey sandwiches, and pico de gallo, just to name a few, along with traditional southern staples like fried green tomatoes, pickled okra, banana pudding, hush puppies, and fried chicken (none of which, however, are attributed to African American culinary history). Where we do not see evidence of integration, however, is in the photos of tailgaters and football fans spread throughout the book. In a cookbook that features narratives and recipes from twelve university towns, only one photograph features a person of color, an unidentified African

American man serving up ribs at Dreamland Bar-B-Que in Tuscaloosa, Alabama. The caption reads "Not much has changed since Dreamland first opened more than 50 years ago," likely a reference to the restaurant's menu, but troubling when positioned below the photo of the only black person in the book, a man who happens to be serving food in a Deep South town.[103] The caption, it seems, is framing more than a barbecue joint. It is a visual reminder of the dogged persistence of racism in the American south. In the rare instances when African Americans are depicted, they remain nameless servants to whites.

The absence of African American perspectives in general cookbooks about barbecue culture and in tailgate-specific books that feature barbecue sections is all the more striking when one considers the rich tradition of this culinary style. These ahistorical considerations of barbecue culture fail to acknowledge the West and Central African (as well as indigenous American and West Indies) origins of grilling and smoking meats that informed the cooking practices of enslaved Africans of the colonial and antebellum South. As historian Michael Twitty notes, "highly spicing meats, the roasting of whole goats, the use of peppery sauces or pepper vinegar . . . the long and slow cooking process, sauces that utilized tomatoes, onions, peppers, and the like, and the social context of barbecue— as a tool to promote social conviviality and community—hearken back to the culture's African roots."[104] In a geographical area in which the intertwined social phenomena of football and barbecue seem to equally inform regional identity, both are presented as white, European traditions. However, "it was enslaved men and their descendants, not the Bubbas of today's Barbecue Pitmasters, that innovated and refined regional barbecue traditions."[105] The expertise and contributions of African Americans are glossed over completely or co-opted, often without adequate credit, in second-wave tailgate cookbooks.

## "We Do Our Roots": Tales Beyond the Tailgate Cookbook

Of course, as noted at the beginning of the chapter, neither these cookbooks nor the cultural practice of tailgating exist in a cultural vacuum. Therefore, it is also important to examine how cookbooks sit both in a broader historical context and amid other cultural sites in which tailgating is represented. In this section, we turn our attention to how racial and ethnic identity are portrayed in film and television depictions of tailgating, as well as how these constructions are understood and celebrated in the lived experiences of tailgaters. Issues of race and ethnicity in these spheres reinforce and occasionally disrupt the dominant discourse found in cookbooks.

Indeed, analysis of cookbooks like that offered by *Southern Living* provides a way both onto the blacktop and into related historical context. Following Doris Witt's precept that work on food requires detailed attention to history, we consider the foundations of racial and ethnic constructions at universities where the spectacle of football has figured prominently in campus culture.[106] Racial segregation at most southern universities actively maintained the whiteness of the football scene, including tailgating spaces. The University of Mississippi stands as a stark case in point. The Confederate flag appeared on the Ole Miss campus in the late 1940s, and along with the Southern anthem, "Dixie," became "an exalted part of the football ritual" in 1948.[107] The flag's appearance coincided with the Dixiecrat revolt against civil rights at that year's Democratic National Convention. Dixiecrats opposed to racial integration broke from the Democratic Party and the Confederate flag reemerged as their political symbol. A number of Ole Miss students participated in this movement, thus helping to bring the flag to campus. As Mississippi was targeted by Civil Rights activists in the 1950s and 1960s, the Ole Miss football program grew in stature and became an increasingly relevant space for expressions of racial intolerance.[108] The flag was embraced by students opposed to racial integration and proudly showcased by the marching band in halftime shows, until protests from student groups and faculty led to the University's 1983 decision to stop actively promoting symbols of the Confederacy. It was at this point that Mississippi stopped distributing Rebel flags before football games and officially licensing products with the symbol.[109] Although the Confederate flag no longer serves as an official symbol of the University, its informal use by fans and merchandisers continues in the twenty-first century. Flags dominate campus spaces around the football stadium, and as late as the 1990s, the Grove—Ole Miss's hallowed tailgating grounds—teemed with Confederate flags in the form of banners hanging from trees, centerpieces on picnic tables, and branded tailgating tents on football Saturdays. Contemporary photos of the Grove reveal that the flag still features in tailgate spaces, albeit in more recessed areas and in smaller forms. In addition to the flag, other symbols of the Confederacy abound—in the University's Confederate-themed official colors, its 'Colonel Reb' mascot (a caricature of an Old South plantation owner—one with which Candy Coleman's romanticization of the region's history is consistent), tailgate decor, and tailgater apparel.[110] Even the University's seemingly innocuous nickname has roots in the era of slavery; a plantation's white mistress was commonly referred to by the title, 'Ole Miss.'[111] As Joshua Newman argues in his book *Embodying Dixie*, Ole Miss football remains a Confederate preserve, maybe more than any other sporting institution in the South. As such, he maintains, this particular form of "whiteness is not only performed at Ole Miss, it is spectacle."[112] Not surprisingly, few African Americans participate in tailgating at the Grove, and those that do are typically seen at the periphery of the campus space, or serving as food workers.[113] Cultural messaging like that found in the narrative content of Coleman's cookbook and implied in the image choices of southern tailgating texts do much to sustain the spectacle.[114]

The racial attitudes that have sustained the use of Confederate symbols on the Oxford, Mississippi campus are evident among football fans and tailgaters at other universities across the South. In *Rammer Jammer Yellow Hammer*, journalist Warren St. John's chronicle of the 1999 season he spent following University of Alabama Crimson Tide football, the author details customs and social attitudes among the RV faithful, including racist-tinged reservations white fans express about Andrew Zow, the Tide's black quarterback. St. John experiences a low point as a lifelong 'Bama fan at a post-game tailgate celebration of an upset victory over the Florida Gators halfway through the season. In the midst of the revelry, a white RVer reacts to breaking news of a black Alabama player's involvement in an illegal speeding ticket fix scheme with racist vehemence, claiming, "stupid [insert racial epithet] are always getting us in trouble." Another fan concurs, saying "she's got a point. Them [racial epithet] always doin' sumpin' stupid."[115] St. John is disturbed by this conversation, as well as his failure to challenge the racial prejudice of the fans. He also notes the contradiction between this prejudice and white fans' delight in a victory secured by black student-athletes—a contradiction that is hardly unique to fans of the Crimson Tide. Tailgate cookbooks do little, if anything, to challenge these manifestations of racism in southern college football tailgate culture.

Exclusionary whiteness is also apparent in the legacy of Native American mascots in tailgating locales across college football, notably on those campuses which have had or continue to use Native American imagery to represent athletic teams. As Jennifer Guilliano compellingly demonstrates in her history of college mascots, "halftime spectacle and

Indian-themed athletic identity were intrinsic aspects of the modern university from the late 1920s onward."[116] At the University of Illinois, 'Chief Illiniwek,' the University's mascot since 1926, has been a much loved aspect of campus culture by the predominantly white student body.[117] The mascot itself no longer performs at home athletic contests, per compliance with an NCAA policy, but images of the mascot remain visible all over Urbana-Champaign, and are a significant part of the tailgating landscape in the form of university-branded products and fan paraphernalia.[118] 'Save the Chief' student groups and 'Humans are not Mascots' protesters both stake out territory at football tailgates to make their cases to the public, with the latter group enduring considerably more resistance.

Stanford University retired its Native American mascot and name in 1971 in the face of mounting social pressure, but one is still likely to see a few references to the old mascot on a stroll through a campus tailgate in Palo Alto. Before a 2016 USC–Stanford matchup, three parties of white tailgaters prominently displayed a flag, blanket, and chair with the discontinued Stanford Indian emblazoned on it. Dawn, an alumna in a separate contingent of tailgaters, viewed the Indian memorabilia as homages from older fans and alumni who remain invested in the pre-counterculture tradition of Stanford football. She supported the name and mascot change when she attended the University in the early 1970s, but explained that students wanted 'Robber Barons' to replace 'Indians' as the official name of Stanford's athletic teams. The University, in an apparent failure to appreciate the student body's sense of irony, went with 'Cardinal' and a corresponding tree mascot instead.[119] As the aforementioned examples demonstrate, the cultural spaces of tailgating, including cookbooks, can sometimes be the locations around which racial ideologies are sustained and even reinforced. Coleman's culinary erasure of indigenous history is part of the same cultural discourse which maintains the use of Native American mascots and racist imagery in tailgate spaces.

As tailgating has grown more popular in the late twentieth- and early twenty-first centuries, we have seen a corresponding growth in fictional and scripted reality TV representations of tailgaters in popular media. Many of these media examples seem predicated on recognition of race- and ethnic-based exclusion in tailgate culture, including recent cookbooks. Films and television shows that feature tailgating scenes often advance themes related to race and ethnicity. A 2013 episode of the animated comedy series *American Dad!* satirizes the racist custom of white tailgaters dressing up as Indian mascots to cheer on their favorite football team.[120] In the film *Silver Linings Playbook*, we see a disruption of whiteness on the blacktop when a group of Indian Americans rolls into the parking lot at the Philadelphia Eagles stadium in a brightly painted bus. Their ethnicity, as well as their food, marks them as other in this setting. A particularly xenophobic group of white fans taunts them about their food, yelling "nasty Indian curry . . . go back to your country," thus sparking a brawl that is eventually broken up by the police.[121] In this media example, ethnic difference marks individuals and their food as intrusive and unwelcome. Fiction is not necessarily reflected in reality, though. A blacktop contrast to this scene occurs at the University of Tennessee, where a large Indian family has been a fixture of the tailgate lots for twenty years, grilling up lamb kabobs, tandoori chicken, and catfish for most home football games. In an overwhelmingly white parade of tailgaters, this family and their contingent of fifty people was easily the most diverse group on campus, and seemed welcomed and appreciated by their Circle Park neighbors. This group and others like it formed the rare exception to a more general rule that we witnessed both across the tailgate spaces and within the cookbooks we examined: racial and ethnic diversity was the outlier in an otherwise white space.

Indeed, the whiteness of professional and collegiate football tailgates is striking in the places where our ethnographic research took us. On the college campuses of Tennessee, Stanford, Oregon, and Louisiana State, as well as in professional stadium parking lots in Buffalo and Foxborough, the majority of participants are white.[122] Again, examples from popular media reinforce what we saw on the blacktop and in our investigation of tailgate cookbooks. This dynamic was not lost on black cast members of MTV's *Guy Code*, who in an episode segment on tailgating machismo quip, "black people tailgate, but white people *tailgate* . . . y'all turn it into an extreme sport," and, "if black people went to a parking lot and started barbecuing, they would call it loitering."[123] Another cast member, a white man, however, reminds the audience that it is a particular form of white, middle-class masculinity that dominates on the blacktop, telling the camera, "I could never tailgate, because I drive a hybrid. You can't show up and just open the trunk of your hybrid and be like 'Hi guys. Anyone want some quinoa? Huh . . . I got a Malbec from 2007." In his comments we see a recognition of the gendered and classed construction of wine and the vegetarian dish of quinoa as too much of a departure from the "cold beer, hot meat" fare of 'real' tailgaters.[124]

The representations of tailgating in mediated popular culture are of a piece with those in cookbooks. While these instructive texts and entertaining sources are significant meaning-makers, none tells the whole story of the lived experiences of tailgaters. What is reported in contemporary cookbooks is reflected on the blacktop to a certain degree (e.g., the primacy of meat, the predominant whiteness), but at times and in certain places, we saw more cultural complexity. Among the many threads of similarity in tailgate spaces across the United States, distinct differences in terms of food and people also exist.

While we found little evidence in tailgating cookbook narratives to unsettle dominant ideologies around race and ethnicity, a walk through the parking lots at the Oakland Coliseum or the Levi's Stadium in Santa Clara challenges those constructions. In these two San Francisco Bay Area locales, the diversity of tailgaters and the food they prepare mirrors that of the region's general population. San Francisco 49ers fans might be adjusting to the tailgating regulations around their team's new home and grumbling about the distance from the stadium at which they have to do their grilling, but they are making the space their own with unique food and custom decorations. In addition to the ubiquitous red-and-gold team flags and tents, US, Greek, Peruvian, and Mexican flags are on display in tailgate spots. Longtime tailgater Frank emigrated to the United States from Peru when he was fourteen years old, by which time he had already been cooking for his mom and younger siblings for five years. Pride in his ethnic roots influences Frank's tailgate menus, most notably when he makes Peruvian-style chicken stew and roasts a whole suckling pig. Twenty-something Raul relies on a local East Bay *carniceria* for chorizo and marinated steak for his carne asada tacos. Kimo, one of the members of the 3rdRail9ers tailgate crew, delves into his Filipino and Hawaiian roots for his signature sesame chicken (dubbed 'crack chicken' for its addictive qualities) and Filipino spareribs—the former is one of three of his mom's dishes that he proudly claims he's improved on (the other two being chicken adobo and lasagna). Of his interest in food, Kimo explained, "the actual act of cooking is okay, more so I enjoy other people enjoying my cooking." Kimo's example illustrates how more diverse tailgate spaces have the potential to disrupt the dominant narratives of masculine expression and move beyond meat-based spectacle and performance to include nurturing others through food.

The Oakland Coliseum was easily the most vibrant tailgating scene we encountered. On any given Sunday, the parking lot around the Raiders

Kimo and his signature sesame chicken, October 2015. *Courtesy of authors.*

home turf (at least until 2019) is a multicultural mix of tailgaters, music (mostly Mexican and hip hop), banners in English and Spanish, and food. With Mexican music blaring from their sound system, Los Malosos, a group of Mexican men who have been tailgating together for fifteen years, can be found in a section just south of the stadium for all Sunday home games. Ramon is usually at the grill, firing up chorizo, tamales, carne asada, tortillas, and carnitas marinated in orange juice and salt ("that's all you need," claims Ramon). One of the younger men in Los Malosos, Ivan, declares, "I don't think there's anybody more loyal than Raiders fans." He loves bringing friends to Raiders games for the first time, especially because of the feeling of camaraderie on the blacktop. Food both helps foster and is a manifestation of communal identity for this group of Latino tailgaters.

A group of Latino tailgaters from the Manteca–Modesto area set up shop in the same area of the Coliseum parking lot for most Raider home games. Louis, a tailgater in his thirties, explains of his group's tailgate fare of chorizo, carne asada, and tacos, "we do our roots." Similarly, the owner of the El Charro restaurant in Turlock, CA sets up professional grilling equipment to cook vast quantities of chorizo, carne asada, chicken, and jalapenos for the many patrons who will stop by for a pregame meal. At Southern University in Baton Rouge, LA, the one HBCU tailgate location we were able to visit, African American tailgaters similarly drew on their regional culinary roots. Sisters Linda and Glinda prepared a pregame spread featuring boiled turkey necks, cornbread, mustard greens, okra, and peach cobbler. Through their tailgate cooking, the gridiron enthusiasts noted above proudly display their ethnic food roots. In doing so, they also call attention to the persistent lack of racial and ethnic representation in contemporary tailgate cookbooks and trouble, albeit in relatively small ways, the normative (white) center of football's pregame ritual.

## Conclusion

More than merely instructing food preparation or policing culinary boundaries, the tailgate cookbooks in our investigation reify racial and ethnic stereotypes and generalizations. Entire cultures are reduced to a single food item, represented through ingredients of questionable authenticity, trivialized, or left out of the narrative altogether, creating further distance between the "culinary local" and the "culinary other."[125] Yet, we discovered that cookbooks also reflect shifting cultural attitudes and greater acceptance of ethnic fare, demonstrating the changing nature and complexity of ethnic constructions in tailgate culture. In regard to authorship, however, tailgate cookbooks remain largely written by white authors for white audiences. Second-wave tailgate cookbooks are similar to publications of the earlier era in this regard. The main shift in authorship is a gendered one; male authors are more common in later tailgate cookbooks, a finding presumably in line with the transition to more blacktop-produced carnivorous fare. African Americans and other people of color are much less in evidence as authors, and African American foodways remain mostly absent from these publications. Those absences in the cookbook literature are challenged by some of what we witnessed on the blacktop at the few stadiums across the country where racial and ethnic diversity held sway. In these small pockets of football revelry, African Americans, Latinos, and people of color more generally, are laying claim to culinary traditions as they participate in one of sport's most popular spectator rituals. In doing so, they push back against the exceedingly narrow racial and ethnic boundaries of tailgate cookbooks.

# 5.

# Culinary Community on the Blacktop

## Introduction

> "... there's some hardcore revelry and excess going on every
> Sunday. But there's also a kinder, gentler and larger shared
> experience that borders on collective consciousness."[1]
>
> —Peter Chakerian

Peter Chakerian's assessment of tailgating strikes at the core of an omni-present contradiction seen across many of the pregame sites explored in this work. The notion of community is central to the ways in which tailgating is represented in various media forms.[2] Communal bonds are also an important component around which many tailgaters express and understand their experiences on the blacktop. Yet other, seemingly competing aspects are evident within tailgate culture, as adversarial ten-dencies share space and coexist alongside displays of fellowship among participants. With food often at its core, we explore this "camaraderie and competition" contradiction, including the many ways that masculinity is both expressed and negotiated.[3]

Our analysis brings five different threads to bear on the discussion. The first, "Battle on the Blacktop: Competition," examines how the Food Network's *Tailgate Warriors* highlighted spirited rivalries and particular constructions of masculinity, obscuring communal aspects so integral to many sites under study in this book. However, as we will also see in this section, our ethnographic observations disrupted this conceptualization of competition, masculinity, and tailgating. Some participants have quite different understandings of their relationships with others and notions of one-upmanship on the blacktop. Constructions of community are explored in other ways in this chapter, including how local cuisine nar-rates place identity. For example, in the section "Fennel Sausage Says Chicago to Me" we examine how certain foods are understood in the context of a city or region's identity. Through the process, tailgaters forge a culinary collective of sorts in which particular cuisine is at the center of community-building. Tailgaters use a cuisine's uniqueness in relation to a particular place to foster community while simultaneously distinguishing *us* from *them* in competitive football circles. We explore this phenomenon in the section "Mascot on the Menu." Often opposing teams consume the culinary symbol of a competitor's mascot (eating alligator when competing against the University of Florida Gators, for example). In doing so tailgaters highlight the sometimes-competitive elements of feasting on the blacktop, and also use food to reaffirm symbolic power over an opponent through eating the other. We also examine the tensions around the community and competition at a tailgate by assessing how participants organize themselves on the blacktop. In "Steaking Out Your Territory," we explore how spatial arrangements are both inclusive and exclusive. Interestingly, in an effort to create community, tailgaters often engage in hyperterritorial behavior, marking off space and claiming it as their own. The final section of this chapter details how cooking and philanthropic endeavors merge in "Tailgating with a Cause." In this chapter's last thread, we explore how the communal bonds and friendships created and sustained between and among male tailgaters complicate dominant understandings of masculinity.

## Battle on the Blacktop: Competition

Tailgating is often cast or perceived as a party and a community event, where giving and sharing is paramount to the experience. It is certainly that, as we witnessed across tailgating spaces around the country and in the way the activity is represented over the span of various media platforms. However, there is also an element of tailgating that is competitive and hierarchical, where winners (those deemed to have the best food or setup) are prized for their good work and sophisticated displays of cookery. A competitive environment that privileges constructions of hegemonic masculinity is featured most prominently in the mediated versions of tailgating, namely the Food Network's *Tailgate Warriors*.

A competitive format forms the foundation on which *Tailgate Warriors* is packaged as a structured, timed, judged, made-for-television cook-off between two teams of four tailgaters, each representing a specific NFL team. Each team is given one hour to prepare two appetizers, one entrée, two side dishes, and one dessert. Dishes are judged on taste, creativity, difficulty, and presentation. The format of the show borrows heavily from the ritual, rhetoric, and standard narrative of an American football game broadcast. From the show's lead-in to its conclusion, host Guy Fieri essentially serves as both play-by-play and color commentator, heightening suspense and tension by continually framing the event in relation to football and competition. Before the "game on the gridiron," Fieri announces, "we're going to have a battle on the blacktop." The site is, according to the host, an "awesome place for a competition."[4] Even corn side dishes go head-to-head in *Tailgate Warriors,* as the culinary clashes in the stadium parking lot further distance cookery from its traditional attachment to the domestic, the private, the feminine.[5]

The format of the packaged competition that is *Tailgate Warriors* infuses cooking practice with the already established cultural milieu of masculinity and football. Fieri calls the cooking action on the blacktop like a commentator while interviewing contestants as they prepare their menu items, and engages in side commentaries with his fellow judges while they critique each tailgate team's play. Fieri incorporates football terminology into his narration through statements such as "each team jumps into action with a confident game plan," "he may have to call an audible," "New Orleans is takin' it down to the wire," "teams are moving fast to beat the clock," and "it's the last drive of what's been an intense competition."[6] At one point in the Packers vs. Seahawks episode, Fieri even uses a telestrator to diagram hot spots on a grill with x's and o's, just as a broadcaster would to highlight an offensive play. Tailgate team members join Fieri in narrative exchanges that blend cookery and football. As Green Bay team member Andy struggles to thicken caramel sauce, Fieri quips, "and dessert wasn't even Andy's assignment. I see some audibles, I see some people changing positions, I've got running backs catching passes." Andy acknowledges his team's adaptations and responds, "you've got to change it as it goes, let the play develop and take the open lane . . . we're . . . switching some things up."[7] The show's competitive structure further fuels a high energy, "one huge party"–like atmosphere on the blacktop outside NFL stadiums, pushing cookery literally and figuratively into public spaces even more removed from the domestic kitchen.[8] In doing so, *Tailgate Warriors* and other shows like it "place cooking firmly in the public sphere and promote a version of masculinity tied to hierarchy, success, power, speed, and stamina."[9]

However, our discussions with tailgaters, observations of them, and other source material trouble the Food Network's construction of pregame festivities in many ways. As we have noted, there are clearly many examples of hegemonic masculinity on display among the tailgating scenes we visited, yet this was far from the only gendered expression men performed on the blacktop before football games. As one observer notes, a communal atmosphere holds sway as "most tailgaters will share a beer with their neighbors in the same way one might borrow a cup of sugar from a neighbor back in the good old days."[10] Relationships forged largely between men, as witnessed in various tailgate venues, do carry a kind of neighborly feel where sharing might well include propane tanks, charcoal, or lighter fluid rather than sugar.

For some, including the 3rdRail9ers of San Francisco, there is little need or desire to engage in a culinary competition, though this was not always the case, and contradictions remain. "We're all competitive guys . . . definitely type A's," concedes Brenn in terms of their approach to tailgating, work, and life in general. Speaking in explicitly gendered terms about grilling and competition, Nick concludes, it is "sort of [an] alpha [male]" activity.[11] After winning several "Tailgater of the Year" competitions, Kimo says of the group's changing orientation, we were "confident in our tailgate sexuality" and thus did "not need to be battling" with others for the top cookery spot.[12] Implied is that the noncompetitive position taken up by the 3rdRail9ers was, in fact, an anomaly among tailgaters more generally, where competitiveness lent credibility. For 3rdRail9ers, however, their culinary skills were not in doubt and thus they need not adopt a competitive stance. "We know we're good," Nick says confidently.[13] Fellow San Francisco tailgater Michael admits to being "real competitive," but his motivations for being so are more complex than simply wanting to be the best. His drive to place food that both looks and tastes extraordinary before family and strangers alike represents his desire to "cook with love." To which Michael adds, "I want you to be fulfilled," it would be "disrespectful" to do otherwise.[14]

Like these San Francisco 49ers fans, other tailgaters with whom we spoke were interested in serving up superb culinary creations, but were less interested in competitive cookery like that seen and promoted on *Tailgate Warriors*. Rather than conceptualize cooking only in masculine terms of performance, competition, and skill, many tailgaters were also invested in using food to nurture and care for others. For them, creating community through food and the simultaneity of competitive and cooperative elements did not appear to be contradictory spaces to occupy. While fellowship among tailgaters can disrupt conventional expressions of manhood and masculinity, we should be mindful of its limits in doing so, as the activity on the blacktop can also reproduce gender norms and expectations.

Communal bonds, often forged between and among men and boys, with food serving as the binding agent, are a common phenomenon at a football tailgate, as well as the many outlets in which the activity is portrayed. The largely homosocial space of a football tailgate fosters a particular understanding of masculinity, while it reinforces gendered arrangements of social power.[15] Men create community with each other at a tailgate and in doing so reaffirm what it means to be 'a man'.

Male bonding is not just a routine occurrence on the blacktop, but a theme seen in popular portrayals of tailgating. For example, in the television sitcom *How I Met Your Mother*, one particular episode centers, in

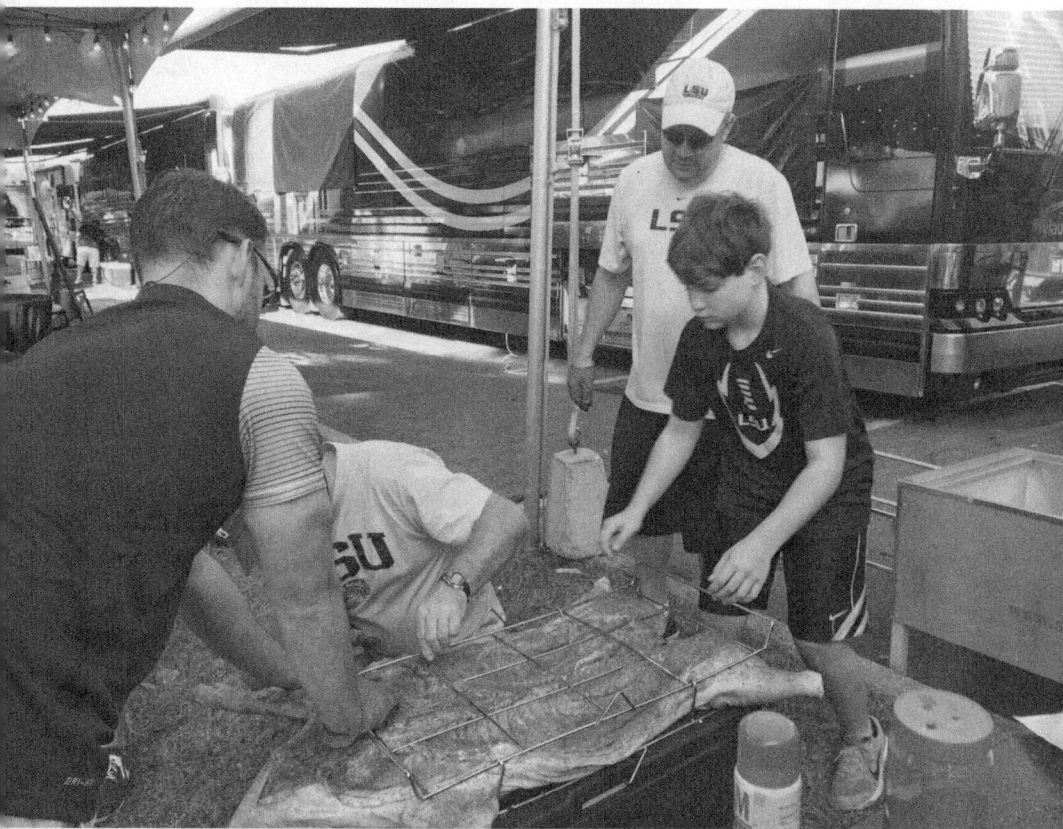

LSU tailgaters preparing a whole pig, November 2016. *Courtesy of Rita Liberti.*

part, on the character Marshall who contends that the most appropriate way to honor the memory of his father on the one-year anniversary of his death is to tailgate at his grave site. As Marshall stands before the grave he reminisces about past tailgating experiences with his father, as the scene cuts to a flashback of the two on the blacktop, years ago, enjoying the pregame activities. Nostalgia occupies a center frame as Marshall's father tells stories to the boy while cooking burgers on the grill.[16] Relationships forged between men are the basis for a "male clustering ritual," with bonds cemented around cookery.[17]

Toyota's football-season-long series of television commercials in 2009 and 2010, "Great Moments in Tailgating History," illustrate how communal bonds among male tailgaters are sometimes formed around constructions of hegemonic masculinity and a concomitant denigration of other gendered expressions.[18] In the eighteen-week series Toyota, hoping to capitalize on the "natural intersection of football and trucks," created forty-five-second segments in which three men in a Toyota truck travel back in time to see how "various tailgating traditions got their start."[19] Whether tracking the origins of the poncho, pompoms, or the portable seat cushion, among other rituals or football-related items, the comedic commercials use the recurring actors in the Toyota truck to place value upon masculinity. In nearly every segment, Frank sits in the backseat filming the action (usually fumbling with his handheld video camera) as his two friends comment on the scene before them. Frank's relatively brief narrative contributions are scorned by his buddies who ridicule or dismiss him for gendered expressions that fall outside narrow boundaries of hegemonic masculinity. When Frank is not admitting to getting pedicures or wearing nylons, he is crying over the beauty of the invented koozie and sympathizing with the animal roasting on a spit, all to the chagrin and disparagement of the other two men. Frank's companions see his words and actions as lacking the markers of rugged masculinity around which men, especially those on the blacktop, should aspire. Hegemonic masculinity is defined, in this series, by what Frank is not and this extends to the food he enjoys. In a final scene of one later episode in which the Toyota truck departs a tailgate lot, Frank is heard saying to the two men in the truck's front seat; "there's a falafel stand on route 87 I'd really like to try."[20] The falafel reference further distances Frank, already considered an outsider, from the boundaries of acceptable masculinity and gender expression. In the Toyota series, tailgating community is built between men, but at the expense of other men and in service to a particular construction of masculinity.

## "Fennel Sausage Says Chicago to Me"

Relationships between and among tailgaters can be fostered or eroded in terms of the ways a city or region's identity is discussed and represented through food. Again, *Tailgate Warriors* did a great deal to reinforce food's uniqueness to place. In the series, the cities participating in the competition and sometimes the regions they inhabit become gendered and classed markers of distinction. Directed by Fieri, the show's judges and tailgate team members engage in banter that sustains city and team identification. The kind of food served and the manner in which it is prepared in *Tailgate Warriors* are the binding agents that establish and reinforce each city's collective identity with its football team, reinforcing gender and class hierarchies in the process.

In the Chicago Bears vs. Buffalo Bills episode, the rugged, gritty, working-class vibes of the two cities provided the ground from which to characterize team members and their behavior, as well as the food. Chicago's team, according to Fieri, is "led by Timmy Shanley, a plumbing contractor from the south side." With respect to the Chicago tailgate squad, Shanley reminds viewers, "we don't dance, we don't sing, we're bears, we're from Chicago, down and dirty blue collar," in case anyone had other ideas about the town's ethos and the tailgate team. Shared assumptions about place identities and perceived traits of those who occupy those spaces need not be spoken as Jay "the Tailgate Guy" DiEugenio (a judge) remarks, in reference to Shanley's team, "these guys roll into Buffalo with a Chicago attitude." For captain Shanley, the team's stoicism explains their attitude and success in the *Tailgate Warriors* competition: "we're a city of broad shoulders" which means "nothin' got inside of us." For at least one judge (Dr. BBQ), the team's success was due to its ability to blend food with constructions of place as he quips, "that thing [fennel sausage] says Chicago to me."[21]

For others, as well, food and the process of creating it symbolized and reaffirmed an urban area's identity in the collective imagination of those within and beyond the city. "Hey brother," Fieri inquires of John, a Buffalo team member, "that's a big bologna sandwich. Is that how you do it in Buffalo?" Unapologetically reclaiming Buffalo's status as a working-class community, John says of the sandwich, "that's how we do it in Buffalo. This is gourmet."[22] In an example from the Packers vs. Seahawks matchup on the blacktop, Fieri comments on "monstro" fritters (referring to their large size) made by the Green Bay team, adding, "if you're going to do a fritter and you're from Lambeau you better roll it like this!"[23] Throughout *Tailgate Warriors* episodes, food comes to represent the urban center's collective identity, strengthening already strong relationships between residents of a specific city, and the professional sport franchise in that location.[24] The Chicago, Buffalo, and Green Bay tailgate activity, including the items on the menu, blend seamlessly with constructions of working-class masculinity that define the cities and the game of football more generally. In this way, *Tailgate Warriors* illustrates that the combination of football and food informs place identification, including construction of classed and gendered identities in those locations.[25]

For other teams, however, the associations among place identity, gender, food, and football were less secure. Most teams did not seem to have to "prove" they were tailgate-worthy, but Seattle was the exception to this general rule. Tanya, a Seattle team member, remained somewhat dubious, even in victory, "I can't believe we won." She continues, "we are so glad to bring a win home for Seattle and to prove that we are actually a tailgating town."[26] In the 49ers vs. Raiders episode, urban identifications were used to differentiate the two teams and in doing so exposed contrasting classed and gendered conceptualizations. Fieri offers, "if you're a San Francisco 49er you know the refined ways of life. I mean I've been to a bunch of 49er games [tailgating] and I've seen people bustin' out sushi and chardonnay." The cultural distance between the two cities, far more than the span of the Bay Bridge, is confirmed later in the episode as Dr. BBQ, admiring his plate of barbeque beans, tri-tip, and potatoes explains, "this is the kind of plate of food I'd expect to get in Oakland."[27]

Perhaps the most interesting episode, in terms of the construction of contrasts and contradictions in the food, football, city, and masculinity formula, is the Vikings vs. Saints matchup. Moreover, in this episode of *Tailgate Warriors* in particular, culinary creations were marked and sustained as different along gendered, as well as racial and cultural lines of distinction. From the start Minnesota's less complicated "heartland kind of menu" was seen as the underdog to the more complex "whole bunch of big food, big flavors" fare expected of the New Orleans team. Even Minnesota team member Jason worried about his squad's "fried and everything on a stick" offerings, saying, "we tried to keep the menu Minnesota and that's kind of a challenge you know." Constructed and operating as polar opposites, the menus, imbued with racialized signifiers, position the bland, white-bread offerings of Minnesota against the spice-filled, exciting cuisine of New Orleans. Much like whiteness, it is within the banality of Minnesota's menu that its power rests, as the exotic New Orleans eatables are marked and cast as other. To further create contrast and distance between the two, Minnesota's "work ethic" as "even-keeled and very solid" is played against the "flare" of New Orleans, its team, and its food. Thus, in this scenario, hierarchical divisions are built from, and rest upon, notions of racialized masculine identity that situate whiteness as stable and self-regulated. Whereas New Orleans is positioned as far from ordered and is instead marked by its tendency toward the chaotic. For at least one observer, however, the New Orleans flare is precisely what distanced the city from a connection to both sport and masculinity. Writing in late 2009 as the Saints marched toward the Super Bowl, Douglas McCollam mused, "it's an odd pairing in a way, this team and this town. Football is a brute game, strictly regimented, born on cold, northern fields and associated with big shouldered cities like Chicago and Pittsburgh. By contrast, New Orleans is a warm and dreamy place, birthplace of jazz, lover of good food, and afternoon naps. America's most feminine city."[28]

In the end, despite the New Orleans team's much anticipated "pigs fly po-boy" entrée (named because people said the Saints would win the Super Bowl when pigs flew), team Minnesota won the matchup. Originally seen as lackluster and monochromatic, their menu eventually won accolades from the judges for its "simplicity" as "good, solid heart-land American food." Moreover, it seems the Minnesota team's ability to cook "like a Viking" (on large grills) helped push their side to victory in a competition in which place meanings, tied to notions of gender, class, and race, were generated and sustained through food.[29]

## Mascot on the Menu

In still other ways, as extensions of cuisine and place identity, food serves to both establish community and create clear and competitive distinctions within it. As we saw in Chapter Four, we actively construct and perform our gendered identities through the food we prepare and consume. More specifically, forms of hegemonic masculinity are established and maintained via the consumption of meat. The eating of meat "connotes power," according to Amy Calvert, as it "signifies domination over nonhumans reducing the latter to consumable flesh."[30] Across a variety of sites we studied, bonds between and among tailgaters were sometimes created and enriched by using food, as symbolized through the opposing team's mascot, as a means to carve out *us* and *them* in relation to a team and a community.

*The Southern Tailgating Cookbook* provides a lengthy description of creative possibilities for "eating your competition." The book's author proclaimed, "on game day, don't settle for beating your opponent," indicating that readers should eat them instead. The narrative noted that some teams have "live versions of their mascots" who are ever-present on game day and an important part of the team's identity. As such, the publication advised, "take the disdain you feel toward the competition and channel it into a delicious and creative meal that will inspire your fellow fans and intimidate the opposition." The publication reminded readers of various mascots across southeast universities and offered up a number of possible culinary creations to "incorporate into your game-day spread." Among them, "any mutton or lamb dish" for the University of North Carolina (Rameses the Ram) and "steak and creamer potato kabobs for Bevo the Longhorn Steer when competing against the University of Texas." Avian mascots presented a bit of a problem since, the author confided, "I certainly wouldn't eat an eagle, owl, or ibis on game day," but not to fret as "any type of poultry can make a plausible substitute."[31]

Beyond cookbooks, actual tailgaters have long been "grilling up the competition."[32] Miami Dolphins fans have been "eating the competition" since at least the 1980s. Ironically for the fans of Miami during the 1990s, tuna steaks were one of their favorite items to grill when the team played the Patriots and then the Jets—a competitive homage to Bill Parcells, who coached both teams during the period and whose nickname was "Tuna."[33] For Louisiana State University fan Bruce Richards, cooking up and "consuming the opponent" is a personal tradition that started in the mid-1990s, and no team's mascot is out of reach. Though when asked if he would hunt a badger if LSU played Wisconsin or gopher for a Minnesota matchup, Richards responded, "nah, for those we'd just make hamburgers . . . that's our catchall category. When in doubt, grind 'em into burgers and eat 'em up."[34]

One of the favorite symbols of an opposition's mascot to be prepared and eaten by LSU fans is "Big Al," the elephant of heated rival University of Alabama. The LSU faithful go to some effort to roast whole pigs, sewing on extra-large ears and a trunk made of pork to create a frighteningly good replica of a baby elephant. When Alabama comes to Baton Rouge to play LSU, hundreds or perhaps thousands of "Cajun microwaves" (large roasting boxes with coals or wood placed above meat

3rdRail9ers gameday menu, October 2015. *Courtesy of authors.*

in the enclosed container) and other cooking contraptions fill tailgating spaces around the stadium. In 2012 a tweet from *ESPN The Magazine* created a social media uproar. It read, "Smoking a baby elephant. To eat. If you can top this, let us know where to find you."[35] Graham Watson at *Yahoo! Sports* was not sure what to make of the tailgating ritual at LSU. You would think, Watson pondered, "baby elephant would be one of those things off limits to folks. I don't think you can just go to your Wal-Mart and pick one up like you do a steak." The author added, "this is right up there with clubbing baby seals and shooting lions for sport," and is "perhaps the most Billy-Bob thing ever." The publication corrected its position and retracted its stereotyped swipe at the South and its people when it learned that the image was actually a pig and not an elephant. That reality "makes us feel a lot better . . . apologies to the tailgaters. Billy-Bob comment withdrawn."[36]

Tailgaters at the University of Oregon also go to great lengths to make "consuming the competition" part of the spectacle on the blacktop. UO tailgater Mike and his crew once butchered a small goat and arranged it to look like a dog for a matchup against the University of Washington Huskies. The one item that's out of bounds for that Oregon crew is, of course, duck.

On at least one occasion, eating the other team's mascot was touted for its nutritional benefits and not just as a symbolic annihilation of the opposition. In a rare consumptive practice not infused with meat and protein, some on the University of Maryland campus advocated that students eat oranges, "but not just any oranges—Otto the Orange, Syracuse's mascot."[37] Though observers wondered how future football matchups against the Panthers and Demon Deacons would play out if the practice of eating the other team's mascot became a pattern.[38]

Competitive rivalries, undergirding particular constructions of masculinity, are expressed in a variety of ways across football tailgating, sometimes through food. In most cases eating the opposition means meat maintains its supremacy at the top of the food chain among many tailgaters. As noted throughout the book, we actively contour our gendered identities through not only what we eat, but how we eat certain foods. The ritual consumption by tailgaters of rival mascots is "symbolic violence through feasting," and accounts for one of the many ways in which masculinity is made by reproducing lines of distinction between *us* and *them*.[39] According to one online entry, whether it is duck for the Oregon game or gator for the Florida contest, it is a tailgating tradition and "it's all in good fun."[40] Indeed, it seems to be that for many tailgaters across the country on game day as opposing team mascots serve up the fun and feast upon which community is cultivated. Importantly, the practice also works to more firmly secure particular understandings of masculinity rooted in competition and dominance as competitors' mascots are to be consumed and eradicated.

## "Steaking" Out Your Territory

Spatial arrangements within and around stadium parking lots matter a great deal to many tailgaters.[41] Similar to mascots on the menu, communities are constructed on the blacktop but with clear lines of distinction between and among parties. Tailgaters often speak of the friendly and open vibe they have or wish to foster with others, but in order to construct that vibe, they very consciously demarcate their space from every other one on the blacktop. Indeed, tailgating spaces are often "walled off" from each other in neat and quite explicit sections with the use of vehicles, trailers, and tents, and even bright yellow caution tape, among other items. It is usually clear when one has left or entered a particular tailgating scene.

Longstanding traditions around space can make tailgaters quite territorial, especially when those customs are unsettled. In part, the tensions surrounding the tailgating landscape are fundamental to the storyline in the 2012 documentary *America's Parking Lot*, featuring Dallas Cowboys fans Cy and Stan (also known as Tiger). The film follows the two men as they negotiate the tumultuous process of the team's move from Texas Stadium to the new Cowboys Stadium (later named AT&T Stadium) in 2009 and 2010. Cy and Tiger's identities as Cowboys fans are as much wrapped up in tailgating as in their love of the team. Cy and Tiger's crew of regulars had commanded the same spot outside of Texas Stadium for over two decades. The association is a long and deep one, so much so the group had their own moniker, "Gate 6 Tailgaters." That's not the only thing, adds Tiger, "we even have our own Koozies." The move to the new stadium ended long-held traditions, as Cy and Tiger's tailgates were now separated by at least two parking lots. Tiger lamented the new arrangement as he underscored the communal elements so integral to the space, "I took enormous pride to say I was part of the Gate 6 Tailgaters. Part of the original group—founders." He adds, "[I'm] not sure what we founded out there. But we did found something; not something tangible, but an intangible spirit that took twenty years to build." However, the communal aspects of the activity were the same points around which competitive antagonisms arose. "It's kind of our God-given right to be in the best parking spot right next to the stadium," Tiger declares, adding, "I'm sure there's a lot of fans who think they're the best, but we think [we are]."

Fans beyond those in Dallas also describe the importance of place in tailgating and the extent to which longtime blacktop revelers will go in competing with others to, ironically enough, create community. San Francisco 3rdRail9er Nick explains that the switch from games played at Candlestick Park to Levi's Stadium caused much consternation among the tailgate faithful. The sense of communal camaraderie among San Francisco tailgaters at the team's previous site at Candlestick park vanished over the course of the first couple of games in the new stadium. So much for the last true village mentality, Nick lamented. Describing the chaotic scene as tailgaters rushed for spots on the blacktop, Nick says, it was "straight up manifest destiny on that first game." Folks who had been parking in the same spot at Candlestick for decades were, in this moment, fighting (sometimes literally) for a new location in which to establish their tailgate. Nick's 3rdRail9ers comrade George continues, "it was like the Oklahoma Land Grab [Rush]," but rather than horses and wagons— cars, trucks, and recreational vehicles in all sizes and shapes made a mad dash for a premiere spot.[42] Hoping to outpace the motorized vehicles, tailgaters jumped the fences and sprinted on foot to secure a suitable location. Invariably the competition resulted in several verbal and physical altercations, but after a "good deal of shuffling" Nick and his crew found a spot with "enough elbow room." It was "golden," he remembers. After the tumult of the stadium opening, tailgaters found "their spot," then "the village started happening." Only after the ground rules had been established and territory had been firmed up could they once again get to a place where "everybody loves each other."[43]

A similar scene plays out prior to football games in Oxford at the University of Mississippi home contests, as revelers vie for desired locations across the Grove. A stand of mature oak and maple trees constitutes the nearly dozen acres of tailgating space where, since 1991, severe restrictions have been placed on motor vehicles entering the location on game days. Early Friday mornings before Saturday afternoon contests, "spot savers" are permitted in to reserve a particular site. As hundreds of people sprint to locations in the Grove, the scene is reminiscent of an adult Easter egg hunt where participants stampede in search of the golden egg, or in this case a spot to tailgate. Red and blue (University of Mississippi colors) garbage cans are the only items, beyond the natural topography of trees, permitted to define individual tailgating spots. Those charged with site reservations are often paid eight to ten dollars an hour for the task of holding a spot, but cannot bring in chairs. Thus "spot savers" must stand or sit in the space until tents are constructed later that night. Over two thousand tents measuring between one- and two-hundred square feet fill the acreage by early Saturday morning, built by one of several local companies employed to construct the canopies.[44] The serious investment in the process of claiming territory, albeit temporarily, is underscored by Christy Knapp of Real Thing Tent: "It's kind of like church," she explained, "you don't sit in someone else's pew."[45]

The relationship between tailgaters and the physical space they occupy is deeper than simply wanting consistently close proximity to a restroom or the benefits of the shade provided under a big tree. For many, a particular location in the areas just outside a football stadium evokes feelings of nostalgia about family and friends. Jim (also known as Dr. Dogz) and his fellow tailgaters outside of Stanford Stadium in Palo Alto, California have occupied the same relatively small site for nearly four decades. Tradition, Jim notes, is important, and though the "wine quality has gotten better over the years," the menu remains constant in terms of what and how much is offered. The hot dogs (always from Costco) are prepared on a very small grill and served in "cradles," which Jim proudly claims is unique across all of Stanford tailgating. Even the apron Jim wears has deep roots and is only the second he has had in decades. The change away from the original apron, with its "PAC 10" insignia, was necessitated only because of the conference renaming to the "PAC 12." Jim and the others enjoy tailgating for a host of reasons, but prime among them is that it "reminds them of what it was like to be undergrads" at the institution. It is those relationships fostered on the campus in the 1970s and in that tailgating spot since that remain their "most cherished memories."[46]

## Tailgating With a Cause

The idea of using the tailgate as a way to fundraise for charity was one rather unexpected practice that we observed among several participants with whom we spoke. Fundraising for charity in order to foster communal bonds or use those existing relationships to promote philanthropy were common practices among groups of men invested in tailgating for a particular cause. In most, if not all cases, those with whom we have spoken who use tailgating to fundraise began their charitable work on a relatively small scale, as a way to assist a friend, family member, or local community organization in need. Sometimes the actual tailgating site, just outside the stadium, provided the location upon which fundraising events occurred. In other instances, tailgaters took their cooking skills on the road to assist any number of charitable organizations in raising funds for various activities and issues. In both situations we pondered the possible gendered aspects of the activity. In particular, our focus centered on how participants talked about and explained cooking for a cause, including how these activities fostered a care-oriented perspective on food—an orientation traditionally assigned to women and femininity.[47]

While the size and sophistication of groups invested in using a football tailgate to fundraise is wide-ranging, men cooking food remains central to the enterprise. Such is the case for Raiders tailgaters Los Malosos, whose charitable activity is less a fundraiser and more an expenditure of time, energy, and money to help those in need. The group loads up their pickup trucks and trailer with an Oakland Raiders logo emblazed on the side panel for an annual trip to Mexico to feed local children in an orphanage near Tijuana. What started as a gesture to feed those in a single facility has turned into an event in which one- to two-thousand people from a local village come by to get a meal served up by members of Los Malosos. Asked about the complications of arranging and carrying out such endeavor, a Los Malosos member noted that the most difficult aspect is taking good-natured ribbing from border patrol agents in San Diego over the hometown Charger rivalry with the Oakland Raiders. The efforts of Los Malosos to "feed everybody" is an extension of how they see themselves as Raiders tailgaters, but also how they, in gathering, cooking, and serving food, care for a community. Acts of nurturing and giving are fundamental to their motivations, troubling dominant understandings of masculinity performed on the blacktop and elsewhere. "It's from the heart," a Los Malosos member concludes.[48]

Similar to Oakland Raiders tailgaters, good deeds and cooking, as well as the camaraderie that grows from participating in charitable events, are the aspects that drive Dwayne Martin and other Louisiana State University tailgate members of the Black Pot Mafia.[49] Friends and others took note of the culinary skills of the Black Pot Mafia and soon asked if they would entertain cooking at fundraising events. With dozens of charitable events on their culinary vita, Martin adds that the group remains committed to continuing the tradition, in part because they really enjoy using their cooking skills to aid others in need. In addition, the prep, which often begins days in advance of an event, provides Black Pot Mafia members with "quality time" to gather and connect with each other, as they cut up onions, pork, celery, sausage, bell peppers, and other items for their signature jambalaya or pastalaya dishes.[50] In this way, the activity serves to further the male bonding narratives we discussed earlier.

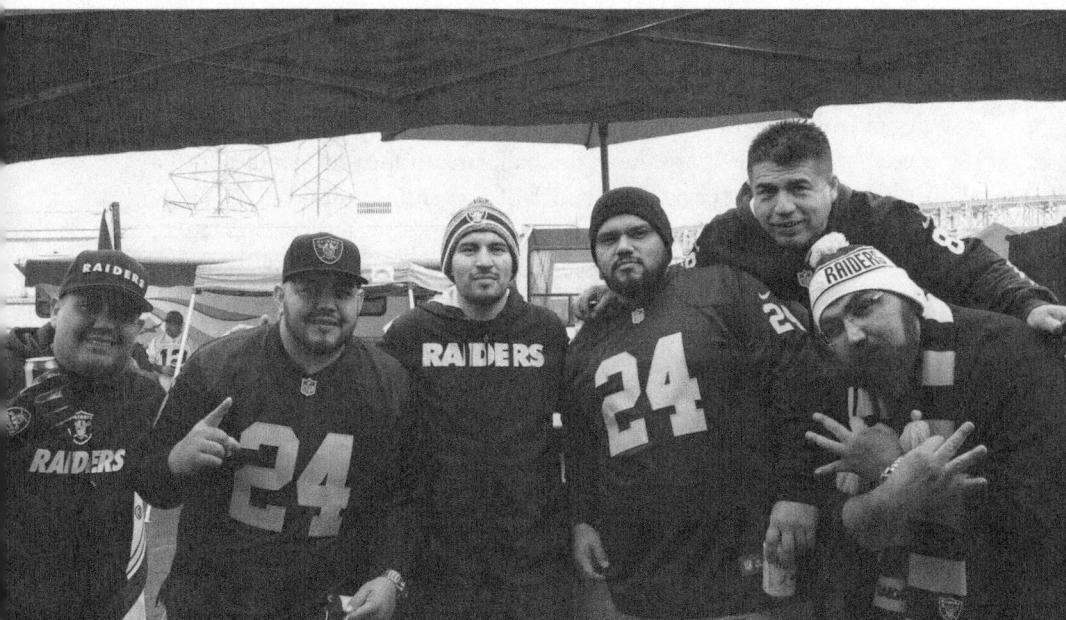

Oakland Raiders tailgaters, Los Malosos, December 2015. *Courtesy of authors.*

While Los Malosos and Black Pot Mafia members take their culinary skills away from the blacktop to fundraise or assist organizations in doing so, others never leave the parking lot in their philanthropic ventures with food. For Joe Fox, a University of Tennessee football fan and tailgater, the impetus for his charitable activities began quite personally, with the death of a close friend. When asked why he uses a football tailgate as the site for a fundraiser drive, Fox noted that his fondest memories of his friend were those on the blacktop on game days. Moreover, Fox adds that as a child he joined female relatives in the kitchen "wanting to learn" from them what he could about cookery. As an extension of those early experiences, hospitality and hosting were integral to how he understood himself, adding, "feeding people feeds my soul." These forces joined together and "Tailgate For A Cause" was born in 2014 on the blacktop just before University of Tennessee football games. Success was immediate with a thousand people attending the first tailgate. That success was also the event's drawback, as Fox quickly acknowledged he could not continue to do all the cooking for home football tailgating events that reached two thousand people in size. Now with a four-member board in place and catered menu (paid for by sponsors), Fox can devote his time to enjoying the party. With over a hundred thousand dollars raised for various charities in four years, that remains his plan going forward.

Like Joe Fox, New York Giants fan Dan Cohen and a group of friends began with a relatively small tailgate philanthropy practice, "born from twelve guys, lamb chops, beer, football, and an idea for good" about a decade ago.[51] What began as a "bunch of guys sitting around eating burgers" has mushroomed into an enormously complex charity event with a "message for good."[52] Now as an established nonprofit organization, the "Section 16H Group" (their original location at the old Giants stadium) has grown to consist of an executive chef who manages the game day menu (which includes, among other culinary items, Chilean sea bass and sushi), a board of directors, live music, event security, and even a bathroom attendant at the port-a-potty for the convenience of guests. Cohen's "Tailgate With A Cause" is trademarked and going forward he hopes to "grow the brand to get more corporate sponsors . . . to host an even bigger/better party." Amid this change, he remains committed to raising money for charities "near and dear" to his and board members' hearts. With fundraising totals in excess of $150,000, Cohen believes the event's success stems from tailgating's quintessential identity as an "American thing" combined with his team's ability to throw a fabulous party in a space (stadium parking lot) "not built for a party." Indeed, the "buzz grows" around football tailgating and philanthropy among New York Giants fans and many others across the country.[53] While philanthropic efforts on the blacktop vary in terms of size and scope, what serves as a core element across each are the bonds created and sustained between men. Furthermore, food acts as the force that fastens and solidifies these relationships among male tailgaters as they further philanthropic endeavors.[54]

## Conclusion

Community is constructed in a variety of ways on the blacktop prior to football games, with cookery serving as a major catalyst in the process. The setting remains one in which participants talk of spending time with family, friends, and those who share an affinity for a football team. While some elements of community-building were steeped in conventional understandings of men and masculinity, others clearly complicate fixed notions of gender. The mediated examples of tailgating, including the Food Network's *Tailgate Warriors*, were clearly invested in a construction of masculinity grounded in competition and dominance. However, the bonds that form community in football tailgating are more complexly layered than simplistic renderings of them delivered via television to viewers. Our observations of tailgaters, as well as their own testimonials throw into relief a range of expressions of masculinity, beyond a set of narrowly defined expectations.

# CONCLUSION

The opening image of a recent television commercial for Chevrolet features a large smoker trailer, being pulled by an even bigger pickup truck. We then see the profile of the male driver within the vehicle's cab. The voiceover clarifies the obvious, stating, "a man and his truck . . . " as the rig is driven into a tailgating scene. The narration continues, " . . . and tofu and veggie burgers and raw kale salad." The narrator informs us that the three food items are "all fine—just not today." This occurs as the truck's driver, now out of the cab, shows off what *is* on the menu: a very large piece of uncooked red meat proudly being held up for a fellow tailgater to see. As we witness numerous tailgaters eating meat off plates piled high with animal protein, we get a final reminder of how and why we arrived in this place. "Introducing high country, the premium Silverado," the narrator intones as the massive vehicle sits amid smoke wafting from numerous grills and smokers.[1]

The scene depicted in the Chevrolet commercial embodies many of the themes and issues discussed in *Gridiron Gourmet*. Masculine signifiers abound in this largely homosocial tailgating space, in this commercial and countless other sites, on the fields and parking lots just outside football stadiums. The supersize truck builds on long held and deeply rooted associations with men and rugged masculinity. The cooking equipment and pieces of red meat join in amplifying expressions of manhood tied to strength, power, excess, independence, and privilege. The setting is marked not only by a close association with hegemonic masculinity, but also with a denigration of, and distancing from, the feminine. Food, in the form of tofu, veggie burgers, and kale symbolizes the feminine, and is constructed as bearing no association with men and masculinity. Importantly, these culinary choices are not simply depicted as foreign to manhood, they are antithetical to it. Thus, as the Chevrolet commercial exemplifies, *Gridiron Gourmet* argues gender is actively constructed and negotiated in this space where food and cooking practices are the ways in which men perform their identity as men. Indeed, the tailgate, a "haunt of the modern male," constitutes one important place, among several in society, where men go to be men.[2]

We believed from the start of this project that tailgating, and the food practices at the core of the activity, offered us rich perspectives on gender constructions and performances outside of football stadiums just prior to the competition on the field of play. Others, however, were less convinced of the site's value. Reaction to our work and the idea of a book on the topic drew a range of reactions from acquaintances, beyond those who study popular culture . Some didn't think there was more to the story than men and meat, drinking and football, while others congratulated us on scoring a research topic that would require us to party at sporting events. Of course, as cultural studies theorists we understand the importance of exploring everyday practices within popular culture, even when conclusions, at least on the surface, appear self-evident. Just as numerous scholars over the past few decades explored the game and the associated gender dynamics being played out in the stadium, tailgating emerges as more than frivolous entertainment. It is a football-related ritual and important example of the ways in which power and privilege play themselves out on the blacktop just outside the arena.

With that said, then, the dearth of scholarly attention paid to tailgating culture, including the cookery at the center of the pursuit, is difficult to explain. Perhaps cookery, traditionally coded as female and gendered feminine, as well as removed to private, largely invisible spaces, was dismissed and ignored precisely for those reasons. These academic gaps are beginning to fill, however, as sport studies scholars and others who study athletics and culture begin to take food seriously.[3] *Gridiron Gourmet* offers a contribution to this fledgling body of knowledge with the hope that it spurs others to consider the power dynamics at work in tailgate culture and cookery's important place in understanding masculinity and the boundaries that give it definition. The numerous ways that manhood and notions of masculinity are represented and negotiated in tailgate spaces through cookery and consumptive practices is worthy of our collective attention. To dismiss this practice as trivial is to permit masculinity and the processes through which it is constructed to go unnamed and thus unexamined.

As we saw, food has long been a central element of football as a social event in the United States. Football's origin stories include references to food's place amid throngs of spectators en route to the game's earliest contests. Even at the turn of the twentieth century, football's ability to entertain was not confined to the moments between the opening and closing whistles. In the hours before, and even after early football games, food and feasting were important parts of a larger all-day event. While men have long held a central place in football tailgating, their relationship to cookery at the center of the activity has evolved over the past half century. From the earliest decades of tailgate history, men moved from happy recipients of neatly wrapped cold cut sandwiches made by wives and mothers to more recent involvement that positions them as central to the activity's core. In twenty-first century America, men and the food they create are often the life of the tailgate party. Writing largely for men about outdoor cookery in 1941, author James Beard noted that for "satisfaction all around" the outdoor picnic should include a wealth of "excellent food . . . good liquor . . . and a large chunk of gayety and good fellowship."[4] Beard might well have penned these words today in relation to the tailgate party, rather than over three quarters of a century ago.

The elements so central to Beard's outdoor party constitute today's tailgate spectacle where men occupy the activity's core space, as they serve up culinary delights and expressions of masculinity. In contemporary tailgating, the vehicles that transport folks to stadium lots, the equipment on which men prepare and cook foodstuffs, and the ways in which those culinary masterpieces are described buttress masculinity, keeping participants a safe distance from the taint of the feminine. Food, equipment, and performance are presented in excess, on a very public stage with hundreds or even thousands of fellow tailgaters looking on or joining in the party on the blacktop. On countless occasions across the tailgating spaces we visited "the grill man or pit master deploys a knife . . . at the very end of his *show*, to carve or chop the animal, and that qualifies as ceremony" [emphasis added].[5] Accessorized with masculine signifiers, men's place is secure. It is, according to Katharina Vester, this "handsomely wrought, masculine gadgetry" and the way it is deployed that makes the man and helps him to reside more comfortably as the king of the culinary space of the tailgate.[6] Indeed, the event's uniqueness, as well as its grand scale, position it as special; the tailgate is no one's idea of cooking mundanity. Importantly, taken together, the equipment and its public presentation foster a tailgating spectacle that embodies, as it reinscribes, gender difference.

The contours of manhood and masculinity are bound as much (or more) to what is being smoked, deep fried, or grilled as they are to the kind of equipment on which the food is cooked. As we have seen, meat, particularly red meat, is king of the tailgate. Rich in symbolism, dead animals, whole or in part, being prepared and cooked at a tailgate connotes a conquest or overpowering.[7] Moreover, meat-eating's deep association with gender, and hegemonic masculinity in particular, fortifies the tailgate as a site often tied to certain kinds of gendered expressions. In fact, as Jeffery Sobal contends, when partaking in activities such as barbecue contests (and tailgating, we would add), men tend to "hyper masculinize meat."[8] The preoccupation with meat and its consumption at the tailgate can, at times, be so outlandish it is difficult to distinguish tongue-in-cheek rhetoric from that meant to be serious. Such is the case with a recent article touting the "meat necklace" to be made and worn at your next party on the blacktop. "Think of the convenience of having your entire meal accompany you wherever you go," the author observed, adding, "think of the envy you'll command—nothing says you're the king or queen of your castle quite like a shimmering bib of cured meat strung around your neck."[9]

*Gridiron Gourmet* moves from the assumptive position that food and culinary practices offer us a window onto a broader political landscape in which our gender identities are constructed and contested. Tailgating culture, as well as the other artifacts that circulate around the space, are more than one-dimensional, however. Racialized discourses join with gender and also pervade tailgating spaces, as evidenced in our exploration of tailgate cookbooks. In some of the earliest tailgate cookbooks of the 1960s through the 1980s, readers embarked on what Zelinsky called, "gastronomic tourism."[10] On these adventures, we were invited to eat the food of the other, but rarely were the cultures or their inhabitants depicted as anything beyond the stereotyped renderings largely white authors and audiences already imagined of racially diverse populations. More recent tailgate cookbooks pull some of the same racist threads through to the present, though inclusion of a wider variety of ethnic fare characterizes recipes within the texts. While more ethnic and racial diversity is apparent in recent cookbooks, the publications reaffirm the white-centric realities that we witnessed at various tailgates across the US. As important cultural products, what important lessons do tailgate cookbooks offer us about the current state of the nation's politics and policies toward immigrant and racially diverse populations? Perhaps contemporary cookbooks present us with what we envision as a palatable way to cross racial and ethnic boundaries in sampling the food of others, without engaging our own racism and privilege in the process.

The symbolic ethnic and racial border crossings within tailgate cookbooks extend, in many ways, to constructions of community on the blacktop. Communal bonds are in constant tension with culinary exclusions and inclusions, each marking the contours of masculinity. The tailgate is simultaneously a competitive and cooperative space in which food plays a central role in how community is envisioned. For example, regional culinary traditions often link tailgaters, forging a fraternity of sorts around the kinds of foods prepared and the place identities associated with those items. Community can also be strengthened by using food to nurture others. These actions can easily be read as resistive to dominant understandings of men and masculinity, ultimately expanding gender boundaries. Conversely, however, competitive hierarchies also mark tailgating spaces where food, specifically the other team's mascot, can be the proving ground for putting distance between tailgaters. In addition to consuming the other, power is also demonstrated via a "conquest of space" in which boundary lines demarcate us and them.[11] Tailgating communities are parking lots filled with contradictions, a competitive brotherhood.

As noted at the start of this book, we attempted to explore a variety of tailgate sites, in terms of how participants represent and experience the activity. With that said, however, our examination of tailgating was not exhaustive, in part, because the ubiquity of the activity throughout so many cultural spaces made it impossible to capture all of the ways the activity is lived and represented. There is much more to tailgating culture and our hope is that others will take to the blacktop to explore this rich site.

We hope that future work in food studies and sports studies will explore how and why tailgating, as it has grown along with football, offers us such a productive space to interrogate gender and power. For us the crux of the matter was always what was happening at the intersection of cookery and masculinity. We never conceptualized the workings of tailgating as apolitical or innocent, a predominantly male space where men simply socialized before and after football contests. It, like so many other exclusively or dominantly male spheres in our world, is imbued with power. As illustrated in *Gridiron Gourmet*, cookery on the blacktop, carried out mainly by men, often establishes and reinforces gender privilege. Status is conferred upon those who adhere to gendered expectations about food and broader culinary practices. The process, in turn, extends to its participants a kind of culinary capital in this majority male foodscape.

It is often the resistive spaces and actors within cultural locations that push us to consider more nuanced understandings of an event or activity, and tailgating is no different. One area of tailgate culture that potentially offers challenges to both hegemonic masculinity and heteronormativity is the activity of those revelers on the blacktop who identify as gay or queer. The experiences and observations of Northwestern University football fan Andrew Bauhs throw into sharp relief the potential to disrupt dominant gendered discourses that circulate around the tailgate. Each year, Bauhs leads a group of gay men in tailgating outside the Northwestern stadium. He cautions that this is far from a usual tailgate as Bauhs must first host a Football 101 course for participants, many of whom know little about the game and are much more excited, he claims, about the Oscars than a Northwestern Wildcats football game. Moreover, he finds it necessary to alert his tailgate party to "go easy on the cologne" so as not to attract bees, "a disclaimer that most tailgate [organizers] don't need to issue."[12] By its very existence, Bauhs' tailgate party is a political act. At one recent festive gathering on the blacktop, "as a cloud of Giorgio Armani hovered over our tailgate [clearly not all participants got the memo about the bees]" Bauhs notes, "a neighboring group of fans . . . couldn't help but notice our unique brand of spirit. With everyone well-appointed in articulately planned purple attire, it was clear this was not a straight affair." The exchange, according to Bauhs, was extremely positive, and to his delight was a great illustration that the "world of sports does not need to be traditionally masculine."[13] While we do not know what was on the menu at Bauhs' tailgate, we can acknowledge that his presence and that of his gay friends creates space to dislodge narrow conceptualizations of masculinity.

Devoted groups of female fans and tailgaters also present potential critical pathways to explore in disrupting hegemonic masculinity on the blacktop. We saw this in *Gridiron Gourmet*, to a certain extent, with individual female tailgaters. In their study of the National Football League's female fans, Obsorne and Coombs conclude that tailgating activity was one of the rare places within their work that underscored gender difference. Interestingly, as one of the study's participants observed, "you know you rarely go to a tailgate where a bunch of women are standing around cooking food. Did you ever notice that? It's always these guys around the barbecue pit, being manly, lighting things on fire, burning meat. The whole thing is, yeah, it definitely is [manly]."[14] This female fan's observations confirmed what we noted as well, eating and cookery within tailgating are important pieces in a gendered performance with men as the main characters. This focused attention, then, on female fans presents another scholarly pathway and a possible critical avenue through which to engage tailgaters' experiences of the activity and its culinary center.

Where are we left, then, in understanding how masculinity is constructed and negotiated in mediated representations and lived experiences of tailgaters? We do believe, in general, tailgating and various activities associated with the activity, bolster traditional conceptualizations of masculinity. This process was not absolute however, as there were spaces of resistance or disruptions to expressions of hegemonic masculinity, providing, as noted, depth and complexity to how gender was expressed and performed. For example, though rare, women's presence on the blacktop was, at times, an occasion that troubled the bonds of fraternity. Festive tailgate leadership and public mastery of the grill were, in these isolated instances, women's work. Moreover, in unsettling gendered ideologies, men, at times, used food to nurture and to give as an expression of sharing and kindness. These examples were exceptions to a more general rule, however, that saw men and rugged masculinity at the center of tailgating activities. *Gridiron Gourmet* concludes that men took culinary cover by hypermasculinizing the space, removing it from any specter of femininity or domestic influence within the surrounds of food and cookery. A power drill for mixing cake batter or a shovel for scrambling eggs—those are the right tools for the job for the gridiron gourmet.

# NOTES

## Introduction

1. *The Simpsons*, season 19, episode 18, "Any Given Sundance," directed by Chuck Sheetz, aired on May 4, 2008 by Fox Broadcasting Company, The Simpsons on FXX, Accessed July 11, 2015, http://www.simpsonsworld.com/video/283769923976.

2. Julia Moskin, "The Chef-Dude is in the House," *New York Times*, (August 11, 2010): D1, D5.

3. *Tailgate Warriors with Guy Fieri*, produced by The Food Network, originally aired on October 17, 2009.

4. The *Oxford English Dictionary* notes this definition of tailgating as first appearing in press in the *Boston Globe* in 1962. "Definitely Dartmouth was Peter Freeman of Westin, sharing a bit of tailgating with Dee and Ann Austin of Arlington," *Boston Globe*, October 28, 1962, 66.

5. *The Simpsons*, "Any Given Sundance."

6. Some of this research has been published in the fields of sport management and marketing. See, for example, J. Drenten, C.O. Peters, T. Leigh, and C.R. Hollenbeck, "Not Just a Party in the Parking Lot: An Exploratory Investigation of the motives underlying the Ritual Commitment of Football Tailgaters," *Sport Marketing Quarterly*, 18 (2009): 92–106; and Tonya Williams Bradford and John F. Sherry, "Domesticating Public Space through Ritual: Tailgating as Vestaval," *Journal of Consumer Research*, 42 (2015): 130–151.

7. James L. Watson and Melissa L. Caldwell (eds), *The Cultural Politics of Food and Eating: A Reader*, (Malden, MA: Blackwell, 2005), 1.

8. C. Wesley Buerkle, "Metrosexuality Can Stuff It: Beef Consumption as (Heteromasculine) Fortification," *Text and Performance Quarterly*, 29 no. 1, (2009): 79–80; Alice Julier and Laura Lindenfeld, "Mapping Men onto the Menu: Masculinities and Food," *Food and Foodways*, 13 (2005): 3.

9. Bob Ashley, Joanne Hollows, Steve Jones, and Ben Taylor, *Food and Cultural Studies*, (London, UK: Routledge, 2004), 153–186.

10. Of particular value and insight were Sherrie A. Inness, *Secret Ingredients: Race, Gender, and Class at the Dinner Table* (New York: Palgrave MacMillan, 2006); Jessamyn Neuhaus, *Manly Meals and Mom's Home Cooking: Cookbooks and Gender in Modern America*, (Baltimore, MD: Johns Hopkins University Press, 2003); Joanne Hollows, "Oliver's Twist: Leisure, Labor, and Domestic Masculinity in *The Naked Chef*," *International Journal of Cultural Studies*, 6 no. 2, (2003); Kathleen Collins, *Watching What We Eat*, (New York: Continuum, 2009); Rebecca Swenson,

"Domestic Divo?: Televised Treatments of Masculinity, Femininity, and Food," *Critical Studies in Media Communication*, 26 no.1 (2009).

11. Carol Adams, *The Sexual Politics of Meat: A Feminist-Vegetarian Critical Theory*, (New York: Continuum, 1990) 34.

12. Collins, *Watching What We Eat*, 4–5; Watson and Caldwell (eds), *The Cultural Politics of Food and Eating*, 1–2.

13. Collins, *Watching What We Eat*, 211–212.

14. Collins, *Watching What We Eat*, 211–212.; Cheri Ketchum, "The Essence of Cooking Shows: How the Food Network Constructs Consumer Fantasies," *Journal of Communication Inquiry*, 29 (2005): 219–220; J. Roshalle, "Cable Capitalizes on America's Favorite Obsession," accessed March 20, 2011, http://www.multichannel.com/article/print/450141-Food_Glorious_Food.php.

15. Pauline Adema, "Vicarious Consumption: Food, Television, and the Ambiguity of Modernity," *Journal of American Culture*, 23 (2004): 116.

16. Katharina Vester, *A Taste of Power: Food and American Identities* (Berkeley: University of California Press, 2015), 14; 107–109; 120–125.

17. Swenson, "Domestic Divo?," 41–49.

18. Julie Moskin, "The Chef-Dude," D5.

19. Michael Oriard, *Reading Football: How the Popular Press Created an American Spectacle*, (Chapel Hill, NC: University of North Carolina Press, 1993), 280.

20. Fabio Parasecoli, *Bite Me: Food in Popular Culture*, (New York: Berg, 2008), 4–5; Kathleen LeBesco and Peter Naccarato (eds), *Edible Ideologies: Representing Food and Meaning*, (Albany, NY: SUNY Press, 2008), 4–6; Brendan Gough, "'Real Men Don't Diet': An Analysis of Contemporary Newspaper Representations of Men, Food, and Health," *Social Science and Medicine*, 64 no. 2 (2007), 326–337.

21. Danielle Gallegos, "Cookbooks as Manuals of Taste," in *Ordinary Lifestyles: Popular Media, Consumption and Taste*, ed. David Bell and Joanne Hollows (New York: Open University Press, 2005), 99; Amy Reddinger, "Eating 'Local': The Politics of Post-Statehood Hawaiian Cookbooks," *Nordic Journal of English Studies* 9 (2010): 67. Quote is from Sherrie A. Inness, *Secret Ingredients: Race, Gender, and Class at the Dinner Table* (New York: Palgrave MacMillan, 2006), 2.

22. Elizabeth Driver, "Cookbooks as Primary Sources for Writing History," *Food, Culture, and Society*, 12 no. 3, (2009): 257–274.

23. Marita Sturken and Lisa Cartwright, *Practices of Looking: An Introduction to Visual Culture*, (New York: Oxford, 2001), 151–183.

24. For more on cultural associations between alcohol and sport, see Michael Messner and Jeffrey Montez de Oca, "The Male Consumer as Loser: Beer and Liquor Ads in Mega Sports Media Events," *Signs*, 30 no. 3, (2005); Sara Gee and Steve Jackson, "Leisure Corporations, Beer Brand Culture, and the Crisis of Masculinity: The Speight's "Southern Man' Advertising Campaign," *Journal of Leisure Studies*, 31 no. 1, (2012); Lawrence Wenner, "In Search of the Sports Bar: Masculinity, Alcohol, Sports, and the Mediation of Public Space," in Genevieve Rail (ed), *Sport in Postmodern Times*, (Albany, NY: SUNY Press, 1998).

25. Irina D. Mihalache, "Of Men and Cupcakes: Baking Identities on Food Network," in Charlene Elliott (ed), *How Canadians Communicate*, (Edmonton, CA: AU Press, 2015), 130.

26. Amy Calvert, "You Are What You (M)eat: Explorations of Meat-eating,

Masculinity, and Masquerade," *Journal of International Women's Studies*, 16 no. 1, (2014): 20.

27. For intriguing insights about food and culture, see Peter Naccarato and Kathleen LeBasco, *Culinary Capital* (New York, NY: Berg, 2012). 28. Michelle Szabo, "'I'm a Real Catch': The Blurring of Alternative and Hegemonic Masculinities in Men's Talk About Home Cooking," *Women's Studies International Forum*, 44 (2014): 229.

29. Vester, *A Taste of Power*, 67.

## Chapter 1

1. Matt Osgood. "War, Beheadings, and Booze: A Brief History of Tailgating," *VICE Sports* (blog), November 14, 2014, accessed January 12, 2018, https://sports .vice.com/en_us/article/war-beheadings-and-booze-a-brief-history of-tailgating.

2. Peter Chakerian, *The Browns Fan's Tailgating Guide* (Cleveland, Ohio: Gray & Company, Publishers, 2008), 19–20; Merrill Baum, "History of Green Bay Packers Tailgating," *AXS*, October 28, 2014, accessed January 5, 2018, https://www.axs.com /history-of-green-bay-packers-tailgating-25505.

3. Walter Levy, *The Picnic: A History* (Walnut Creek, CA: AltaMira Press, 2013), 83.

4. Michael Oriard, *Reading Football: How the Popular Press Created an American Spectacle* (Chapel Hill: University of North Carolina Press, 1993), 189–276.

5. Pamela Grundy and Benjamin G. Rader, *American Sports: From the Age of Folk Games to the Age of Televised Sports*, 7th ed. (New York: Routledge, 2015), 90–92.

6. Ronald A. Smith, *Sports and Freedom: The Rise of Big-Time College Athletics* (New York: Oxford University Press, 1988), 84.

7. Eugene Richards, "Foot-Ball and Its Opponents," *Yale Medical Journal*, 1 (Nov. 1894–June 1895): 221.

8. Patrick B. Miller, "To 'Bring the Race Along Rapidly': Sport, Student Culture, and Educational Mission at Historically Black Colleges during the Interwar Years," in *The Sporting World of the Modern South*, ed. Patrick Miller (Champaign: University of Illinois, 2002), 129–152.

9. "Meharry and Fisk Game," *Nashville Globe*, November 24, 1911, 1.

10. Michael Oriard, *King Football: Sport & Spectacle in the Golden Age of Radio & Newsreels, Movies & Magazines, The Weekly & Daily Press* (Chapel Hill: University of North Carolina, 2001), 328–363.

11. "College Spirit Will Dominate Saturday," Pittsburgh Courier, October 23, 1926, 7.

12. Oriard, *King Football*, 329.

13. Richard O. Davies, *Sports in American Life: A History*, 2nd ed. (Malden, Massachusetts: Wiley-Blackwell, 2012), 54–59.

14. Brian M. Ingrassia, *The Rise of the Gridiron University: Higher Education's Uneasy Alliance with Big-Time Football* (Lawrence: University Press of Kansas, 2012), 139–170.

15. "Yale Beat Harvard In Last Big Game," *New York Times*, November 20, 1904, 1; Thomas G. Bergin, *The Game: The Harvard-Yale Football Rivalry, 1875–1983* (New Haven, Connecticut: Yale University Press, 1984), 113.

16. William H. Jones, *Recreation and Amusement Among Negroes in Washington, D.C.: A Sociological Analysis of the Negro in an Urban Environment* (Westport, CT: Negro University Press, 1927), 76.

17. "Yale Beat Harvard in Last Big Game," 1.

18. "Transportation to Field," *Yale Daily News*, November 16, 1898, 1, accessed March 5, 2016, http://digital.library.yale.edu/cdm/compoundobject/collection /yale-ydn/id/175934/rec/3560.

19. Oriard, *Reading Football*, 61–62.

20. "Plans for the Big Game," *The Sun* (New York City), November 15, 1891, 18.

21. Oriard, *Reading Football*, 248–249.

22. "A Football-Mad Throng," *New York Times*, November 25, 1906, 2.

23. S.D. Ehrhart, Artist. *Thanksgiving scene in ye old Plymouth colony / Ehrhart*. Massachusetts Plymouth, 1912. N.Y.: Published by Keppler & Schwarzmann, Puck Building. Photograph. https://www.loc.gov/item/2013650005/; For a brief description of *Puck*, see https://www.senate.gov/artandhistory/art/puck/puck_intro.htm. Notably, this politically oriented publication, in its popularization of the social aspects of the Thanksgiving Day football games, promoted the troubling stereotypes of Native Americans of the day.

24. While there are a number of book-length treatments dedicated to football's past and present, see the following for examples that more specifically analyze gender constructions in football: Oriard, *Reading Football*; Oriard, *King Football*; Jeffrey Montez de Oca, *Discipline and Indulgence: College Football, Media, and the American Way of Life During the Cold War* (New Brunswick, NJ: Rutgers University Press, 2013); Thomas P. Oates, Football and Manliness: An Unauthorized Feminist Account of the NFL (Champaign, IL: University of Illinois Press, 2017); Kurt Edward Kemper, *College Football and American Culture in the Cold War Era* (Champaign, IL: University of Illinois Press).

25. "Sigourney," *The Ottumwa Courier*, October 26, 1905, 7.

26. "Meals at University Club," *Yale Daily News*, November 22, 1902, 1, accessed March 3, 2016, http://digital.library.yale.edu/cdm/compoundobject/collection/yale -ydn/id/85533/rec/1; Oriard, *Reading Football*, 248–251.

27. "Harvard Game Luncheon at the Dining Club," *Yale Daily News*, November 21, 1906, 2, accessed March 3, 2016, http://digital.library.yale.edu /cdm/compoundobject/collection/yale-ydn/id/142207/rec/1361.

28. "Harvard Game Luncheon at the Dining Club."

29. "Football Luncheon at Commons," *Yale Daily News*, November 23, 1906, 1, accessed March 3, 2016, http://digital.library.yale.edu/cdm/compoundobject /collection/yale-ydn/id/142217/rec/19.

30. Richard C. Crepeau, *NFL Football: A History of America's New National Pastime* (Champaign: University of Illinois Press, 2014), 3–8.

31. "Here We Are Behind Green Bay's Packers," *Green Bay Press-Gazette*, September 13, 1924, 11.

32. "Football Picnic," *The Fort Wayne Journal-Gazette*, September 18, 1919, 2.

33. Nancy Grimes, "Football Heads Social Events," *Portsmith Daily News*, November 12, 1933, 4.

34. Marjorie, "For the Hero of the Gridiron," *The Philadelphia Inquiry*, November 8, 1903, 3.

35. John Sayle Watterson, *College Football: History, Spectacle, Controversy* (Baltimore: The John Hopkins University Press, 2000), 99–100.

36. "State University," *The Lincoln Star* (Nebraska), October 22, 1916, 3.

37. David K. Wiggins, "The Biggest 'Classic' of Them All: The Howard and

Lincoln Thanksgiving Day Football Games, 1919–1929," in *Rooting for the Home Team: Sport, Community, and Identity*, ed. Daniel A. Nathan (Champaign, IL: University of Illinois Press, 2013), 36–53.

38. J. LeCount Chestnut, "Nation's Society Captured Washing for 'Classic,'" *Chicago Defender*, December 9, 1922, 8.

39. Nettie George Speedy, "Society," *Chicago Defender*, October 19, 1902, 5.

40. Benjamin G. Rader, "'The Greatest Drama in Indian Life,' Experiments in Native American Identity and Resistance at the Haskell Institute Homecoming of 1926," *Western Historical Quarterly* 35 (Winter 2004): 429–450. Haskell Institute opened in 1884 as a federally controlled boarding school for Native Americans. The school was part of the US government's attempt to "civilize" and "assimilate" Indian children into Euro-American culture by forcibly removing them from their families to attend off-reservation boarding schools designed to teach them English, expose them to Christianity, and provide them with a vocational trade. In the process, Indian children often suffered greatly and the cultural genocide of North American indigenous peoples was further perpetuated. Though Athletics at Indian boarding schools such as Haskell and the Carlisle Institute (PA) were used by white administrators as a means of socializing students into American culture, Indian students frequently experienced them as a refuge and means of resistance in an oppressive, racist environment. Read in this context, the inaugural Haskell homecoming is remarkable for its promotion of Indian culture—including food—in the midst of a white sporting tradition. See also, John Bloom, "'Show What an Indian Can Do': Sports, Memory, and Ethnic Identity at Federal Indian Boarding Schools," *Journal of American Indian Education* (Spring 1996): 33–48; Haskell Indian Nations University, *School History*, accessed July 11, 2018, https://www.haskell.edu/about/history/.

41. "Tigers Beat Columbia in First Big Game," *The Evening World* (New York), October 25, 1902, 1.

42. A.L. Jackson, *Chicago Defender*, December 15, 1923, 12.

43. "Around Green Bay," *Green Bay Press-Gazette*, September 27, 1920, 1.

44. "Lunch for the Game," *Yale Daily News*, November 20, 1920, 2, accessed March 10, 2016, http://digital.library.yale.edu/cdm/compoundobject/collection /yale-ydn/id/95234/rec/162.

45. "Make Read's Your Goal for the Football Lunch," *The Bridgeport Telegram*, October 29, 1924, 13.

46. "The Yale–Harvard Game," *The Yale Daily News*, November 24, 1922, 3, accessed March 10, 2016, http://digital.library.yale.edu/cdm/compoundobject /collection/yale-ydn/id/98053/rec/1.

47. "Of One Thing or Another," *Princeton Alumni Weekly* XXIX, no. 10 (November 30, 1928): 312.

48. "Triumph of Blue and Gold," *San Francisco Chronicle*, December 1, 1899, 2.

49. "A Football-Mad Throng," *New York Times*, November 25, 1906, 2.

50. "John Jacob Astor has Thirty-One Cars," *Evening Star* (Washington, DC), July 22, 1906, 4, accessed March 20, 2016, http://chroniclingamerica.loc.gov/lccn /sn83045462/1906-07-22/ed-1/seq56/#date1=1905&index=0&rows=20&words =ASTOR+CARS+HAS+JACOB+JOHN+ONE+THIRTY+THIRTYONE&search Type=basic&sequence=0&state=&date2=1907&proxtext=John+Jacob+Astor+has +thirty+one+cars&y=13&x=9&dateFilterType=yearRange&page=1.

51. "A Football-Mad Throng," 2.

52. Cotten Seiler, *Republic of Drivers* (Chicago: University of Chicago Press, 2008), 41; Seiler, *Republic of Drivers*, 43.

53. Ocania Chalk, *Black College Sport* (New York: Dodd, Mead and Co., 1976), 210.

54. "Football Owes Place to Auto, Asserts Dealer," *Oakland Tribune*, October 24, 1926, 0–3.

55. "Nearby Colleges to Draw Many "Motor-Grid Hounds" To Imbroglios Next Fall," *The Evening News* (Harrisburg, PA), September 26, 1924, 11.

56. "In Automobiles as in Football—'All American' is the Word!" *The News Palladium*, November 19, 1927, 11.

57. "Football and Autos Mingle," *Los Angeles Sunday Times*, November 18, 1923 [Part VI], 3.

58. "Miss Roosevelt in Upset?" *New York Times*, November 22, 1904, 1.

59. "Rye Takes a Day Off and Levies on Autos," *New York Times*, November 20, 1904, 7.

60. Seiler, *Republic of Drivers*, 43.

61. "Late Rally Ties Game for Harvard," *New York Times*, November 9, 1919, S1.

62. "In Praise of the Motor Picnic," *Truth* (Special Motor Supplement), July 24, 1907, 4.

63. Walter Levy, *The Picnic: A History* (Lanham, Maryland: AltaMira Press, 2013), 83.

64. Westbrook Pegler, "Yale Democracy Comes to Light in Game with Georgia," *Chicago Daily Tribune*, October 15, 1928, 1.

65. Dorothy Greig, "*Rah! Rah! Rah! Siss, Boom, Bah!* We're Off To The Game!" *Plattsburgh (NY) Daily Republican*, November 23, 1938, 2.

66. "Football Picnic Kit," *The Press and Sun-Bulletin* (Binghamton, NY), October 29, 1931, 9.

67. Candy Coleman, *Pigskin Picnics* (Mt. Pocono, PA: C.C. Enterprises, 1980).

68. Michael Oriard, *King Football: Sport & Spectacle in the Golden Age of Radio & Newsreels, Movies & Magazines, The Weekly & The Daily Press* (Chapel Hill: University of North Carolina Press, 2001), 1–8.

69. Kristin L. Matthews, "One Nation Over Coals: Cold War Nationalism and the Barbecue," *American Studies* 50, no. 3/4 (2009): 8.

70. "Outdoor Cooking," *LIFE*, July 20, 1953, 49–54, 56.

71. Matthews, "One Nation Over Coals," 23.

72. Melanie De Proft, et al., *The Hungry Man's Outdoor Grill Cookbook* (Chicago, IL: Spencer Press, Inc., 1953), 25.

73. "America is Bit by the Barbecue Bug," *LOOK*, July 12, 1955, 57.

74. Ted Hatch, "For the Male Cook in All His Glory!" *American Home*, June 1940, 34.

75. "Outdoor Cooking," *LIFE*, 49.

76. James Beard, *Cook It Outdoors* (New York: M. Barrows and Company, Inc., 1941), vii.

77. "Man and His Beef," *LOOK*, September 6, 1955, 63.

78. "Barbecue Outfit Folds Into Suitcase," *Popular Mechanics*, July 1946, 158.

79. "Rear-Engine Car Boasts Kitchen," *Popular Science*, September 1947, 159.

80. Alfred R. Zipser, Jr., "Outdoor Cooking a Sizzling Trade," May 1, 1955, 1.

81. Helen Evans Brown and James A. Beard, *The Complete Book of Outdoor Cookery* (New York: Doubleday & Company, 1955), 8.

82. "The New American Domesticated Male," *Life*, January 4, 1954, 43.

83. Culinary Arts Institute, *The Hungry Man's Outdoor Grill Cookbook* (Grosset & Dunlap, 1954), 59.

84. Quoted in Matthews, "One Nation Over Coals," 22.

85. Sally Weiner, "The Art of the Barbecue," *New York Times*, July 19, 1953, SM24.

86. Horace Sutton, "Football Stadium," *Sports Illustrated*, October 25, 1954, 38.

87. Sutton, "Football Stadium."

88. Sutton, "Football Stadium."

89. Tim Miller, *Barbecue: A History* (Lanham, Maryland: Rowman and Littlefield, 2014), 34–42.

90. Mildred Sutherd, "Football Picnics Popular With Saturday Fans," *Herald and Review* (Decatur, Illinois), October 30, 1955, Sect. 3, 1.

91. "Start Early for the Game and Take Along a Football Picnic," *Sunset*, October 1958, 124.

92. Jean Hewitt, "Kublebvaka Isn't the Fullback's Name—It's the Main Course at a Tailgate Picnic," *New York Times*, November 7, 1966, 62.

93. "Rah! Rah! For a Football Picnic," *The Orlando Sentinel* (Orlando, FL), November 7, 1968, 77.

94. "Tips on 'Tailgate Picnics,'" *Florence Morning News* (Florence, South Carolina), November 5, 1967, 14; "Homecoming Suggestion," *The Baltimore Sun*, November 3, 1966, D4.

95. "Let's Have a Party, Penn State Fans," *Call-Chronicle* (Allentown, Pa), October 6, 1974, F-1.

96. "Pre-Football Picnic—Indoors!" *The Daily Journal* (Vineland, New Jersey), October 1, 1969, 17.

97. "Station Wagon Popularity Hits a Downhill Stretch," *New York Times*, April 4, 1965, 136.

98. "Shades of Past Football Glory: N.Y.U. Will Play Georgetown," *New York Times*, November 21, 1964, 21.

99. Helen E. Fleischmann, *Sagehens Retriever Club Tailgate Cookbook* (St. Helena, CA: Herdell Printing, Inc., 1967); April Herbert, *The Tailgate Cookbook: A Practical Handbook of Delightful Meals for Campers, Travelers, and Sport Enthusiasts* (New York: Funk & Wagnalls: 1970).

100. Peter Andrews, "An Enquiry Into the Present State Of Old College Try," *New York Times*, October 10, 1971, Section 10, 1. Of note is the fact that this article appears on the Travel and Resorts section of the paper and thus is a telling reminder that those for whom the piece may have appealed were well beyond simply fans of football.

101. Patricia McCormack, "Football Tailgate Parties," *The Times* (San Mateo, California), September 25, 1974, 12.

102. Lipsyte, "Chowderheads' Year," 66. See also, "Jets Fans Hitch Their Chuck Wagons to Front-Office Stars," *New York Times*, December 18, 1966, S3.

103. Jim Morris, "Football Tailgate Parties, Some Plain, Some Fancy," *The Tribune* (Seymour, Indiana), November 14, 1980, 16.

104. "Action Want Ads, Personals: We Need," *The Long Islander, Huntington, New York*, September 28, 1978, 29.

105. Jerry Kirshenbaum, "Pigskins Preceded by Pâté on Asphalt," *Sports Illustrated*, December 6, 1971, 96.

106. Kirshenbaum, "Pigskins Preceded by Pâté."

107. Kirshenbaum, "Pigskins Preceded by Pâté," 96, 101.

108. Mark Moss, *The Media and Models of Masculinity* (Lanham: Maryland: Lexington Books, 2011), 97; Michael S. Kimmel, *Manhood in America: A Cultural History*, 2nd ed. (New York: Oxford University Press, 2006), 173–181.

109. Kimmel, *Manhood in America*, 173.

110. Bruce Feirstein, *Real Men Don't Eat Quiche* (New York: Pocket Books, 1982), 10; Feirstein, *Real Men Don't Eat Quiche*, 9; Feirstein, *Real Men Don't Eat Quiche*, 75.

111. Moss, *The Media and Models of Masculinity*, 94–97; Kimmel, *Manhood in America*, 203. We recognize that tailgates are not—nor have they ever been—all-male spaces. However, our observations on the blacktop and analysis of popular culture representations of the activity indicate that men occupy a central role in this fan ritual.

112. Katharina Vester, A Taste of Power: Food and American Identities (Berkeley: University of California Press, 2015), 134.

113. Marguerite Michaels, "The Other Super Bowl," *Time*, October 15, 1973, 89.

114. Michaels, "The Other Super Bowl."

115. Michaels, "The Other Super Bowl."

116. For a more thorough discussion of early tailgate cookbooks see Chapter Five.

117. Jill Gerston, "49ers Name Woman, 26, To Key Post," *New York Times*, February 3, 1974, Section 5, 9. This story is ironic in that the 49ers were applauded as breaking gender barriers with the hire, yet the promotions and public relations tasks assigned to Robin Mitchell remained distanced from actual play on the field, as she was relegated to organizing pregame and halftime shows among other duties.

118. Irene Rothschild, Life Among the Tailgaters at the Yale Bowl, *New York Times*, October 28, 1979, Section 23, 2.

119. Louise Lague, "If You Run Out of Ideas for Tailgate Picnics," *Gannett Westchester Newspapers*, October 24, 1981, D9.

120. Lague, "If You Run Out of Ideas."

121. Coleman, *Pigskin Picnics*, 2.

122. Coleman, *Pigskin Picnics*, 45.

123. *The Mid American Tailgaters Cookbook* (Olathe, Kansas: Cookbook Publishers, Inc., 1985), E.

124. *The Mid American Tailgaters Cookbook.*

125. Isabel Wilkerson, "Signs of Fall in Michigan: Faces of Maize or Green," *New York Times*, October 13, 1986, accessed May 14, 2017, http://www.nytimes.com/1986/10/13/us/signs-of-fall-in-michigan-faces-of-maize-or-green.html.

126. Bryan Miller, "Tailgate Feasts," *New York Times*, October 23, 1983, accessed May 14, 2017, http://www.nytimes.com/1983/10/23/magazine/tailgate-feasts.html.

127. Miller, "Tailgate Feasts."

128. "PM Takes You Tailgating," *Popular Mechanics*, October 1979, 116–117, 181.

129. "WENDY'S and WPHD-FM present 'The Beef is Here,'" *The Griffin* (Canisius College), September 14, 1984, 11.

130. S. Lee Kanner, "Sporting Gear: Portable Cooker in a Suitcase, *New York Times*, June 16, 1980, C11.

131. Patricia McCormack, "Tailgate Parties Redefine Football Games, *The Citizen, Auburn, NY*, October 18, 1981, 12.

132. McCormack, "Tailgate Parties Redefine Football Games."

133. Nathan Cobb, "The King of BC's Tailgaters: Richard Carlson Serves a Feast from his Ford," *Boston Globe*, October 28, 1981, 1.

134. Alan C. Miller, "Tailgaters Featured on All-Madden Team: Football Broadcaster Loves the Parties as Much as the Games," *Los Angeles Times*, October 17, 1991, accessed January 6, 2018, http://articles.latimes.com/1991-10-17/sports/sp-774 _1_john-madden.

135. John Madden with Peter Kaminsky, *John Madden's Ultimate Tailgating* (New York: Viking Press, 1998), 1. Madden's prominent standing in the football world is reflected, in part, in the book's appeal to reviewers. See, for example, Larry Stewart, "The Hot Corner," *LA Times*, September 17, 1998, accessed July 15, 2018; Phil Cornell, "John Madden Calls the Signals in a Cookbook," *Chicago Tribune*, October 21, 1998, accessed July 15, 2018; Cece Sullivan "Tailgate Cookbook is Typical Madden," *Sun Sentinel* (Florida), October 1, 1998, accessed July 15, 2018.

136. Madden, *John Madden's Ultimate Tailgating*, 9.

137. Madden, *John Madden's Ultimate Tailgating*, 15, 19, 27, 17, 5. In a nod to previous tailgate cookbooks whose emphasis was as centrally focused on meat as it should have been in Madden's view, the author says, "There are a lot of books of floater recipes, but this cookbook is an all-sinker book," (p. 1).

138. Madden, *John Madden's Ultimate Tailgate*.

139. The College Football Hall of Fame is an example of a corporate sport museum that uses a range of exhibition techniques to convey its version of college football history and brand the sport as a desirable product. See Murray Phillips, *Representing the Sporting Past in Museums and Halls of Fame*, ed. (New York: Routledge, 2012), 10–11.

140. These observations are drawn from the authors' visit to the College Football Hall of Fame in Atlanta, Georgia on May 30, 2016.

141. Wall Text, "Coca-Cola Fan's Game Day," College Football Hall of Fame, Atlanta, Georgia.

142. Joseph N. Cooper, et al, "The State of Intercollegiate Athletics at Historically Black Colleges and Universities (HBCUs): Past, Present, & Persistence, *Journal of Issues in Intercollegiate Athletics*, 7 (2014): 319–321; Patrick B. Miller, "To Bring the Race Along Rapidly: Sport, Student Culture, and Educational Mission at Historically Black Colleges During the Interwar Years," *History of Education Quarterly* 35, no. 2 (1995): 111–135.

# Chapter 2

1. These observations are drawn from the author's (Liberti's) conversations with security personnel outside of LSU Tiger Stadium. Baton Rouge, LA., November 5, 2016.

2. Bud Johnson, LSU tailgater, quoted in Loran Smith, *Spread Formation: Tailgating and Home Recipes from College Football Greats* (Atlanta: Whitman Publishers, LLC, 2014), 89.

3. "Tiger Stadium Motor Home/RV Parking," *Louisiana State University Athletics*, September 20, 2017, accessed January 13, 2018, http://www.lsusports.net/ViewArticle .dbml?ATCLID=205425260.

4. Mark, in conversation with the author, Liberti (field notes), Tiger Stadium, Baton Rouge, LA, November 5, 2016.

5. Candace West and Don H. Zimmerman, "Doing Gender," *Gender & Society* 1, no. 1 (1987): 125–151.

6. "Tailgating Turned Up to 11," youtube video, 1:07, Accessed September 24, 2011, https://www.youtube.com/watch?v=OgadZiuhc9Q.

7. James B. Twitchell, *Where Men Hide* (New York: Columbia University Press, 2006), 179.

8. David Joachim, *The Tailgater's Cookbook* (New York: Broadway Books, 2005), 7.

9. Bob Sloan, *The Tailgating Cookbook: Recipes for the Big Game* (San Francisco: Chronicle Books, 2005), 58.

10. *The Simpsons*, season 19, episode 18, "Any Given Sundance," directed by Chuck Sheetz, aired on May 4, 2008 by Fox Broadcasting Company, The Simpsons on FXX, Accessed July 11, 2015, http://www.simpsonsworld.com/video/283769923976.

11. Ray Lampe *The NFL Gameday Cookbook* (San Francisco, California: Chronicle Books, 2008), 13.

12. *Tailgate Warriors*, season 2, episode 2, "49ers vs. Raiders," directed by Daniel Dvorak [cameraman], aired on October 27, 2010 by Food Network.

13. *Tailgate Warriors*, season 1, episode 1, "Chicago Bears vs. Buffalo Bills," directed by Anthony Rogriguez [director of photography], aired on October 17, 2009 by Food Network.

14. *Tailgate Warriors*, "Chicago Bears vs. Buffalo Bills."

15. Richard A. Rogers, "Beasts, Burgers, and Hummers: Meat and the Crisis of Masculinity in Contemporary Television Advertisements," *Environmental Communication* 2, no. 3 (2008): 288.

16. *Tailgate Warriors*, "Chicago Bears vs. Buffalo Bills."

17. *Tailgate Warriors*, "Chicago Bears vs. Buffalo Bills."

18. Joanne Hollows, "Oliver's Twist: Leisure, Labor and Domestic Masculinity in *The Naked Chef*," *International Journal of Cultural Studies* 6, no. 2 (2003): 232.

19. Kenny Johnson, in conversation with the author, Liberti (field notes), Ralph Wilson Stadium, Orchard Park, New York, October 4, 2015.

20. Harriet Wheatly Riggs, "Cooking on Six Cylinders," *Travel*, 132 (October, 1969): 65–67.

21. Rebecca Swenson, "Domestic Divo? Television Treatments of Masculinity, Femininity, and Food." *Critical Studies in Media Communication* 26, no. 1 (2009): 40. On grilling and public performance also see: Kristen L. Matthews, "One Nation Over Coals: Cold War Nationalism and the Barbecue," *American Studies* 50, no. 3/4 (2009): 22; Jeffery Sobal, "Men, Meat, and Marriage: Models of Masculinity," *Food & Foodways* 13, no. 1/2 (2005): 144.

22. Michael Pollan, *Cooked: A Natural History of Transformation* (New York: The Penguin Press, 2013), 155.

23. Pollan, *Cooked*, 128.

24. Mario Batali, *Mario Tailgates NASCAR Style: The Essential Cookbook for NASCAR Fans*" (Charlotte: Sporting News, 2006), 34.

25. Nick Benigno, Interview with authors, Pleasanton, California, January 30, 2016.

26. Hollows, "Oliver's Twist," 242.

27. Pableaux Johnson, *ESPN Gameday Gourmet* (New York: ESPN Books, 2007), 13.

28. David Bowers and Sharon Bowers, *Bake It Like A Man: A Real Man's Cookbook* (New York: William Morrow & Company, 1999), as cited in Katharina Vester, *A Taste of Power: Food and American Identities* (Berkeley: University of California Press, 2015), 66.

29. Jennifer Jensen Wallach, *How America Eats: A Social History of U.S. Food & Culture* (Lanham, MD: Rowman & Littlefield, 2013), 112.

30. Peter Chakerian, *The Browns Fan's Tailgating Guide* (Cleveland, Ohio: Gray & Company, Publishers, 2008), 12; Zachary Schisgal, *A Man A Can, A Tailgate Plan: 50 Easy Game-Time Recipes That Are Sure to Please* (Emmaus, Pennsylvania: Rodale Book, 2006), i.

31. Chakerian, *Browns Fan's*, 12–13.

32. Signe Hansen, "Society of the Appetite: Celebrity Chefs Deliver Consumers," *Food, Culture, & Society* 11, no. 1 (2008): 50 51.

33. Batali, *Mario Tailgates NASCAR Style*, 12; Lampe, *The NFL Gameday Cookbook*, 12.

34. *Tailgate Warriors*, "49ers vs. Raiders."

35. Tim Miller, "The Birth of the Patio Daddy-O: Outdoor Grilling in Postwar America," *Journal of American Culture* 33, no. 1 (2010): 8.

36. "Bud Light Ultimate Tailgate Car," youtube video, :30, September 14, 2010, https://www.youtube.com/watch?v=OsMHezUKzsc.

37. Herschel, in conversation with the author, Veri (field notes), Neyland Stadium, Knoxville, TN, September 12, 2015.

38. Sean, in conversation with the authors, Veri and Liberti (field notes), Oakland Coliseum, Oakland, CA, December 6, 2015.

39. Jack, in conversation with author Liberti (field notes), Gillette Stadium, Foxborough, MA, October 2, 2016.

40. Mitch Hall, in conversation with author Veri (phone interview), September 23, 2015.

41. *Tailgate Warriors*, season 2, episode 3, "Vikings vs. Saints," directed by Daniel Dvorak [cameraman], aired on November 3, 2010 by Food Network.

42. Niel, in conversation with authors Liberti and Veri, (field notes), Stanford Stadium, Palo Alto, CA, September 17, 2016.

43. Glinda, in conversation with author Liberti (field notes), Southern University, Baton Rouge, LA, November 5, 2016.

44. Greg Melville, "Nail the Tailgate Party," *Men's Life Today*, accessed January 14, 2018, http://www.menslifetoday.com/work/entertainment/tailgate_guide/index.php.

45. *Tailgate Warriors*, "Vikings vs. Saints."

46. Pollan, *Cooked*, 67.

47. Pollan, *Cooked*, 67.

48. *Tailgate Warriors*, "49ers vs. Raiders."

49. *Tailgate Warriors*, "Chicago Bears vs. Buffalo Bills."

50. Hollows, "Oliver's Twist," 241.

51. *Tailgate Warriors*, "49ers vs. Raiders."

52. *Tailgate Warriors*, "Chicago Bears vs. Buffalo Bills."

53. Dana Polan, *Jane Campion* (London, UK: British Film Institute, 2001), 1; Mark Gallagher, "What's So Funny About *Iron Chef*?" *Journal of Popular Film & Television* 31, no. 4 (2004): 176.

54. Swenson, *"Domestic Divo?"* 49–50; Maria J. Veri and Rita Liberti, *"Tailgate Warriors*: Exploring Constructions of Masculinity, Food, and Football," *Journal of Sport & Social Issues* 37, no. 3 (2013): 232.

55. *Tailgate Warriors*, "Vikings vs. Saints."

56. *Tailgate Warriors*, "Chicago Bears vs. Buffalo Bills."

57. Thomas A. Adler, "Making Pancakes on Sunday: The Male Cook in Family Tradition," *Western Folklore* 40, no. 1 (1981): 45–54; Alice Julier and Laura Lindenfield, "Mapping Men onto the Menu: Masculinities and Food," *Food & Foodways* 13, no. 1/2 (2005): 1–16.

58. Adler, "Making Pancakes on Sunday," 51.

59. *Tailgate Warriors*, "49ers vs. Raiders."

60. Mark Meister, "Cultural Feeding, Good Life Science, and the TV Food Network," *Mass Communication and Society* 4, no. 2 (2001): 174.

61. Adler, "Making Pancakes on Sunday," 48.

62. Julier & Lindenfield, "Mapping Men onto the Menu," 2.

63. Michael Jones, Interview with authors, Oakland, California, October 22, 2010.

64. Swenson, "Domestic Divo," 44.

65. Benigno, interview.

66. Benigno, interview.

67. Swenson, "Domestic Divo," 47.

68. Chakerian, *The Browns Fan's Tailgating Guide*, 49.

69. Lampe, *The NFL Gameday Cookbook*, 24.

70. Johnson, *ESPN Gameday Gourmet*, 19.

71. Doug Uhlenbrock, "Motorhomes: the Ultimate Tailgating Machine," *RV Daily Report*, October 22, 2010, accessed January 7, 2019, https://rvdailyreport.com/owner/motohomes-the-ultimate-tailgating-machine/.

72. "Go RVing Kicks off 2008 With a Super Week," *Recreation Vehicle Industry Association*, January 31, 2008, accessed November 1, 2017, http://www.rvia.org/?ESID=pReleases&PRID=2&SR=21.

73. Warren St. John, *Rammer Jammer Yellow Hammer: A Journey into the Heart of Fan Mania* (New York: Crown Publishers, 2004), 9.

74. Walter Levy, *The Picnic: A History* (Lanham, Maryland: AltaMira Press, 2014), 84.

75. St. John, *Rammer Jammer Yellow Hammer*, 8.

76. A slide-out is an add-on to a motorhome that moves outward to provide more interior space.

77. Kevin, in conversation with author Liberti (field notes), Oakland Coliseum, Oakland, CA, September 17, 2017.

78. Jesse, in conversation with author Liberti (field notes), Oakland Coliseum, Oakland, CA, September 17, 2017.

79. Mike, in conversation with author Veri (field notes), Autzen Stadium, Eugene, OR, October 29, 2016.

80. Karen Robinson-Jacobs, "Decades after teaming up with college football, Dr. Pepper serves up more Larry," *Dallas News*, September 2016, accessed November 1, 2017, https://www.dallasnews.com/business/sports-business/2016/09/02/dr-pepper-bets-big-campy-concessions-guy-college-ball.

81. "College Football: Presenting the Tailgate 2000," *iSpot.tv*, accessed November 1,

2017, https://www.ispot.tv/ad/ArAj/dr-pepper-college-football-presenting-the
-tailgate-2000.

82. "Mountain Home Man Creates Fire Truck Tailgate Smoker," *Arkansasmatters*
*.com*, accessed January 14, 2018, http://www.arkansasmatters.com/news/mountain
-home-man-creates-fire-truck-tailgate-smoker/199858033.

## Chapter 3

1. Carol J. Adams, *The Sexual Politics of Meat: A Feminist-Vegetarian Critical
Theory* (New York: Continuum, 1990), 25–38.

2. Jeffrey Sobal, "Men, Meat, and Marriage: Models of Masculinity," *Food &
Foodways*, 13 (2005): 137.

3. Adams, *Sexual Politics*, 33; Sobal, "Men, Meat and Marriage," 137; Katharina
Vester, *A Taste of Power: Food and American Identities* (Oakland, CA: University of
California Press, 2015), 125.

4. Adams, *Sexual Politics*, 14; Bettina Heinz and Ronald Lee, "Getting Down
to the Meat: The Symbolic Construction of Meat Consumption," *Communication
Studies* 49, no. 1 (1998): 91.

5. Adams, *Sexual Politics*, 27–34; Thomas Adler, "Making Pancakes on Sunday:
The Male Cook in Family Tradition," *Western Folklore* 40, no. 1 (1981): 47; Daniel
Block, "Saving Milk through Masculinity: Public Health Officers and Pure Milk,"
*Food and Foodways* 13 (2005): 133; Tim Miller, "The Birth of the Patio Daddy-O:
Outdoor grilling in Postwar America," *Journal of American Culture* 33, no. 1 (2010):
8; Sobal, "Men, Meat and Marriage," 137.

6. Michael Pollan, *Cooked: A Natural History of Transformation* (New York: The
Penguin Press, 2013), 13.

7. Pollan, *Cooked*, 54–55.

8. Peter Naccarato and Kathleen LeBesco, *Culinary Capital* (London: Berg,
2012), 1–2.

9. Steven Raichlen, *Man Made Meals: The Essential Cookbook for Guys* (New
York: Workman Publishing Co, 2014), 10.

10. Risto Moisi and Mariam Beruchashvili, "Mancaves and Masculinity,"
*Journal of Consumer Culture* 16, no. 3 (2016): 658.

11. *Tailgate Warriors*, season 2, episode 1, "Packers vs. Seahawks," directed by
Daniel Dvorak [cameraman], aired on October 20, 2010 by Food Network.

12. *Tailgate Warriors*, "Packers vs. Seahawks."

13. *Tailgate Warriors*, season 2, episode 2, "49ers vs. Raiders," directed by Daniel
Dvorak [cameraman], aired on October 27, 2010 by Food Network.

14. *Tailgate Warriors*, "49ers vs. Raiders."

15. *Tailgate Warriors*, season 2, episode 3, "Vikings vs. Saints," directed by Daniel
Dvorak [cameraman], aired on November 3, 2010 by Food Network.

16. *Tailgate Warriors*, "49ers vs. Raiders."

17. *Tailgate Warriors*, "49ers vs. Raiders."

18. *Tailgate Warriors*, "49ers vs. Raiders."

19. *Tailgate Warriors*, "Packers vs. Seahawks."

20. Patrick McGann, "Eating Muscle: Material Semiotics and a Manly Appetite,"
in *Revealing Male Bodies*, ed. Nancy Tuana, William Cowling, Maurice Hamington,
and Greg Johnson (Bloomington, IN: Indiana University Press, 2002), 83–99.

21. *The Simpsons*, season 19, episode 18, "Any Given Sundance," directed by Chuck Sheetz, aired on May 4, 2008 by Fox Broadcasting Company, The Simpsons on FXX, Accessed July 11, 2015, http://www.simpsonsworld.com/video/283769923976.

22. Siegel, Robert D., dir. *Big Fan*. 2009; United States: First Independent Pictures. Amazon Prime Instant Video, https://www.amazon.com/dp/B06XJ1ZVY7?ref_=imdbref_tt_wbr_piv&tag=imdbtag_tt_wbr_piv-20.

23. Anspaugh, David, dir. *Rudy*. 1993; TriStar Pictures. Amazon Prime Video, https://www.amazon.com/dp/B00171R0OO?ref=sr_1_1_acs_kn_imdb_pa_dp&qid=1516500394&sr=1-1-acs&autoplay=0.

24. "Pepsi Tailgate commercial," youtube video, :30, Accessed July, 11, 2015, https://www.youtube.com/watch?v=yjMN_b6Acz4.

25. Mark A. Newcombe, Mary B. McCarthy, James M. Cronin, and Sinead N. McCarthy, "'Eat Like a Man': A Social Constructionist Analysis of the Role of Food in Men's Lives," *Appetite* 59 (2012): 392.

26. Bob Sloan, *The Tailgating Cookbook: Recipes for the Big Game*, (San Francisco: Chronicle Books, 2005), 59.

27. Pableaux Johnson, *ESPN Gameday Gourmet: More Than 80 All-American Tailgate Recipes* (New York: ESPN, 2007), 1.

28. Johnson, *ESPN Gameday Gourmet*, 77.

29. Debbie Moose, *Fan Fare: A Playbook of Great Recipes for Tailgating or Watching the Game at Home* (Boston, MA: The Harvard Common Press, 2007), 115.

30. McGann, "Eating Muscle," 89.

31. Douglas Brownlie and Paul Hewer, "Prime Beef Cuts: Culinary Images for Thinking Men," *Consumption, Markets and Culture* 10, no.3 (2007): 343.

32. James B. Twitchell, *Where Men Hide*, (New York: Columbia University Press, 2006), 176.

33. John Madden with Peter Kaminsky, *John Madden's Ultimate Tailgating* (New York: Penguin, 1998), 9.

34. Madden and Kaminsky, 32.

35. Madden and Kaminsky, 32.

36. Sloan, *The Tailgating Cookbook*, 52.

37. Johnson, *ESPN Gameday Gourmet*, 5.

38. Herschel, in conversation with the author Veri (fieldnotes), Neyland Stadium, Knoxville, TN, September 9, 2015.

39. Mike, in conversation with the authors (fieldnotes), Ralph Wilson Stadium, Buffalo, NY, October 4, 2015.

40. Nancy, in conversation with the authors (fieldnotes), Stanford Stadium, Palo Alto, Stanford, September 17, 2016.

41. Mike, in conversation with the author Veri (fieldnotes), Autzen Stadium, Eugene, Oregon, October 30, 2016.

42. Dan, in conversation with the author, Veri (fieldnotes), Autzen Stadium, Eugene, Oregon, October, 29, 2016.

43. Dan, discussion.

44. Adler, "Making Pancakes on Sunday," 47; Amy Bentley, "From Culinary Other to Mainstream American: Meanings and Uses of Southwestern Cuisine," *Southern Folklore* 55, no. 3 (1998): 241.

45. *Tailgate Warriors*, "49ers vs. Raiders."

46. Mario Batali, *Mario Tailgates NASCAR Style: The Essential Cookbook for NASCAR Fans* (Charlotte, North Carolina: Sporting News, 2006), 139.

47. Sloan, *The Tailgating Cookbook*, 102.

48. *Guy Code*, season 2, episode 10, "Online dating, going to the doctor, and tailgating," directed by H. Grandison, aired on September 3, 2012 by MTV.

49. C. W. Buerkle, "Metrosexuality Can Stuff It: Beef Consumption as (Heteromasculine) Fortification," *Text and Performance Quarterly* 29 no.1 (2009): 81–82.

50. Moose, *Fan Fare*, 118.

51. Johnson, *ESPN Gameday Gourmet*, 84.

52. Batali, *Mario Tailgates NASCAR Style*, 84.

53. *Southern Living: The Official SEC Tailgating Cookbook*, (New York: Oxmoor House, 2012), 178.

54. C.W. Buerkle, "Metrosexuality Can Stuff It: Beef Consumption as (Heteromasculine) Fortification," *Text and Performance Quarterly* 29, no.1 (2009): 78.

55. Rebecca Swenson, "Domestic Divo? Televised Treatments of Masculinity, Femininity, and Food," *Critical Studies in Media Communication* 26, no.1 (2009): 39.

56. Jessamyn Neuhaus, *Manly Meals and Mom's Home Cooking: Cookbooks and Gender in Modern America* (Baltimore, MD: The Johns Hopkins University Press, 2003), 191–218.; Sherrie Inness, *Dinner Roles: American Women and Culinary Culture* (Iowa City, IA: University of Iowa Press, 2001), 20–28.

57. Neuhaus, *Manly Meals*, 197

58. Joanne Hollows, "The Bachelor Dinner: Masculinity, Class and Cooking in *Playboy*, 1953–1961," *Continuum: Journal of Media & Cultural Studies* 16 (2002): 143.

59. Hollows, 146.

60. Hollows, 146.

61. Vester, *Taste of Power*, 68.

62. Lampe, *NFL Tailgating Cookbook*, 12, 100; Johnson, *ESPN Gameday Gourmet*, 43, 135, 34; Peter Chakerian, *The Browns Fan's Tailgating Guide* (Cleveland, Ohio: Gray & Company Publishers, 2008), 102.

63. Sloan, *The Tailgating Cookbook*, 112.

64. Johnson, *ESPN Gameday Gourmet*, 88–89.

65. Batali, *Mario Tailgates NASCAR style*, 15.

66. Allegations of sexual harassment and assault by women against chef/restauranteur Mario Batali have revealed a history of sexual misconduct. See Irene Plagianos and Kitty Greenwald, "Mario Batali Steps Away From Restaurant Empire Following Sexual Misconduct Allegations," *NY Eater*, Dec 11, 2017: https://ny.eater.com/2017/12/11/16759540/mario-batali-sexual-misconduct-allegations ; Christine Hauser, Kim Severson and Julia Moskin, "Mario Batali Steps Away From Restaurants Amid Sexual Misconduct Allegations," *NY Times*, Dec 11, 2017 https://www.nytimes.com/2017/12/11/dining/mario-batali-sexual-misconduct.html?_r=0. For more on misogyny in the restaurant world, see Tom Colicchio, Nov 8, 2017, "An Open Letter to (Male) Chefs," Medium, https://medium.com/@tcolicchio/an-open-letter-to-male-chefs-742ca722e8f2.

67. "Tailgate Doctor," youtube video, :30, Accessed July 11, 2015, https://www.youtube.com/watch?v=B6w0KReNmpk.

68. "Tailgate," *iSpot.tv*, :30, Accessed July 11, 2015, https://www.ispot.tv/ad/7M5x/honda-eu2000-tailgate#.

69. *Southern Living*, 6.

70. *Southern Living*, 214.

71. Susan Bordo, *Unbearable Weight: Feminism, Western Culture, and the Body*, (Oakland, CA: University of California Press, 1993), 125.

72. Vester, *Taste of Power*, 15.

73. *Portlandia*, season 4, episode 4, "The Pull-Out King," directed by J. Krisel, aired on March 20, 2014 by Sundance Channel.

74. Heinz and Lee, "Getting Down to the Meat," 90–91.

75. Batali, *Mario Tailgates NASCAR Style*, 158.

76. Batali, *Mario Tailgates*, 166, 160.

77. Sloan, *The Tailgating Cookbook*, 178.

78. Vester, *Taste of Power*, 14–15.

79. Johnson, *ESPN Gameday Gourmet*, 6.

80. Johnson, *ESPN Gameday Gourmet*, 137.

81. Johnson, *ESPN Gameday Gourmet*, 153.

82. Buerkle, "Metrosexuality Can Stuff It," 81–82.

83. Sloan, *The Tailgating Cookbook*, 53.

84. Sloan, *The Tailgating Cookbook*, 100.

85. Moose, *Fan Fare*, 60.

86. Moose, *Fan Fare*, 132.

87. Ray Lampe, *The NFL Gameday Cookbook* (San Francisco: Chronicle Books, 2008), 32.

88. Lampe, *The NFL Gameday Cookbook*, 99.

89. Lampe, *The NFL Gameday Cookbook*, 186.

90. Sloan, *The Tailgating Cookbook*, 101.

91. Sloan, *The Tailgating Cookbook*, 101.

92. Amy Calvert, "You Are What You (M)eat: Explorations of Meat-Eating, Masculinity and Masquerade" *Journal of International Women's Studies* 16, no.1 (2014): 24.

93. See, for example, Jennifer Brady and Matthew Ventresca's "'Officially a Vegan Now': On Meat and Renaissance Masculinity in Pro Football," *Food and Foodways* 22, no. 4 (2014): 300–321, for an analysis of media coverage of NFL player Arian Foster's vegan announcement.

94. Heinz and Lee, "Getting Down to the Meat," 91.

95. See Emily Sohn, "Evidence Grows Kinking Grilled Meat and Cancer, but You Can Lower the Risk," *The Washington Post*, June 3, 2017, accessed July 11, 2018, https://www.washingtonpost.com/national/health-science/evidence-grows-linking-grilled-meat-and-cancer-but-you-can-lower-the-risk/2017/06/02/f946078c-4549-11e7-a196-a1bb629f64cb_story.html?utm_term=.0611b0eb96c1.

96. Adams, *Sexual Politics*, 34.

97. *Tailgate Warriors*, "Bears vs. Buffalo Bills."

98. Buerkle, "Metrosexuality Can Stuff It," 82; Heinz and Lee, "Getting Down to the Meat," 95.

99. Newcombe et al, "'Eat Like a Man'," 392.

# Chapter 4

1. Peter Naccarato and Kathleen LeBesco, *Culinary Capital* (London: Berg, 2012), 12; Liora Gvion, "What's Cooking in America? Cookbooks Narrate Ethnicity: 1850–1990," *Food, Culture and Society* 12, no. 1 (2009): 54–56. Rachel Slocum, "Race in the Study of Food," *Progress in Human Geography*, 35 (2010): 303–327. Rafia Zafar, "The Signifying Dish: Autobiography and History in Two Black Women's Cookbooks," *Feminist Studies* 25 (1999): 449–469; Doris Witt, *Black Hunger: Soul Food and America* (Minneapolis, MN: University of Minnesota Press, 2004).

2. Sherrie A. Inness, *Secret Ingredients: Race, Gender, and Class at the Dinner Table* (New York: Palgrave MacMillan, 2006), 2.

3. Inness, *Secret Ingredients*.

4. Rosalyn Collings Eves, "A Recipe for Remembrance: Memory and Identity in African-American Women's Cookbooks," *Rhetoric Review* 24 (2005): 280–297; Zafar, "The Signifying Dish," 449–469. Toni Tipton-Martin, *The Jemima Code: Two Centuries of African American Cookbooks* (Austin, TX: University of Texas Press, 2015); Megan J. Elias, *Food on the Page: Cookbooks and American Culture* (Philadelphia: University of Pennsylvania Press, 2017).

5. Tipton-Martin, *The Jemima Code*; Eves, "Recipe for Remembrance," 282–285; Slocum, "Race in the Study of Food," 306–308; Anne L. Bower (Ed), *African American Foodways: Explorations of History and Culture* (Champaign, IL: University of Illinois Press, 2007).

6. Gvion, "What's Cooking in America?" 54.

7. Danielle Gallegos, "Cookbooks as Manuals of Taste," in *Ordinary Lifestyles: Popular Media, Consumption and Taste*, ed. David Bell and Joanne Hollows (New York: Open University Press, 2005), 99.

8. Katharina Vester, *A Taste of Power: Food and American Identities* (Berkeley: University of California Press, 2015), 2.

9. Slocum, "Race in the Study of Food," 305–306; Tipton-Martin, *The Jemima Code*, 2–3; Zafar, "Signifying Dish," 454.

10. John Egerton, "Foreword: A Gallery of Great Cooks," in Tipton-Martin, *The Jemima Code*, ix-xi; Tipton-Martin, *The Jemima Code*, 1–9; Barbara Haber, "Foreword: Why Cookbooks Matter," in Tipton-Martin, *The Jemima Code*, xiii-xv; Zafar, "Signifying Dish," 452.

11. Tipton-Martin, *The Jemima Code*, 4.

12. Liora Gvion and Naomi Trostler, "From Spaghetti and Meatballs through Hawaiian Pizza to Sushi: The Changing Nature of Ethnicity in American Restaurants," *Journal of Popular Culture* 41 (2008): 955–958; Shun Lu and Gary Alan Fine, "The Presentation of Ethnic Authenticity: Chinese Food as a Social Accomplishment," *The Sociological Quarterly* 36 (1995): 536; Amy Reddinger, "Eating 'Local': The Politics of Post-Statehood Hawaiian Cookbooks," *Nordic Journal of English Studies* 9 (2010): 85–86.

13. Gvion, "What's Cooking in America," 59.

14. Tipton-Martin, *The Jemima Code*, 39–40.

15. For examples of these images and their cultural influence, see, among others, Brian D. Behnken and Gregory D. Smithers, *Racism in American Popular Media: From Aunt Jemima to the Frito Bandito* (Santa Barbara, California: Praeger, 2015);

Witt, *Black Hunger*; Patricia A. Turner, *Ceramic Uncles and Celluloid Mammies: Black Images and their Influence on Culture* (New York: Anchor-Doubleday, 1994). Witt, *Black Hunger*, 21–53; Tipton-Martin, *The Jemima Code*, 2–4. The Aunt Jemima stereotype operates in much the same way as myths of natural black athletic superiority. As African American athletic accomplishments became more prominent in the twentieth century, white supremacists needed a way to account for those successes while maintaining institutionalized white dominance. Claims that black athleticism was "natural" and linked to race-based differences functioned to discredit the agency of black athletes, obscure their efforts to perfect a craft, and uphold the fallacy of race as biology. Paradoxically, this use of stereotypes recognizes black labor, while at the same time demeaning it. See, for example., Patrick B. Miller, "The Anatomy of Scientific Racism: Racialist Responses to Black Athletic Achievement," *Journal of Sport History* 25 (1998); Laurel Davis, "The Articulation of Difference: White Preoccupation with the Question of Racially Linked Genetic Differences Among Athletes," *Sociology of Sport Journal* 7 (1990).

16. Witt, 54.

17. Gvion and Trostler, "From Spaghetti and Meatballs through Hawaiian Pizza to Sushi," 955; Elias, *Food on the Page*, 78–79.

18. Linda Keiler Brown and Kay Mussell, "Introduction," in *Ethnic and Regional Foodways in the United States: The Performance of Group Identity* (Knoxville, University of Tennessee Press, 1984), 4; Gvion and Trostler, "From Spaghetti and Meatballs through Hawaiian Pizza to Sushi, 955.

19. Zafar, "Signifying Dish," 455; Vertamae Smart-Grosvenor, *Vibration Cooking, or, the Travel Notes of a Geechee Girl* (NY: Ballantine Books, 1991), 3.

20. Eves, "Recipe for Remembrance," 284; Zafar, "Signifying Dish," 451; Tipton-Martin, *The Jemima Code*, 80.

21. Tipton-Martin, *The Jemima Code*, 79–107; Eves, "Recipe for Remembrance," 283; Zafar, "Signifying Dish," 455; Slocum, "Race in the Study of Food," 306.

22. Tipton-Martin, *The Jemima Code*, 79; For a nuanced discussion of the relationship between blacks and chicken that ranges well beyond stereotype and stigma, see Psyche Williams-Forson's *Building Houses Out of Chicken Legs: Black Women, Food, and Power* (Chapel Hill, NC: The University of North Carolina Press, 2006), in which the author examines the role chicken has played in the lives of black women throughout history.

23. Elias, *Food on the Page*, 143–144.

24. Gvion and Trostler, "From Spaghetti and Meatballs through Hawaiian Pizza to Sushi," 962–963.

25. Gvion and Trostler, "From Spaghetti and Meatballs through Hawaiian Pizza to Sushi," 964.

26. Tipton-Martin, *The Jemima Code*, 109; Witt, *Black Hunger*, 7.

27. Gvion, "What's Cooking in American?" 53.

28. Marilyn Halter, *Shopping for Identity: The Marketing of Ethnicity* (New York: Random House, 2000), 107.

29. Lu and Fine, "The Presentation of Ethnic Authenticity," 536.

30. Hyla O'Conner, *The Complete NFL Cookbook* (New York: Plume Publishing, 1981).

31. Malavasi quoted in O'Conner, *The Complete NFL Cookbook*, 12.

32. O'Conner, *The Complete NFL Cookbook*, 7.

33. Matthew Frye Jacobson, *Roots Too: White Ethnic Revival in Post-Civil Rights America* (Cambridge, MA: Harvard University Press, 2006), 2.

34. Halter, *Shopping for Identity*, 9. Molly O'Neill, "New Mainstream: Hot Dogs, Apple Pie, and Salsa," *The New York Times*, March 11, 1992, C1, accessed May 7, 2018, https://www.nytimes.com/1992/03/11/garden/new-mainstream-hot-dogs-apple-pie -and-salsa.html; Alex Seitz Wald, "Actually, Salsa Dethroned Ketchup 20 Years Ago," *The Atlantic*, October 17, 2013, accessed May 7, 2018, https://www.theatlantic.com /national/archive/2013/10/actually-salsa-dethroned-ketchup-20-years-ago/309844/.

35. O'Connor, *The Complete NFL Cookbook*; April Herbert, *The Tailgate Cookbook* (New York: Fund and Wagnalls, 1970), see especially pages 14–48; Nan Perry, et al., The Souper Bowl of Recipes (Stafford, Virginia: Northwoods Press, Inc., 1980).

36. Amy Reddinger, "Eating 'Local': The Politics of Post-Statehood Hawaiian Cookbooks," *Nordic Journal of English Studies* 9 (2010): 74.

37. Candy Coleman, *Pigskin Picnics* (Mt. Pocono, Pennsylvania: C.C. Enterprises, 1980), 3.

38. Candy Coleman, *Pigskin Picnics*, 12.

39. Candy Coleman, *Pigskin Picnics*, 7.

40. Candy Coleman, *Pigskin Picnics*, 19.

41. *Tailgate Cooking and Other Gastronomical Horrors*, (Minneapolis, Minnesota: Twin Cities Federal, 1972).

42.

43. Elena Machado Sáez, "Bittersweet (Be)Longing: Filling the Void of History in Andrea Levy's *Fruit of the Lemon*," *Anthurium: A Caribbean Studies Journal* 4 (2006): 3.

44. Reddinger, "Eating Local," 72.

45. Fleischmann, *Sagehen's Retreiver Club Tailgate Cookbook*, 94.

46. *Picnics & Tailgate Parties* (Menlo Park, California: Lane Publishing Company, 1982), 47.

47. *Picnics & Tailgate Parties*, 9.

48. *Picnics & Tailgate Parties*, 9.

49. Reddinger, "Eating Local," 86.

50. Reddinger, "Eating Local," 73; Dottie Dekko, *Cooking for Kicks: The Sport of Tailgating* (Detroit, Michigan: Sprague Publishing Company, 1978): 135.

51. Reddinger, "Eating Local," 135.

52. April Herbert, *The Tailgate Cookbook* (New York: Funk & Wagnalls, 1970), 19–20; Lu and Fine, "The Presentation of Ethnic Authenticity," 541.

53. Indeed, white Americans from the mainland continue to be dismissive of Hawaiian statehood, as illustrated by US Attorney General Jeff Sessions' derisive reference to a federal judge in Hawaii as "a judge sitting on an island in the Pacific" in April 2017. See, Charlie Savage, "Sessions Dismisses Hawaii as 'an Island in the Pacific,'" *New York Times*, April 21, 2017, A15.

54. Gvion, "What's Cooking in America?" 54.

55. O'Connor, *The Complete NFL Cookbook*, 112.

56. Dekko, *Cooking for Kicks*, 28.

57. Tipton-Martin, *The Jemima Code*, 2, 40; Elias, *Food on the Page*, 78.

58. Kristen L. Matthews, "One Nation Over Coals: Cold War Nationalism and the Barbecue," *American Studies* 50 (2009): 19.

59. Tipton-Martin, *The Jemima Code*, 11. Indeed, Tipton-Martin's book, along

with Psyche A. Williams-Forson's, *Building Houses Out of Chicken Legs: Black Women, Food, & Power* remain two of the few academic treatments of African American foodways.

60. Lu and Fine, "The Presentation of Ethnic Authenticity," 538.

61. Young Rae Oum, "Authenticity and Representation: Cuisines and Identities in Korean-American Diaspora," *Postcolonial Studies* 8, no. 1 (2005): 116.

62. Young Rae Oum, "Authenticity and Representation," 116.

63. Lu and Fine, "The Presentation of Ethnic Authenticity," 536.

64. Herbert, *The Tailgate Cookbook*, 61–64.

65. Fleischmann, *Sagehen's Retreiver Club Tailgate Cookbook*, 57.

66. Fleischmann, *Sagehen's Retreiver Club Tailgate Cookbook*, 91.

67. Perry, *Souper Bowl of Recipes*, 85.

68. Herbert, *The Tailgate Cookbook*, 93.

69. Perry, *Souper Bowl of Recipes*, 6.

70. O'Connor, *The Complete NFL Cookbook*, 105.

71. Herbert, *The Tailgate Cookbook*, 44.

72. Sherrie A. Inness, *Dinner Roles: American Women and Culinary Culture* (Iowa City: University of Iowa Press, 2001), 24–26.

73. *Picnics & Tailgate Parties*, 48.

74. Susan Wyler, *Tailgate Parties: 24 Menus for Gourmet Picnics and Outdoor Entertaining* (Nevada City, California: Harmony Books, 1984), 71.

75. Wyler, *Tailgate Parties*, 22–23.

76. Gvion & Trostler, "From Spaghetti and Meatballs through Hawaiian Pizza to Sushi," 957.

77. Pauline Adema, "Vicarious Consumption: Food, Television and the Ambiguity of Modernity," *Journal of American & Comparative Cultures* 23 (2000): 113–123.

78. Peter Chakerian, *The Browns Fan's Tailgating Guide* (Cleveland, Ohio: Gray & Company, Publishers, 2008), 15.

79. Though not specific to football, we include Batali's text for its popularity and similarity to books focused on gridiron tailgating.

80. Mario Batali, *Mario Tailgates NASCAR Style: The Essential Cookbook for NASCAR Fans* (Charlotte, North Carolina: Sporting News, 2006), 153.

81. Marla Dickerson, "Race to the Border; NASCAR Hopes to Court Hispanic Fans," *Los Angeles Times*, March 6, 2005, accessed May 7, 2018, http://articles .latimes.com/2005/mar/06/business/fi-nascar6; Greg Beacham, "NASCAR Races After Latino Market with TV Series," *The San Diego Union-Tribune*, March 28, 2013, accessed May 7, 2018, http://www.sandiegouniontribune.com/sdut-nascar-races -after-latino-market-with-tv-series-2013mar28-story.html.

82. Batali, *Mario Tailgates NASCAR Style*, 29.

83. Joanne Hollows, "Oliver's Twist: Leisure, Labor and Domestic Masculinity in *The Naked Chef*," *International Journal of Cultural Studies* 6 (2003): 235.

84. Bob Sloan, *The Tailgating Cookbook: Recipes for the Big Game* (San Francisco: Chronicle Books, 2005), 44.

85. Ray Lampe, *The NFL Gameday Cookbook* (San Francisco: Chronicle Books, 2008), 147.

86. John Madden and Peter Kaminsky, *John Madden's Ultimate Tailgating* (New York: Penguin, 1998), 105–125.

87. Madden and Kaminsky, 6.

88. Pableaux Johnson, *ESPN Gameday Gourmet: More Than 80 All-American Tailgate Recipes* (New York: ESPN, 2007), 3.

89. Johnson, *ESPN Gameday Gourmet*, 69.

90. Johnson, *ESPN Gameday Gourmet*, 46.

91. Amy Bentley, "From Culinary Other to Mainstream American: Meanings and Uses of Southwestern Cuisine," *Southern Folklore* 55, no. 3 (1998): 238–252; Nola McKey, "My Oh My! Fritos Pie!" *Texas Highways*, June 2011, accessed July 5, 2018, http://texashighways.com/food-drink/item/779-my-oh-my-fritos-pie; The Kitchen Sisters, "The Birth of the Frito," *NPR Morning Edition*, October 18, 2007, accessed August 1, 2017, https://www.npr.org/2007/10/18/15377830/the-birth-of-the-frito.

92. For a good discussion on resistive movements against the "Frito Bandito" character see: Brian D. Behnken and Gregory D. Smithers, *Racism in American Popular Media: From Aunt Jemima to the Frito Bandito* (Santa Barbara, California: Praeger, 2015), 120–122.

93. Behnken and Smithers, 25.

94. Williams-Forson, *Building Houses Out of Chicken Legs*, 3.

95. Bentley, "From Culinary Other to Mainstream American," 244. Recently, however, the link between Mexicans and the Latino foods that Americans have embraced has been emphasized for nefarious purposes. Late in the 2016 presidential campaign, *Latinos for Trump* founder Marco Gutierrez used the taco as a signifying dish to stoke racist fears when he proclaimed, "My culture is a very dominant culture. It is imposing and it's causing problems. If you don't do something about it, you're going to have taco trucks on every corner." See, for example., Phillip Bump, "The National Economic Implications of a Taco Truck on Every Corner," *The Washington Post*, September 2, 2016, accessed July 3, 2018, https://www.washingtonpost.com /news/the-fix/wp/2016/09/02/the-national-economic-implications-of-a-taco-truck -on-every-corner/?utm_term=.d262f49f32a7; John Paul Brammer, "Taco Trucks on Every Corner? That'd Really Make America Great Again," *The Guardian*, September 2, 2016, accessed July 3, 2018, https://www.theguardian.com/commentisfree/2016/sep /02/taco-truck-on-every-corner-trump-mexican-marco-gutierrez.

96. It is also shared by a number of politicians, social commentators—and voters. Bentley cites conservative nationalist Pat Buchanan's 1996 pledge to build a wall on the US-Mexico border. It didn't help him secure the Republican presidential nomination, but on the campaign trail twenty years later, Donald Trump resorted to similar vitriolic "Build a Wall" rhetoric en route to securing an unlikely Republican nomination and White House electoral win. Eleanor Clift, "Pat Buchanan: Donald Trump Stole My Playbook," *Daily Beast*, June 1, 2016, accessed January 13, 2018, https://www.thedailybeast.com/pat-buchanan-donald-trump-stole-my -playbook; Emily Messner, *The Washington Post*, "The Debate," (blog), accessed January 13, 2018, http://blogs.washingtonpost.com/thedebate/2006/03/wall_or _no_wall.html.

97. Smith, *Spread Formation*, title page.

98. Smith, *Spread Formation*, 37.

99. Smith, 29.

100. Smith , 40.

101. Smith , 114.

102. Smith, 19.

103. *Southern Living*, 28.

104. Michael W. Twitty, "The Colonial Roots of Southern Barbecue: Re-Creating the Birth of an American Culinary Staple," *Afroculinaria.com*, July 4, 2012, https://afroculinaria.com/2012/07/14/the-colonial-roots-of-southern-barbecue-re-creating-the-birth-of-an-american-culinary-staple/.

105. Michael W. Twitty, "Barbecue is an American Tradition—of Enslaved Africans and Native Americans," *The Guardian*, July 4, 2015, accessed July 9, 2018, https://www.theguardian.com/commentisfree/2015/jul/04/barbecue-american-tradition-enslaved-africans-native-americans.

106. Witt, *Black Hunger*, 6.

107. Douglas Lederman, "Old Times Not Forgotten: A Battle Over Symbols Obscures U. of Mississippi's Racial Changes," *The Chronicle of Higher Education*, October 23, 1993, A52.

108. Joshua I. Newman, *Embodying Dixie*, 224; Lederman, "Old Times Not Forgotten," A53; Logan Strother, et al., "The Confederate Flag Largely Disappeared After the Civil War. The Fight Against Civil Rights Brought It Back," *The Washington Post*, June 12, 2017, accessed January 13, 2018, https://www.washingtonpost.com/news/monkey-cage/wp/2017/06/12/confederate-symbols-largely-disappeared-after-the-civil-war-the-fight-against-civil-rights-brought-them-back/?utm_term=.d80d0bfc51bb.

109. Lederman, "Old Times Not Forgotten," A52.

110. Although officially retired in 2003, the Colonel Reb mascot endures. It still features prominently on the Ole Miss campus and in the Grove on game days, and its retirement spurred the creation of the Colonel Reb Foundation, a student-led group lobbying to reinstate the mascot. See https://www.colonelreb.org/saving-colonel-reb; https://www.nbcnews.com/news/us-news/confederacy-still-haunts-campus-ole-miss-n820881.

111. Newman, *Embodying Dixie*, 231–232; Charles Frederick, *A Good Day to Be Here: Tailgating in the Grove at Ole Miss*, Indiana University, 1999.

112. Newman, *Embodying Dixie*, 222.

113. Turner, *A Good Day to Be Here*, 62.

114. It bears mentioning that in 2017, emboldened by the Trump presidency, there has been a resurgence of Confederate flag use, notably among white supremacist groups and those who protest the removal of Confederate monuments. Among tailgaters, cultural illiteracy at best, and outright racism at worst, can be read in the presence of Confederate flags, as well as Indian mascot banners and other material reminders of America's racist past in tailgating spaces around the country. See, for example, Vann R. Newkirk II, "Growing Up in the Shadow of the Confederacy," *The Atlantic*, August 22, 2017, accessed January 13, 2018, https://www.theatlantic.com/politics/archive/2017/08/growing-up-in-the-shadow-of-the-confederacy/537501/ and Louis Moore, "Sports Won't Save US: Sports, Race, and Charlottesville," *Sport in American History* (blog), August 21, 2017, https://ussporthistory.com/2017/08/21/sports-wont-save-us-sports-race-and-charlottesville/.

115. John St. Warren, *Rammer Jammer Yellow Hammer* (New York: Broadway Paperbacks, 2004), 149.

116. Jennifer Guilliano, *Indian Spectacle: College Mascots and the Anxiety of Modern America* (2015), 13.

117. 2016 statistics indicate that the student body at the University of Illinois is approximately 44% white, 15% Asian, 5% African American, and 9% Hispanic. See,

"Office of Inclusion & Intercultural Relations," accessed January 13, 2018. https://oiir.illinois.edu/about/demographics.

118. Megan Rogers, "Mascot Makeover," *Inside Higher Ed*, December 10, 2013, accessed January 15, 2018, https://www.insidehighered.com/news/2013/12/10/most-colleges-adjust-moving-away-native-american-mascots; Guilliano, Indian Spectacle, 109–110.

119. Mark Simonian, "Voters Axe Indian Mascot; Robber Barons Selected," *The Stanford Daily*, December 5, 1975, accessed July 7, 2018, https://stanforddailyarchive.com/cgi-bin/stanford?a=d&d=stanford19751205-01.2.2#.

120. *American Dad!* "Kung Pao Turkey," directed by Rodney Clouden, (November 24, 2013; Los Angeles: Fox Network).

121. *Silver Linings Playbook*, directed by David O. Russell (New York, New York: The Weinstein Company, 2013), DVD.

122. A review of our field notes reminded us of the lack of diversity we saw on the blacktop at these tailgate locations. Common observations: "overwhelmingly white" (University of Tennessee), "all tailgate lots predominantly white" (Buffalo), "very white" (Stanford), "the vast majority of tailgaters were white" (Louisiana State University), "very white—saw maybe two people of color in tailgate areas around stadium" (University of Oregon).

123. His quip isn't at all off the mark, as evidenced by the now infamous #BBQBecky incident in which a white woman called the police to report a group of black people barbecuing at Lake Merritt in Oakland, CA. See Laura M. Holson, "Hundreds in Oakland Turn Out to BBQ While Black," *The New York Times*, May 21, 2018, accessed July 8, 2018, https://www.nytimes.com/2018/05/21/us/oakland-bbq-while-black.html and "BBQ Becky: Woman Photoshopped into Black History After Barbecue Complaint," *BBC News Newsbeat*, May 18, 2018, accessed July 8, 2018, https://www.bbc.com/news/newsbeat-44167760.

124. *Guy Code*, "Online dating, Going to the Doctor, and Tailgating," directed by Howard Grandison, (September 3, 2012; New York City: MTV2).

125. Gvion, "What's Cooking in America," 58.

## Chapter 5

1. Peter Chakerian, *The Browns Fan's Tailgating Guide* (Cleveland, Ohio: Gray & Company Publishers, 2008), 13.

2. The notion of tailgating as forging community is underscored in the academic literature as well. See, Deborah Kerstetter et al, "The Multiple Meanings Associated with the Football Tailgating Ritual," in *Proceedings of the 2010 Northeastern Recreation Research Symposium* (Bolton Landing, New York), 38–44, accessed December 31, 2017, https://www.nrs.fs.fed.us/pubs/gtr/gtr_nrs-p-94.pdf; Jeffrey James, G. Steven Breezeel, and Stephen Ross, "A Two-Stage Study of the Reasons to Begin and Continue Tailgating," *Sport Marketing Quarterly* 10, no. 4 (2001): 212–222.

3. Jenna Drenten, et al., "Not Just a Party in the Parking Lot: An Exploratory Investigation of the Motives Underlying the Ritual Commitment of Football Tailgaters," *Sport Marketing Quarterly* 18, no. 2 (2009): 92.

4. *Tailgate Warriors*, season 1, episode 1, "Bears vs. Buffalo Bills," directed by Anthony Rogriguez [director of photography], aired on October 17, 2009 by Food Network.

5. Rebecca Swenson, "*Domestic Divo?* Televised Treatments of Masculinity, Femininity and Food," *Critical Studies in Media Communication* 26, no. 1 (2009): 50–51; Drenten et al., "Not Just a Party in the Parking Lot," 99–100; Sherrie A. Inness, *Dinner Roles: American Women and Culinary Culture* (Iowa City: University of Iowa Press, 2001): 52–70.

6. *Tailgate Warriors*, season 2, episode 3, "Vikings vs. Saints," directed by Daniel Dvorak [cameraman], aired on November 3, 2010, by Food Network; *Tailgate Warriors*, "Packers vs. Seahawks."

7. *Tailgate Warriors*, "Packers vs. Seahawks."

8. *Tailgate Warriors*, "Packers vs. Seahawks."

9. Swenson, "*Domestic Divo*," 49.

10. Chakerian, *The Browns Fan's Tailgating Guide*, 15.

11. Nick Benigno, interview with authors, Pleasanton, California, January 30, 2016.

12. Kimo, interview with the authors, Pleasanton, California, January 30, 2016.

13. Nick Benigno, Interview with authors, Pleasanton, California, January 30, 2016.

14. Michael Jones, Interview with authors, Oakland, California, October 22, 2010.

15. Richard A. Rogers, "Beasts, Burgers, and Hummers: Meat and the Crisis of Masculinity in Contemporary Television Advertisements," *Environmental Communication* 2, no. 3 (2008): 296. We are not arguing that tailgates were/are exclusively all-male spaces. Our claim that tailgates are homosocial sites is largely in reference to contemporary tailgating. This is not to say that women are not present, but as our fieldnotes attest, we did encounter many spaces that were all-male. Women do participate in the festivities on the blacktop, but they are usually in the minority, and when they are present, it is often at the periphery of the tailgate.

16. *How I Met Your Mother*, season 7, episode 13, "Tailgate," directed by P. Fryman, aired on January 2, 2012 by CBS.

17. James B. Twitchell, *Where Men Hide* (New York: Columbia University Press, 2006), 179.

18. For a bit of a history on the series of commercials see, "Great Moments in Tailgate History," http://cargocollective.com/bobfremgen/Great-Moments-in -Tailgating-History, accessed January 21, 2018.

19. "Toyota—NBC//Great Moments in Tailgating History," http://www.czako.com /mike_czako_%7C_HISTORY_OF_TAILGATING.html, accessed January 8, 2018.

20. "Great Moments in Tailgating History," see "Episode 15, 6 Foot Sandwich," for the falafel discussion. All other episodes in the series can be found on this site.

21. *Tailgate Warriors*, "Chicago Bears vs. Buffalo Bills."

22. *Tailgate Warriors*, "Chicago Bears vs. Buffalo Bills."

23. *Tailgate Warriors*, "Packers vs. Seahawks."

24. Daniel A. Nathan, *Rooting for the Home Team: Sport, Community, and Identity* (Champaign, IL: University of Illinois Press, 2013): 1–15.

25. John Bale, *Sports Geography* (New York: NY: Routledge, 2003): 161–177; Greg Ramshaw and Tom Hinch, "Place Identity and Sport Tourism: The Case of the Heritage Classic Ice Hockey Event," *Current Issues in Tourism* 9, no. 4–5 (2006): 401.

26. *Tailgate Warriors*, "Packers vs. Seahawks."

27. *Tailgate Warriors*, season 2, episode 2, "49ers vs. Raiders," directed by Daniel Dvorak [cameraman], aired on October 27, 2010 by Food Network.

28. *Tailgate Warriors*, "Vikings vs. Saints."

29. *Tailgate Warriors*, "Vikings vs. Saints."

30. Amy Calvert, "You Are What You (M)eat: Explorations of Meat-eating, Masculinity and Masquerade," *Journal of International Women's Studies* 16, no. 1 (2014): 22.

31. Taylor Mathis, *The Southern Tailgating Cookbook: A Game-Day Guide for Lovers of Food, Football, and the South* (Chapel Hill: University of North Carolina Press, 2013), 146–148.

32. Paul Lukas, "Grilling Up the Competition," *ESPN*, November 12, 2009, 2, accessed November 25, 2017, http://www.espn.com/espn/page2/story/_/page/lukas %2F091112/sportCat/ncf.

33. Sarah Talalay, "Dolfans Can Stomach Opposition," *SunSentinel* November 22, 1999, accessed November 25, 2017http://articles.sun-sentinel.com/1999-11-22/sports /9911220207_1_kick-competition-dolphins-nfl-gatorade-punt.

34. Quoted in Lukas, "Grilling Up the Competition."

35. Cork Gaines, "LSU Fans Are Cooking Pigs Disguised As Baby Elephants Prior To Showdown With Alabama," *Business Insider*, November 3, 2012, accessed January 16, 2018, http://www.businessinsider.com/photos-lsu-fans-cooking-pigs -disguised-as-baby-elephants-2012-11.

36. Graham Watson, "The Tailgating menu at LSU includes 'baby elephant' **UPDATED**," *Yahoo! Sports*, November 3, 2012, accessed November 28, 2017, https://sports.yahoo.com/blogs/dr-saturday/tailgating-menu-lsu-includes-baby -elephant-171722235--ncaaf.html.

37. Seth Rosenthal, "Maryland Suggests You Eat Syracuse's Mascot," *SBNATION*, November 3, 2013, accessed November 30, 2017, https://www.sbnation.com/lookit /2013/11/5/5069408/maryland-suggests-you-eat-syracuses-mascot-orange.

38. Rosenthal, "Maryland Suggests"

39. Tonya Williams Bradford and John F. Sherry, Jr. "Grooving in the Ludic Foodscape: Bridled Revelry in Collegiate Tailgating," *Journal of Consumer Culture* 17, no. 3 (2017): 785.

40. "OkieTigerTK," *Tigerfan*, August 3, 2011, accessed November 30, 2017, http://www.tigerfan.com/threads/at-home-tailgate-party.99787/.

41. Chakerian, *The Browns Fan's Tailgating Guide*, 15.

42. George Astin, interview with the authors, Pleasanton, California, January 30, 2016.

43. Nick Benigno, interview with the authors, Pleasanton, California, January 30, 2016.

44. James K. Gentry, "Tailgating Goes Above and Beyond at the University of Mississippi," *New York Times*, October 31, 2014, accessed November 12, 2017, https://www.nytimes.com/2014/11/01/sports/ncaafootball/tailgating-goes-above -and-beyond-at-the-university-of-mississippi.html.

45. Knapp quoted in James K. Gentry, "Tailgating Goes Above and Beyond at the University of Mississippi," *New York Times*, October 31, 2014, accessed January 16, 2018, https://www.nytimes.com/2014/11/01/sports/ncaafootball/tailgating-goes -above-and-beyond-at-the-university-of-mississippi.html?_r=0.

46. Jim (also known as Dr. Dogz), in conversation with the author, Veri (field notes), Stanford Stadium, Palo Alto, California, September 17, 2016.

47. Michelle Szabo, "Men Nurturing Through Food: Challenging Gender Dichotomies Around Domestic Cooking," *Journal of Gender Studies* 23, no. 1 (2014): 20.

48. A Los Malosos member, in conversation with the authors (field notes), Oakland Alameda Coliseum, Oakland, California, December 6, 2015.

49. Dwayne C. Martin, email message to author (Liberti), November 13, 2017.

50. Martin, email to author.

51. "The Tailgate With A Cause," accessed December 13, 2017, https://thetailgate .squarespace.com/#upcoming-events-1.

52. Dan Cohen, phone interview with the author (Liberti), November 30, 2017.

53. Cohen, interview. The University of Tennessee and the New York Giants are aware of Joe Fox and Dan Cohen's respective activities, and in both cases have reached agreements around a range of issues that can at times mean the organizations look the other way as the blacktop is used by tailgaters to raise money for charity.

54. We are mindful of the critical observations made by scholars concerning the politics of philanthropy, specifically Samantha King's analysis of the "current preoccupation with consumer-oriented philanthropic solutions to social prob- lems." See Samantha King, *Pink Ribbons, Inc.: Breast Cancer and the Politics of Philanthropy* (Minneapolis: University of Minnesota Press, 2006), xi. Our aim is not to intentionally sidestep the important issues King and others raise about philan- thropy. The politics of tailgate philanthropy, though not the focus of our work, are worth exploring, especially given the numerous places in which fundraising on the blacktop is occurring.

## Conclusion

1. "Chevy Silverado, Wheat Grass," YouTube Video, :30, June 1, 2014, https:// www.youtube.com/watch?v=jFGepTFffVY.

2. James B. Twitchell, *Where Men Hide* (New York: Columbia University Press, 2006), 22–23.

3. See, for example: Katarzyna Joanna Herd, "Colour my Falafel Blue: Football Branding in Swedish Food Industry—An Ethnographic Approach," *Fork to Farm: International Journal of Innovative Research and Practice* 2, no. 1 (2015): 1–6; Jennifer Brady and Matthew Ventresca, "'Officially A Vegan Now': On Meat and Renaissance Masculinity in Pro Football," *Food and Foodways* 22, no 4 (2014): 300–321.

4. James Beard, *Cook It Outdoors* (New York: M. Barrows and Company, Inc., 1941), viii.

5. Michael Pollan, *Cooked: A Natural History of Transformation* (New York: The Penguin Press, 2013), 128.

6. Katharina Vester, *A Taste of Power: Food and American Identity* (Berkeley: University of California Press, 2015), 121.

7. Lynda Birke, *Feminism, Animals, and Science: The Naming of the Shrew* (Philadelphia: Open University Press, 1994), 21.

8. Jeffery Sobal, "Men, Meat, and Marriage: Models of Masculinity," *Food & Foodways* 13, no. 1 & 2 (2005): 137.

9. Amelia Rayno, "Meat Necklace Exemplifies Extreme Tailgating," *Honolulu Star Advertiser*, November 7, 2017, http://www.staradvertiser.com/2017/11/07 /food/meat-necklace-exemplifies-extreme-tailgating/.

10. Wilbur Zelinsky, "The Roving Palate: North America's Ethnic Restaurant Choices," *Geoforum* 16, no. 1 (1985): 51.

11. Nir Avieli, "Grilled Nationalism: Power, Masculinity, and Space in Israeli Barbeques," *Food, Culture, and Soicety* 16, no. 2 (2013): 306.

12. Andrew Bauhs, "Gay College Football Fan's Goal: Visit all 130 Major Stadiums," *Outsports*, August 29, 2017, https://www.outsports.com/2017/8/29/16171288/gay -college-football-fan-andrew-bauhs-stadium-tour.

13. Bauhs, "Gay College Football Fan's Goal."

14. Anne Cunningham Osborne and Danielle Sarver Coombs, *Female Fans of the NFL: Taking Their Place in the Stands* (New York: Routledge, 2016), 135–136.

# BIBLIOGRAPHY

Adams, Carol. *The Sexual Politics of Meat: A Feminist-Vegetarian Critical Theory*. New York: Continuum, 1990.

Adema, Pauline. "Vicarious Consumption: Food, Television, and the Ambiguity of Modernity." *Journal of American Culture* 23 (2004): 113–123.

Adler, Thomas A. "Making Pancakes on Sunday: The Male Cook in Family Tradition." *Western Folklore* 40 (1981): 45–54.

Ashley, Bob, Joanne Hollows, Steve Jones, and Ben Taylor. *Food and Cultural Studies*. London, UK: Routledge, 2004.

Avieli, Nir. "Grilled Nationalism: Power, Masculinity, and Space in Israeli Barbeques." *Food, Culture, and Society* 16 (2013): 301–320.

Bale John. *Sports Geography*. New York, NY: Routledge, 2003.

Beard, James. *Cook It Outdoors*. New York: M. Barrows and Company, Inc., 1941.

Behnken, Brian D. and Gregory D. Smithers. *Racism in American Popular Media: From Aunt Jemima to the Frito Bandito*. Santa Barbara, CA: Praeger, 2015.

Bentley, Amy. "From Culinary Other to Mainstream American: Meanings and Uses of Southwestern Cuisine." *Southern Folklore* 55 (1998): 238–252

Bergin, Thomas G. *The Game: The Harvard-Yale Football Rivalry, 1875–1983*. New Haven, CT: Yale University Press, 1984.

Birke, Lynda. *Feminism, Animals, and Science: The Naming of the Shrew*. Philadelphia: Open University Press, 1994.

Block, Daniel. "Saving Milk through Masculinity: Public Health Officers and Pure Milk." *Food and Foodways* 13 (2005): 115–134.

Bordo, Susan. *Unbearable Weight: Feminism, Western Culture, and the Body*. Oakland, CA: University of California Press, 1993.

Bower, Anne L., ed. *African American Foodways: Explorations of History and Culture*. Champaign, IL: University of Illinois Press, 2007.

Bradford, Tonya Williams and John F. Sherry, Jr.. "Domesticating Public Space through Ritual: Tailgating as Vestaval." *Journal of Consumer Research* 42 (2015): 130–151.

Bradford, Tonya Williams and John F. Sherry, Jr. "Grooving in the Ludic Foodscape: Bridled Revelry in Collegiate Tailgating." *Journal of Consumer Culture* 17 (2017): 774–793.

Brady, Jennifer and Matthew Ventresca. "'Officially A Vegan Now': On Meat and Renaissance Masculinity in Pro Football." *Food and Foodways* 22 (2014): 300–321.

Brown, Linda Keiler and Kay Mussell., eds. *Ethnic and Regional Foodways in the United States: The Performance of Group Identity* (Knoxville, University of Tennessee Press, 1984).

Brownlie, Douglas and Paul Hewer. "Prime Beef Cuts: Culinary Images for Thinking Men." *Consumption Markets and Culture* 10 (2007): 229–250.

Buerkle, C. Wesley. "Metrosexuality Can Stuff It: Beef Consumption as (Heteromasculine) Fortification," *Text and Performance Quarterly* 29 (2009): 77–93.

Calvert, Amy. "You Are What You (M)eat: Explorations of Meat-eating, Masculinity, and Masquerade." *Journal of International Women's Studies* 16 (2014): 18–33.

Chalk, Ocania. *Black College Sport*. New York: Dodd, Mead and Co., 1976.

Coleman, Candy. *Pigskin Picnics*. Mt. Pocono, PA: C.C. Enterprises, 1980.

Collins, Kathleen. *Watching What We Eat*. New York: Continuum, 2009.

Cooper, Joseph N., J. Kenyatta Cavil, and Geremy Cheeks. "The State of Intercollegiate Athletics at Historically Black Colleges and Universities (HBCUs): Past, Present, & Persistence, *Journal of Issues in Intercollegiate Athletics* 7 (2014): 307–332.

Crepeau, Richard C. *NFL Football: A History of America's New National Pastime*. Champaign: University of Illinois Press, 2014.

Davies, Richard O. *Sports in American Life: A History*. 2nd ed. Malden, MA: Wiley-Blackwell, 2012.

Davis, Laurel. "The Articulation of Difference: White Preoccupation with the Question of Racially Linked Genetic Differences Among Athletes." *Sociology of Sport Journal* 7 (1990): 179–187.

Drenten, Jenna, Cara Okieshen Peters, Thomas Leigh, and Candice R. Hollenbeck. "Not Just a Party in the Parking Lot: An Exploratory Investigation of the Motives Underlying the Ritual Commitment of Football Tailgaters." *Sport Marketing Quarterly* 18 (2009): 92–106.

Driver, Elizabeth. "Cookbooks as Primary Sources for Writing History." *Food, Culture, and Society* 12 (2009): 257–274.

Eves, Rosalyn Collings. "A Recipe for Remembrance: Memory and Identity in African-American Women's Cookbooks." *Rhetoric Review* 24 (2005): 280–297

Fleischmann, Helen E. *Sagehen's Retriever Club Tailgate Cookbook*. Suisun City, CA: Sagehen's Retriever Club, 1967.

Gallagher, Mark. "What's So Funny About *Iron Chef?*" *Journal of Popular Film & Television* 31 (2004): 176–184.

Gallegos, Danielle. "Cookbooks as Manuals of Taste." In *Ordinary Lifestyles: Popular Media, Consumption and Taste*, edited by David Bell and Joanne Hollows, 99–112. New York: Open University Press, 2005.

Gee, Sara and Steve Jackson. "Leisure Corporations, Beer Brand Culture, and the Crisis of Masculinity: The Speight's 'Southern Man' Advertising Campaign." *Journal of Leisure Studies* 31 (2012): 83–102.

*Gooseberry Patch Game-Day Fan Fare*. Columbus, OH: Gooseberry Patch, 2012.

Gough, Brendan. "'Real Men Don't Diet': An Analysis of Contemporary Newspaper Representations of Men, Food, and Health." *Social Science and Medicine* 64 (2007): 326–337.

Guilliano, Jennifer. *Indian Spectacle: College Mascots and the Anxiety of Modern America*, 2015.

Grundy, Pamela and Benjamin G. Rader. *American Sports: From the Age of Folk Games to the Age of Televised Sports*. 7th ed. New York: Routledge, 2015.

Gvion, Liora. "What's Cooking in America? Cookbooks Narrate Ethnicity: 1850–1990." *Food, Culture and Society* 12 (2009): 53–76.

Gvion, Liora and Naomi Trostler. "From Spaghetti and Meatballs through Hawaiian Pizza to Sushi: The Changing Nature of Ethnicity in American Restaurants." *Journal of Popular Culture* 41 (2008): 950–974.

Halter, Marilyn. *Shopping for Identity: The Marketing of Ethnicity*. New York: Random House, 2000.

Hansen, Signe. "Society of the Appetite: Celebrity Chefs Deliver Consumers." *Food, Culture, & Society* 11 (2008): 49–67.

Heinz, Bettina and Ronald Lee. "Getting Down to the Meat: The Symbolic Construction of Meat Consumption." *Communication Studies* 49 (1998): 86–99.

Herd, Katarzyna Joanna. "Colour my Falafel Blue: Football Branding in Swedish Food Industry—An Ethnographic Approach." *Fork to Farm: International Journal of Innovative Research and Practice* 2 (2015): 1–6.

Hollows, Joanne. "Oliver's Twist: Leisure, Labor, and Domestic Masculinity in *The Naked Chef.*" *International Journal of Cultural Studies* 6 (2003): 229–248.

Hollows, Joanne. "The Bachelor Dinner: Masculinity, Class and Cooking in *Playboy*, 1953–1961." Journal of Media & Cultural Studies 16 (2002): 143–155.

Ingrassia, Brian M. *The Rise of the Gridiron University: Higher Education's Uneasy Alliance with Big-Time Football*. Lawrence: University Press of Kansas, 2012.

Inness, Sherrie A. *Dinner Roles: American Women and Culinary Culture*. Iowa City, IA: University of Iowa Press, 2001.

Inness, Sherrie A. *Secret Ingredients: Race, Gender, and Class at the Dinner Table*. New York: Palgrave MacMillan, 2006.

James, Jeffrey, G. Steven Breezeel, and Stephen Ross. "A Two-Stage Study of the Reasons to Begin and Continue Tailgating." *Sport Marketing Quarterly* 10 (2001): 212–223.

Jacobson, Matthew Frye. *Roots Too: White Ethnic Revival in Post-Civil Rights America*. Cambridge, MA: Harvard University Press, 2006.

Julier, Alice and Laura Lindenfeld. "Mapping Men onto the Menu: Masculinities and Food." *Food and Foodways*, 13 (2005): 1–16.

Kerstetter, Deborah, et al. 2012. "The Multiple Meanings Associated with the Football Tailgating Ritual." In *Proceedings of the 2010 Northeastern Recreation Research Symposium*, 38–44. Newtown Square, PA: US Department of Agriculture, Forest Service, Northern Research Station.

Ketchum, Cheri. "The Essence of Cooking Shows: How the Food Network Constructs Consumer Fantasies." *Journal of Communication Inquiry* 29 (2005): 217–234.

Kimmel, Michael S. *Manhood in America: A Cultural History*. 2nd ed. New York: Oxford University Press, 2006.

King, Samantha. *Pink Ribbons, Inc.: Breast Cancer and the Politics of Philanthropy*. Minneapolis: University of Minnesota Press, 2006.

LeBesco, Kathleen and Peter Naccarato, eds. *Edible Ideologies: Representing Food and Meaning*. Albany, NY: SUNY Press, 2008.

Levy, Walter. *The Picnic: A History*. Walnut Creek, CA: AltaMira Press, 2013.

Lu, Shun and Gary Alan Fine. "The Presentation of Ethnic Authenticity: Chinese Food as a Social Accomplishment." *The Sociological Quarterly* 36 (1995): 535–553.

Mathis, Taylor. *The Southern Tailgating Cookbook: A Game-Day Guide for Lovers of Food, Football, and the South*. Chapel Hill: University of North Carolina Press, 2013.

Matthews, Kristin L. "One Nation Over Coals: Cold War Nationalism and the Barbecue." *American Studies* 50 (2009): 5–34.

McGann, Patrick. "Eating Muscle: Material Semiotics and a Manly Appetite." In *Revealing Male Bodies*, edited by Nancy Tuana, William Cowling, Maurice Hamington, and Greg Johnson, 83–99. Bloomington, IN: Indiana University Press, 2002.

Meister, Mark. "Cultural Feeding, Good Life Science, and the TV Food Network." *Mass Communication and Society* 4 (2001): 165–182.

Messner, Michael and Jeffrey Montez de Oca. "The Male Consumer as Loser: Beer and Liquor Ads in Mega Sports Media Events." *Signs* 30 (2005): 1879–1909.

Mihalache, Irina D. "Of Men and Cupcakes: Baking Identities on Food Network." In *How Canadians Communicate*, edited by Charlene Elliott, 129–144. Edmonton, CA: AU Press, 2015.

Miller, Patrick B. "The Anatomy of Scientific Racism: Racialist Responses to Black Athletic Achievement." *Journal of Sport History* 25 (1998): 119–151.

Miller, Patrick B. "To 'Bring the Race Along Rapidly': Sport, Student Culture, and Educational Mission at Historically Black Colleges during the Interwar Years." In *The Sporting World of the Modern South*, edited by Patrick B. Miller, 129–152. Champaign: University of Illinois Press, 2002.

Miller, Tim. *Barbecue: A History*. Lanham, MD: Rowman and Littlefield, 2014.

Miller, Tim. "The Birth of the Patio Daddy-O: Outdoor Grilling in Postwar America." *Journal of American Culture* 33 (2010): 5–11.

Moisi, Risto and Mariam Beruchashvili. "Mancaves and Masculinity." *Journal of Consumer Culture* 16 (2016): 656–676.

Moss, Mark. *The Media and Models of Masculinity*. Lanham, MD: Lexington Books, 2011.

Naccarato, Peter and Kathleen LeBesco. *Culinary Capital*. London: Berg, 2012.

Nathan, Daniel A. *Rooting for the Home Team: Sport, Community, and Identity*. Champaign, IL: University of Illinois Press, 2013.

Neuhaus, Jessamyn. *Manly Meals and Mom's Home Cooking: Cookbooks and Gender in Modern America*. Baltimore, MD: Johns Hopkins University Press, 2003.

Newcombe, Mark A., Mary B. McCarthy, James M. Cronin, and Sinead N. McCarthy. "'Eat Like a Man': A Social Constructionist Analysis of the Role of Food in Men's Lives." *Appetite* 59 (2012): 391–398.

Oriard, Michael. *King Football: Sport & Spectacle in the Golden Age of Radio & Newsreels, Movies & Magazines, The Weekly & Daily Press*. Chapel Hill: University of North Carolina Press, 2001.

Oriard, Michael. *Reading Football: How the Popular Press Created an American Spectacle*. Chapel Hill, NC: University of North Carolina Press, 1993.

Osbourne, Anne Cunningham and Danielle Sarver Coombs. *Female Fans of the NFL: Taking Their Place in the Stands*. New York: Routledge, 2016.

Oum, Young Rae. "Authenticity and Representation: Cuisines and Identities in Korean- American Diaspora." *Postcolonial Studies* 8 (2005): 109–125.

Parasecoli, Fabio. *Bite Me: Food in Popular Culture*. New York: Berg, 2008.

Phillips, Murray, ed. *Representing the Sporting Past in Museums and Halls of Fame*. New York: Routledge, 2012.

Polan, Dana. *Jane Campion*. London, UK: British Film Institute, 2001.

Pollan, Michael. *Cooked: A Natural History of Transportation*. New York: The Penguin Press, 2013.

Rader, Benjamin G. "'The Greatest Drama in Indian Life,' Experiments in Native American Identity and Resistance at the Haskell Institute Homecoming of 1926." *Western Historical Quarterly* 35 (2004): 429–450.

Ramshaw, Greg and Tom Hinch. "Place Identity and Sport Tourism: The Case of the Heritage Classic Ice Hockey Event." *Current Issues in Tourism* 9 (2006): 399–418.

Reddinger, Amy. "Eating 'Local': The Politics of Post-Statehood Hawaiian Cookbooks." *Nordic Journal of English Studies* 9 (2010): 67–87.

Rogers, Richard A. "Beasts, Burgers, and Hummers: Meat and the Crisis of Masculinity in Contemporary Television Advertisements." *Environmental Communication* 2 (2008): 281–301.

Sáez, Elena Machado. "Bittersweet (Be)Longing: Filling the Void of History in Andrea Levy's *Fruit of the Lemon*." *Anthurium: A Caribbean Studies Journal* 4 (2006): 1–14.

Seiler, Cotton. *Republic of Drivers*. Chicago, IL: University of Chicago Press, 2008.

Slocum, Rachel. "Race in the Study of Food." *Progress in Human Geography* 35 (2010): 303–327.

Smith, Ronald A. *Sports and Freedom: The Rise of Big-Time College Athletics*. New York: Oxford University Press, 1988.

Sobal, Jeffery. "Men, Meat, and Marriage: Models of Masculinity." *Food & Foodways* 13 (2005): 135–158.

St. John, Warren. *Rammer Jammer Yellow Hammer: A Journey into the Heart of Fan Mania*. New York: Crown Publishers, 2004.

Sturken, Marita and Lisa Cartwright. *Practices of Looking: An Introduction to Visual Culture*. New York: Oxford, 2001.

Swenson, Rebecca. "Domestic Divo?: Televised Treatments of Masculinity, Femininity, and Food." *Critical Studies in Media Communication* 26 (2009): 36–53.

Szabo, Michelle. "'I'm a Real Catch': The Blurring of Alternative and Hegemonic Masculinities in Men's Talk About Home Cooking." *Women's Studies International Forum* 44 (2014): 228–235.

Tipton-Martin, Toni. *The Jemima Code: Two Centuries of African American Cookbooks*. Austin, TX: University of Texas Press, 2015.

Turner, Patricia A. *Ceramic Uncles and Celluloid Mammies: Black Images and their Influence on Culture*. New York: Anchor-Doubleday, 1994.

Twitchell James B. *Where Men Hide*. New York: Columbia University Press, 2006.

Vester, Katharina. *A Taste of Power: Food and American Identities*. Berkeley: University of California Press, 2015.

Wallach, Jennifer Jensen. *How America Eats: A Social History of US Food & Culture*. Lanham, MD: Rowman & Littlefield, 2012.

Watson, James L. and Melissa L. Caldwell, eds. *The Cultural Politics of Food and Eating: A Reader*. Malden, MA: Blackwell, 2005.

Watterson, John Sayle. *College Football: History, Spectacle, Controversy*. Baltimore: The John Hopkins University Press, 2000.

Wenner, Lawrence. "In Search of the Sports Bar: Masculinity, Alcohol, Sports, and the Mediation of Public Space." In *Sport in Postmodern Times*, edited by Genevieve Rail, 301–332. Albany, NY: SUNY Press, 1998.

West, Candace and Don H. Zimmerman. "Doing Gender." *Gender & Society* 1 (1987): 125–151.

Wiggins, David K. "The Biggest 'Classic' of Them All: The Howard and Lincoln Thanksgiving Day Football Games, 1919-1929." In *Rooting for the Home Team: Sport, Community, and Identity*, edited by Daniel A. Nathan, 36–53. Champaign: University of Illinois Press, 2013.

Williams-Forson, Psyche. *Building Houses Out of Chicken Legs: Black Women, Food, and Power* Chapel Hill, NC: The University of North Carolina Press, 2006.

Witt, Doris. *Black Hunger: Soul Food and America*. Minneapolis, MN: University of Minnesota Press, 2004.

Zafar, Rafia. "The Signifying Dish: Autobiography and History in Two Black Women's Cookbooks." *Feminist Studies* 25 (1999): 449–469.

Zelinsky, Wilbur. "The Roving Palate: North America's Ethnic Restaurant Choices," *Geoforum* 16 (1985): 51–72.

## Cookbooks

Batali, Mario. *Mario Tailgates NASCAR Style: The Essential Cookbook for NASCAR Fans*. Charlotte: Sporting News, 2006.

Bowers, David and Sharon Bowers. *Bake It Like A Man: A Real Man's Cookbook*. New York: William Morrow & Company, 1999.

Chakerian, Peter. *The Browns Fan's Tailgating Guide*. Cleveland, Ohio: Gray & Company Publishers, 2008.

Dekko, Dottie. *Cooking for Kicks: The Sport of Tailgating*. Detroit, Michigan: Sprague Publishing Company, 1978.

Herbert, April. *The Tailgate Cookbook*. New York: Fund and Wagnalls, 1970.

Joachim, David. *The Tailgater's Cookbook*. New York: Broadway Books, 2005.

Johnson, Pableaux. *ESPN Gameday Gourmet*. New York: ESPN Books, 2007.

Lampe, Ray. *The NFL Gameday Cookbook*. San Francisco: Chronicle Books, 2008.

Madden, John and Peter Kaminsky. *John Madden's Ultimate Tailgating*. New York: Viking Press, 1998.

Moose, Debbie. *Fan Fare: A Playbook of Great Recipes for Tailgating or Watching the Game at Home*. Boston, MA: The Harvard Common Press, 2007.

O'Conner, Hyla. *The Complete NFL Cookbook*. New York: Plume Publishing, 1981.

*Picnics & Tailgate Parties*. Menlo Park, California: Lane Publishing Company, 1982.

Raichlen, Steven. *Man Made Meals: The Essential Cookbook for Guys*. New York: Workman Publishing Co., 2014.

Schisgal, Zachary. *A Man A Can, A Tailgate Plan: 50 Easy Game-Time Recipes That Are Sure to Please*. Emmaus, Pennsylvania: Rodale Books, 2006.

Sloan, Bob. *The Tailgating Cookbook: Recipes for the Big Game*. San Francisco: Chronicle Books, 2005.

*Southern Living: The Official SEC Tailgating Cookbook*. New York: Oxmoor House, 2012.

Smith, Loran. *Spread Formation: Tailgating and Home Recipes from College Football Greats*. Atlanta: Whitman Publishers, LLC, 2014.

*Tailgate Cooking and Other Gastronomical Horrors*. Minneapolis, MN: Twin Cities Federal, 1972.

Wyler, Susan. *Tailgate Parties: 24 Menus for Gourmet Picnics and Outdoor Entertaining*. Nevada City: Harmony Books, 1984.

# INDEX

## A

abalone, 64, 83

Adams, Carol, 6–7

advertisements: automobile-football relationship, 26–29, 68, 69–70; barbecue promotions, 32; culinary racism, 97, 98, 169n15; gameday merchandising, 29; sexual objectification, 86; tailgating culture, 11, 76–77, 84, 86; vegetarian fare, 91. *See also* television commercials

African American cuisine, 97–100, 105–6, 114–15, 122, 123

African Americans, 46, 114–17, 119. *See also* Historically Black College and University (HBCU) football-playing institutions; race and ethnicity

alcohol: costs, 4; as gender signifier, 5, 12, 40, 73; tailgate cookbooks, 84

alligator meat, 71, 126

all-male spaces, 37, 39, 44, 78, 160n111, 176n15

*American Dad!* (television series), 118–19

*American Home*, 31

Americanized cuisine, 97, 100, 106, 107, 111–13

*America's Parking Lot* (documentary), 137

animal protein. *See* meat; specific animal protein

antebellum South, 102

applesauce, 104, 106

Armenian cuisine, 107

assimilation, cultural, 23, 97, 100–101, 113, 157n40

AT&T Stadium, 137

Atlanta, Georgia, 45

Auburn, New York, 43

Aunt Jemima character, 97, 98, 112, 169n15

authentic food traditions, 106, 109–10, 120–22

automobile-football relationship, 25–30, 32–38, 67–70

automobile picnics: gameday merchandising, 29; gender constructs, 32–36, 38–45; historical perspective, 4, 16, 25–30, 32–38, 67–68; portable grills, 31, 32, 33–34, 36–38, 54; pregame festivities, 3–4, 20, 32–38; take-out lunches, 24–25. *See also* tailgating culture

## B

baby back ribs, 3, 71, 79

baby elephants, 134–36

baccalà, 101

backyard grilling culture. *See* grills/grilling culture; outdoor cooking

bacon: cooking equipment and gadgets, 54; ethnic cuisine, 104, 106; as gender signifier, 90; popularity, 74; tailgate specialties, 3, 50, 65, 71, 79, 80

baked beans, 40, 63, 90

barbecue culture: advertisements, 30–32; African American cuisine, 106, 114–15; gender constructs, 52–62, 73; people of color, 114–15, 175n123; signifying ingredients and stereotypes, 106–7. *See also* ethnic cuisine; grills/grilling culture; tailgating culture

Batali, Mario: on cooking equipment and gadgets, 57; ethnic cuisine, 109; on grilling, 56, 85; on planning and preparation, 67; sexual innuendo, 85–86; sexual misconduct, 86, 167n66; tailgate cookbooks, 83, 88, 109; on vegetarian fare, 88

Baton Rouge, Louisiana, 61, 122

Bauhs, Andrew, 150

#BBQBecky incident, 175n123

Beard, James, 8, 31, 147
Bedouin culture and cuisine, 104, 108
beer: communal bonds and friendships, 128, 142; as gender signifier, 11–12, 40, 52, 83, 90, 91, 119; German cuisine, 113; tailgate cookbooks, 85; tailgating equipment and gadgets, 57–58; television commercials, 91; traditional tailgate fare, 42
Bentley, Amy, 112
*Big Fan* (film), 76
bite-sized food portions, 78
black athleticism, 169*n*15
black ethnic cuisine, 97–100, 105–6, 114–15, 122, 123
black-owned presses, 98–99
Black Pot Mafia, 4, 140, 141
blacktop cookery. *See* automobile picnics; pregame festivities; stadium parking lots; tailgating culture
boarding schools, 157*n*40
Boston College, 43
brats/bratwurst, 44, 59, 63, 71, 74, 80, 85, 113
Brodkorb, Bernie and Lois, 39–40
Bromberek, Bob, 54
*The Browns Fan's Tailgating Guide*, 109
Buchanan, Pat, 173*n*96
Bucknell University, 23
Bud Light, 57–58, 91
Buffalo Bills tailgating parties and competitions: competition menus, 64; customized cooking equipment, 3, 54–55, 57, 64, 79–80; food presentation, 65; masculine signifiers, 76, 131–32; meat as gender signifier, 76; meatless dishes, 92; place identity, 131–32; white-centric culture, 119, 175*n*122
buffalo meat, 23, 38
"Build a Wall" rhetoric, 173*n*96
burgers. *See* hamburgers
by-men-for-men cookbooks, 84, 88–89, 109–11

## C

California, 102–3
Calvert, Amy, 133

Candlestick Park, 138
Canisius College, 42
car cookery, 3, 54–55, 57–58
Carlisle Institute, 157*n*40
Carlson, Richard, 43
casseroles, 89, 90
cast iron skillets, 60
celebrity chefs, 7, 65–66, 73. *See also* Batali, Mario; Fieri, Guy
Chakerian, Peter, 125
charcoal-fired grills, 33–34, 36, 37, 38, 52, 53. *See also* barbecue culture; grills/grilling culture
charitable fundraising, 139–42, 178*n*53
Chevrolet commercial, 145
Chicago Bears tailgating parties and competitions, 54, 64, 76, 93, 131, 132
*Chicago Daily Tribune*, 29
*Chicago Defender*, 23
chicken: African American cuisine, 170*n*22; chicken wings, 3, 43, 54, 62, 71, 81; customized cooking equipment, 3, 54; ethnic cuisine, 103, 105, 107, 113, 119, 120, 122; fried chicken, 33, 34, 62, 99, 114; gendered cooking, 42; as gender signifier, 83–84, 90; preparation techniques, 66, 80; tailgate cookbooks, 83, 114; tailgate menus, 3–4, 38, 50, 74, 79
Chiffon margarine, 37
Child, Julia, 7
chili powder, 79, 107, 108
Chowderheads, 36–37
Chowder Society, 36–37
*The Citizen*, 43
civil rights movement, 38
Claiborne, Craig, 8
class distinctions: automobile-football relationship, 28–29; food-portion size importance, 78; football athletics, 16–17; immigrant and ethnic cuisine, 111; place identity and local cuisine, 131–33; pregame festivities, 23, 111
Coca-Cola, 46
Cohen, Dan, 142, 178*n*53
Cold War America, 30–33

Coleman, Candy, 41, 102–3, 109, 116–17, 118
Coliseum Arena (Oakland), 68–69
college football, 5, 16–21, 67–68, 116, 119
College Football Hall of Fame, 45–46, 114, 161n139
College Station, Texas, 87
Colonel Reb Foundation, 174n110
Colonel Reb mascot, 116, 174n110
Columbia, South Carolina, 84
Columbia University, 24
commercials. *See* advertisements; television commercials
commodity racism, 97–98, 112, 169n15
communal bonds and friendships, 125–26, 128–30, 133–43, 148–49
competitions. *See* rivalries and competitions; team competition
*The Complete NFL Cookbook* (O'Connor), 100–101, 105, 107
Confederate flag and symbols, 103, 116–17, 174n114
cookbooks: African American cuisine, 97, 98–100, 105–6; by-men-for-men genre, 84, 88–89, 109–11; culinary racism, 96, 97–100, 102–6, 114–15, 117, 148, 169n15; cultural significance, 11, 95–108, 115–16; gender constructs, 40, 41, 44–45, 77–78, 84–91, 96, 109–11, 122–23; historical perspective, 96–100; misogynistic discourse, 85–86; outdoor grilling culture, 32; racial and ethnic diversity, 13, 95–108, 148; retrograde masculinity, 84, 86–89; sexual innuendo, 84–87; vegetables and non-meat sides, 88–92. *See also* tailgate cookbooks
cooking equipment and gadgets: car cookery, 3, 54–55, 57–58; consumerism, 65–66; gendered cooking, 52–62, 65–66, 145, 147; meat preparation, 78–82
*Cooking for Kicks* (Dekko), 105–6
corn: cornbread, 122; grilled corn, 88; popcorn, 58; roasted corn, 77; side dishes, 127; steamed corn on the cob, 92; tailgate menus, 62, 64
corn chips, 111–12
corn dogs, 81
Costco, 139
Cowboys Stadium, 137
crab meat, 110
Crimson Tide football, 117
cross-cultural understandings, 102
culinary-based media, 4, 6, 7–8, 65, 108–9, 128. *See also Tailgate Warriors*
culinary celebrities, 7–8. *See also* Batali, Mario; Fieri, Guy
culinary complexity, 62–67, 83
culinary racism, 96, 97–100, 102–6, 114–15, 117, 148, 169n15
culinary symbols, 126, 133–36
cultural illiteracy, 102–3, 105, 108, 174n114
curry powder, 98, 103, 104, 106, 107
customized cooking equipment, 3, 54–62, 65–66, 78–82, 145, 147
customized vans, 69
custom-made brands, 93

## D

Dallas Cowboys, 137
deep fryers, 52, 80–81
DeFilippo, Gene and Anne, 112–13
Dekko, Dottie, 105–6
Del Greco, Al and Lisa, 113
Democratic Party, 116
DiEugenio, Jay, 131
Dixiecrats, 116
domestic versus tailgate cookery, 55–57, 63–66, 84–85, 88–92, 127. *See also* gendered cooking; masculinity
Doolin, C. E., 111–12
Dr. BBQ. *See* Lampe, Ray
Dr. Dogz, 139, 177n46
Dreamland Bar-B-Que, 115
drills, 57
Dr. Pepper, 69–70
duck: mascots as culinary symbols, 14, 136; tailgate menus, 4, 50, 71
Duck bus, 69, 80–81

# E

"eating the competition". *See* mascots
elephants, 134–36
elk, 63, 74, 75
*Embodying Dixie* (Newman), 117
*Emeril Live!*, 7, 8
Engine 66 tailgate machine, 70
engine manifolds, 55
equal rights movements, 38
*ESPN Gameday Gourmet* cookbook
(Johnson), 56, 84, 89, 111
*ESPN The Magazine*, 135
*Esquire*, 8, 84
ethnic cuisine: authentic food traditions, 106, 109–10, 120–22; cookbooks, 96–106, 148; cross-cultural
understandings, 102–6, 120–22;
culinary racism, 96, 97–100,
102–6, 114–15, 117, 148, 169n15;
first-wave tailgate cookbooks, 99,
100–108, 112–13; ghettoization
and othering, 96, 97, 99, 101, 102,
103–6; historical perspective,
96–100; integration and inclusion,
108–15, 122–23, 148; place identity
and local cuisine, 132–33; revivalist
period, 100–102; second-wave tailgate cookbooks, 100, 108–15; signifying ingredients and stereotypes,
98, 99–115, 119, 132–33
European immigrants, 97, 100–102
Ewbank, Weeb, 36

# F

false narratives, 102–3
Family Motor Coach Association
(FMCA), 67
*Fan Fare* (Moose), 77, 83, 90
fava beans, 92
federally controlled boarding schools,
157n40
Feirstein, Bruce, 39
female-only football luncheons, 22–23
femininity and cooking: culinary racism, 97–100, 169n15; domestic versus tailgate cookery, 55–57, 63–66,
84–85, 88–92, 127; Food Network
programming, 7; food studies, 6,

145–46; football tailgating culture,
33–36, 38, 39–41, 45, 60–62, 150–51,
176n15; gameday breakfasts and
luncheons, 22–23; gender signifiers,
13, 72–73, 89–92, 127, 145; grilling
culture, 30–31, 33, 60–62, 77, 80,
83; as marginalized other, 60, 73,
83, 86, 89–92; misogynistic discourse, 83–84, 85, 89–90; non-meat
foods, 13, 72–73, 145; pregame
festivities, 5, 32–36, 38–45; sexual
objectification, 84–87
Fieri, Guy: background information, 4,
8; customized cooking equipment,
53–54, 57; gendered cooking, 60,
73–75; place identity and local cuisine, 131–33; as play-by- play and
color commentator, 75, 90, 127; on
special ingredients, 83; tailgating
competitions, 63–66, 73–75; on
vegetarian fare, 92. *See also Tailgate
Warriors*
film representations, 12, 75, 115, 118–19
Finley, Rob, 70
fire trucks, 70
first-wave tailgate cookbooks, 99,
100–108, 112–13
fish, 83, 89, 91, 110, 114, 119, 134. *See
also* seafood
Fisk University, 26
Fleischmann, Helen E., 104, 107
Fogelson, Susie, 8
food-gender relationships, 39, 40
Food Network, 4, 7, 54, 57, 63–66, 125.
*See also Tailgate Warriors*
food television. *See* culinary-based
media; *Tailgate Warriors*; television
programming
football: automobile-football relationship, 25–30, 67–70; ethnic food
heritage and identity, 100–102;
food studies, 146; meat-football
relationship, 75–91; popularity, 30;
racial segregation, 116–17; sexual
innuendo, 84; vegetable-football
analogy, 88, 89
football athletics, 5, 16–21, 67–68,
116–17, 119, 169n15

football clubs and leagues, 21–22

football picnics: gameday merchandising, 29; gender constructs, 32–36, 38–45; historical perspective, 5, 15–16, 25–30, 32–38; planning and preparation, 42; portable grills, 31, 32, 33–34, 36–38, 54; pregame festivities, 3–4, 5, 19–20, 32–38, 146–47; racial and ethnic diversity, 45–46; take-out lunches, 24–25. *See also* tailgate cookbooks; tailgating culture

football tailgating culture. *See* tailgating culture

football-tailgating relationship, 76–77

Ford Motors, 29

Fort Wayne, Indiana, 22

Foxboro, Massachusetts, 58

Fox, Joe, 141–42, 178*n*53

*Fresh Air*, 87

fried chicken, 33, 34, 62, 99, 114

Frito Bandito, 112

Frito-Lay, 112

Fritos, 111–12

fryers, 52, 80–81

fusion cooking, 99

## G

gameday breakfasts and luncheons, 21, 22–24, 34

*Game-Day Fan Fare*, 87

*Gameday Gourmet*, 89

gameday merchandising, 29

Gate 6 Tailgaters, 137

gay community, 150

gay liberation movement, 38

gender constructs: barbecue culture, 73; charitable fundraising, 139–42, 178*n*53; cookbooks, 40, 41, 44–45, 77–78, 84–91, 96, 109–11, 122–23; equal rights movements, 38; food-gender relationships, 39, 40; football athletics, 16–18; gameday breakfasts and luncheons, 21, 22–23, 34; grilling culture, 11, 13, 30–33, 38, 42–45, 77–88, 145; meat consumption, 6–7, 30–31, 71–93, 133–36, 145, 147–48; non-meat

foods, 13, 72–73, 88–92, 119, 145; outdoor cooking, 52–62, 73, 77–80, 147; place identity and local cuisine, 125–26, 131–33, 149; pregame festivities, 3–4, 20, 21, 22–23, 30, 32–45, 49–62, 146–47; sex-based segregation, 22–23; spicy ingredients and foods, 108; tailgating cookbooks, 40, 41, 84–91

gendered cooking: cooking equipment and gadgets, 52–62, 65–66; culinary complexity, 62–67; feminine signifiers, 13, 72–73, 145; Food Network programming, 7–8; historical perspective, 15–19; masculine signifiers, 3, 8, 11, 12, 52–58, 65–66, 145, 147–48; meat consumption, 6–7, 13, 30–31, 71–93, 145, 147–48; media representations, 13, 60, 73, 84–85, 93; multiple-ingredient rubs and sauces, 79; non-meat foods, 88–92; tailgating culture, 3–6, 8–14, 33–45, 49–62, 71–93, 119, 125–36, 145–51, 176*n*15; television commercials, 11, 52, 57–58, 76–77, 91, 130; television programming, 129–33. *See also Tailgate Warriors*

gender equality, 38

German cuisine, 113

ghettoization and othering, 96, 97, 99, 101, 103–6

good deeds and cooking, 139–42

Great Depression, 30

Greek cuisine, 113

Green Bay Packers tailgating parties and competitions: competition menus, 63, 74, 75, 127, 131–32; historical perspective, 15, 21–22, 24; masculine signifiers, 83; vegetarian fare, 90, 92

*Green Bay Press-Gazette*, 24

Green Bay, Wisconsin, 21–22

griddles, 52

Griese, Bob, 107, 113

grills/grilling culture: by-men-for-men cookbooks, 84, 109–11; customized cooking equipment, 52–62, 78–80; elaborate outdoor cooking equipment, 42–43; gender constructs, 11, 13, 30–33, 38, 52–62, 73, 77–88, 145; historical perspective, 30–31; media representations, 53; people of color, 114–15; portable grills, 31, 32, 33–34, 36–38; sexual innuendo, 84–87; spectacles and performance, 56, 63, 68–70, 73–77, 146–47; vegetables, 90–91. *See also* ethnic cuisine; rivalries and competitions; tailgating culture

"grill-zilla," 53

Gross, Terry, 87

Grove at Ole Miss, 5, 87, 116–17, 138

Guilliano, Jennifer, 117–18

gumbo, 4, 50, 62, 71

Gutierrez, Marco, 173*n*95

*Guy Code* (television series), 83, 119

*Guy's Big Bite*, 8

## H

Hagemeister Park, 15, 24

hamburgers: advertisements, 11; charitable fundraising, 142; communal bonds and friendships, 130; as gender signifier, 76, 77, 80, 83, 85, 145; grilling culture, 32, 33, 37, 38, 79; mascots as culinary symbols, 134; prevalence, 71; sexual innuendo, 86; tailgate cookbooks, 106–7; tailgating competitions, 63; television commercials, 86. *See also* meatless dishes

Harvard University, 17, 18, 21, 28

Haskell Institute, 23, 157*n*40

hatchets, 54

Hawaiian culture and cuisine, 104–5, 171*n*53

hegemonic masculinity: challenges, 150–51; communal bonds and friendships, 130; food writing themes, 85; meat consumption, 13, 74, 133–36, 145, 147–48; rivalries and competitions, 126; tailgating culture, 10, 45, 93, 128, 130, 149–50; televised cookery, 65, 128; vegetables/vegetarian fare, 91, 145

helmets, 54

Herbert, April, 106–7

heterosexuality, 84, 85, 86–87

hibachi grilling, 33–34, 37

"Hindu-style" spices, 104

Historically Black College and University (HBCU) football-playing institutions, 17, 18, 23, 24, 26, 46, 61–62, 114

homophobia, 84

Honda commercial, 86

hot dogs: corn dogs, 81; as gender signifier, 75, 80; grilling culture, 32, 38, 76, 80, 139; prevalence, 71, 79; sexual innuendo, 85; tailgating competitions, 63; as traditional tailgating cuisine, 139

Hotel Duncan, 25

Howard University, 17, 18, 23, 24

*How I Met Your Mother* (television series), 129–30

hubcaps, 54

*Hungry Man's Outdoor Grill Cookbook*, 31

hyperterritorialism, 126

## I

immigrant and ethnic cuisine. *See* ethnic cuisine; race and ethnicity

indigenous populations. *See* Native Americans

indoor versus outdoor cookery, 55–57, 63–66, 84–85, 88–92

Inness, Sherrie, 11

*Iron Chef*, 64–65

ironing boards, 55

Italian cuisine, 101, 109–10, 112–13

## J

Jack's (fast-food burger chain), 86

jalapeños, 107

"Jambalaya Girl," 60

Jaworski, Ron, 101

Jets Parking and Chowder Society, 36–37

Jim Crow America, 97

*John Madden's Ultimate Tailgating*, 44–45, 110–11

Johnson, Kenny (Pinto Kenny), 3, 54–55, 57

Johnson, Pableaux, 56, 78, 84, 85, 89, 111

**K**

kale, 145
Keota, Iowa, 21
Key, Wade, 107
Kimmel, Michael, 38
Kirshenbaum, Jerry, 37
Knapp, Christy, 139
Kuligowski, Mary, 113

**L**

Lagasse, Emeril, 7, 8
Lake Merritt, 175n123
Lambeau Field, 83
Lampe, Ray, 53, 74, 75, 76, 90, 92, 110, 131, 132
Latinx cuisine, 109, 121–22
Lawrence, Kansas, 23
Levi's Stadium, 120, 138
Lewis, Edna, 99
LGBT community, 150
*LIFE*, 31, 32
*The Lincoln Star*, 22–23
Lincoln University, 23, 24
lobster, 71
local cuisine. *See* place identity
*LOOK*, 31
Los Angeles Rams, 101
*Los Angeles Times*, 27–28
Los Malosos, 4, 121–22, 140, 141
Louisiana State University, 4, 49–50, 119, 134–36, 140, 175n122
luaus, 104–5

**M**

Madden, John, 44–45, 78, 110–11
magazines. *See* media coverage and representations
Malavasi, Ray, 101
manifolds, car engine, 55
*Mario Tailgates NASCAR Style* (Batali), 57, 109
Martin, Dwayne, 140
mascots: as culinary symbols, 14, 126, 133–36, 149; racist imagery, 103, 112, 117–18, 119, 174n114;

University of Mississippi, 116, 174n110
masculine signifiers: culinary complexity, 62–67; customized cooking equipment, 3–4, 54–62, 65–66, 145, 147; food-gender relationships, 39, 40; grilling culture, 11, 13, 30–32, 38, 42–45, 52–58, 77–80, 145; Italian cuisine, 109–10; meat consumption, 6–7, 11–13, 30–31, 40, 44–45, 71–93, 133–36, 145, 147–48; meat-football relationship, 75–91; media portrayals, 12, 63–65; motorized vehicles, 16, 26–28, 67–70, 145; spicy ingredients and foods, 108; tailgating competitions, 42, 73–76; televised cookery, 8, 63–65. *See also* rivalries and competitions
masculinity: by-men-for-men cookbooks, 84, 88–89, 109–11; charitable fundraising, 139–42, 178n53; communal bonds and friendships, 125–26, 128–30, 133–43, 148–49; cooking equipment and gadgets, 52–58, 65–66; ethnic identity, 101, 109–10; Food Network programming, 7–8; food studies, 6, 39, 145–51; football athletics, 16–19; meat consumption, 6–7, 30–31, 71–93, 133–36, 145, 147–48; racialized masculinity, 132–33; retrograde masculinity, 84, 86–89; rivalries and competitive spirit, 125–36; sexual innuendo, 84–87; spectacles and performance, 56, 63, 68–70, 73–77, 120, 146–47; tailgating culture, 3–5, 8–14, 33–45, 49–62, 71–93, 125–36, 145–51; working-class masculinity, 131–33. *See also* hegemonic masculinity; tailgate cookbooks; *Tailgate Warriors*
McCollam, Douglas, 133
meat: customized cooking equipment, 54–62, 78–82; established hierarchy, 82–83; as gender signifier, 6–7, 11–13, 30–31, 40, 44–45, 71–93, 133–36, 145, 147–48; grilling culture, 30–31, 33–34, 145; meat-football

relationship, 75–91; misogynistic discourse, 84, 85; multiple-ingredient rubs and sauces, 79; pregame festivities, 3–4; preparation techniques, 80; sexual innuendo, 84–87; signature custom-made brand, 93; size importance, 78; tailgating competitions, 42, 73–76; television commercials, 57–58, 76–77. *See also* barbecue culture; grills/grilling culture; rivalries and competitions; tailgating culture

meatless dishes, 13, 72–73, 88–92, 119, 145. *See also* vegetables/vegetarian fare

media coverage and representations: automobile-football relationship, 25–29, 68, 69–70; communal bonds and friendships, 125–26; ethnic cuisine, 104; gameday luncheons, 21; gendered cooking, 13, 60, 73, 84–85, 93; grilling culture, 53; sexual objectification, 86; tailgating culture, 11–12, 32–34, 36–38, 40–43, 76–77, 86, 118–19, 129–33; Thanksgiving Day football games, 20. *See also* meat; *Tailgate Warriors*; television programming; visual media representations

Meharry Medical College, 17, 26

Melville, Greg, 62

*Men's Life Today*, 62

#MeToo movement, 86

Mexican cuisine, 103, 107, 108, 110–12, 121–22, 173*n*95

Miami Dolphins, 134

Michigan, 41–42

Michigan State University, 41–42

*Mid American Tailgaters Cookbook*, 41

Middle Eastern culture and cuisine, 104, 108

The Minneapolis Twin City Federal Bank, 103

Minnesota Vikings tailgating parties and competitions, 37–38, 39, 64, 74, 92, 132–33

misogynistic discourse, 84, 85

Mitchell, Robin, 40, 160*n*117

Moose, Debbie, 77, 83, 90

Morris, Jim, 37

motor car picnics. *See* automobile picnics

motorhomes, 49–51, 67–70, 117

Moulton, Sara, 7

movie portrayals, 12

MTV, 83, 119

multiethnic cuisine, 98. *See also* ethnic cuisine

multiple-ingredient rubs and sauces, 79

## N

The Naked Chef, 109

NASCAR tailgates, 77, 109

*Nashville Globe*, 17

Nashville, Tennessee, 26

National Football Foundation, 45, 114

National Football League (NFL), 4, 100–101, 119

National Public Radio (NPR), 87–88

Native Americans, 23, 102–3, 117–18, 119, 157*n*40. *See also* mascots

New England Patriots tailgates, 58, 119

New Haven, Connecticut, 5, 15, 18–19, 21, 24–25, 26. *See also* Yale University

New Iberia, Louisiana, 4

Newman, Joshua, 117

New Orleans Saints tailgating competition, 64, 74, 92, 132–33

newspapers. *See* media coverage and representations

New York City, 19

New York Giants, 37, 76, 142, 178*n*53

New York Jets, 36

*New York Times*: on automobile-football relationships, 25, 26, 28; celebrity chef profiles, 4; outdoor cooking equipment, 42–43; outdoor grilling culture, 32; on pregame festivities, 19; on tailgate parties, 35, 36, 40

*The NFL Gameday Cookbook* (Lampe), 53, 90, 110

nomadic people and feasts, 104, 108

non-meat foods, 13, 72–73, 88–92, 119, 145. *See also* vegetables/vegetarian fare

North Carolina State University, 46
Northwestern University, 150

## O

Oakland, California, 4, 175*n*123
*Oakland (CA) Tribune*, 26
Oakland Coliseum, 120–22
Oakland Raiders tailgating parties and competitions: culinary complexity, 63–64, 65, 83; customized cooking equipment, 53, 57, 58, 64; ethnic cuisine, 120–22; meat preparation, 74–75; motorhomes, 68–69; traditional tailgating cuisine, 74, 90, 132. *See also* Los Malosos; Madden, John; *Tailgate Warriors*
O'Connor, Hyla, 100, 105
off-reservation boarding schools, 157*n*40
The Ohio State University tailgates, 114
Old South, 102, 114–15, 117, 134–36
Ole Miss. *See* University of Mississippi
Olguin, Gustavo, 111
Oliver, Jamie, 109
Oriard, Michael, 10, 21
*Orlando Sentinel*, 34
Osgood, Matt, 15
outdoor cooking: elaborate culinary equipment, 42–43; gender constructs, 52–62, 73, 77–80, 147; indoor versus outdoor cookery, 55–57, 63–66; masculine signifiers, 11, 13, 30–32, 52–58, 77–88. *See also* barbecue culture; grills/grilling culture; tailgating culture
outdoor eating. *See* picnics
oversize vehicles, 40
Oxford, Mississippi, 117, 138

## P

Palo Alto, California, 60–61, 139
Parcells, Bill, 134
parking lots. *See* tailgating culture
people of color, 113–15, 123, 175*n*123. *See also* African Americans; race and ethnicity
Pepsi, 76–77
periodicals. *See* media coverage and representations

Peruvian cuisine, 120
Phelan, Don, 36–37
Philadelphia Eagles, 101, 119
*The Philadelphia Inquiry*, 22
philanthropic fundraising, 139–42, 178*n*53
picnics: gameday merchandising, 29; gender constructs, 5, 32–36, 38–45; historical perspective, 5, 15–16, 25–30, 32–38; planning and preparation, 42; portable grills, 31, 32, 33–34, 36–38, 54; pregame festivities, 3–4, 5, 19–20, 32–38, 146–47; racial and ethnic diversity, 45–46; take-out lunches, 24–25. *See also* tailgate cookbooks; tailgating culture
*Picnics & Tailgate Parties* (Sunset), 104
*Pigskin Picnics* (Coleman), 41, 102–3
pineapple, 64, 98, 105, 106
Pinto Kenny. *See* Johnson, Kenny (Pinto Kenny)
*Pittsburgh Courier*, 17
place identity, 125–26, 131–33, 149. *See also* spatial arrangements
Plains' Indians, 23
*Playboy*, 8, 84–85, 86
polenta, 101
Polish cuisine, 101
Pollan, Michael, 55–56, 63, 73
popcorn, 58
*Popular Mechanics*, 31, 42, 43
popular media. *See* media coverage and representations; television programming; visual media representations
*Popular Science*, 31
pork: baby back ribs, 3, 71, 74–75; ethnic cuisine, 105, 107, 113; as gender signifier, 83; marinades, 79; mascots as culinary symbols, 134–36; popularity, 74–75, 83; pulled pork, 3, 54; spareribs, 110, 120; stew, 44; tenderloin, 64
portable grills, 31, 32, 33–34, 36–38, 54
*Portlandia*, 12, 87–88
Portsmith, Ohio, 22
poultry. *See* chicken; duck; turkey

power tools, 57

*Prairie Home Companion*, 87

pregame festivities: class distinctions, 23, 111; communal bonds and friendships, 125–26, 128–30, 133–43, 148–49; fan participation, 33–38; gameday breakfasts and luncheons, 21, 22–24, 34, 146–47; gameday picnic merchandising, 29; gender constructs, 3–4, 20, 21, 22–23, 30, 32–45, 49–62, 160*n*117; historical perspective, 5, 15–25; planning and preparation, 67; popularity, 37–40; private homes, 21, 22; racial and ethnic diversity, 23, 120–22; recreational vehicles (RVs), 67–70; restaurants and take-out lunches, 24–25; team competition, 42, 54, 63–66, 73–76; traditional cuisine, 36, 40–42, 50, 60–62, 120–22. *See also* automobile picnics; stadium parking lots; tailgating culture

*Princeton Alumni Weekly*, 25

Princeton, New Jersey, 24

Princeton University, 19, 24, 25, 28, 45

privilege, white, 102–3, 117–18

professional football, 21–22, 68, 119

*Puck*, 20

Purdue University, 113

## Q

queer community, 150

quinoa, 91, 119

## R

race and ethnicity: authentic food traditions, 106, 109–10, 120–22; cookbooks, 13, 95–108; cross-cultural understandings, 102–6, 120–22; culinary racism, 96, 97–100, 102–6, 114–15, 117, 148, 169*n*15; ethnic revivalist period, 100–102; first-wave tailgate cookbooks, 99, 100–108, 112–13; football athletics, 17, 114; gendered cooking, 61–62; place identity and local cuisine, 132–33; pregame festivities, 23, 120–22; racialized masculinity, 132–33;

second-wave tailgate cookbooks, 100, 108–15; tailgating culture, 11, 12, 45–46, 95–96, 99–115, 120–23, 148, 175*n*122; visual media representations, 115–16, 118–19. *See also* ethnic cuisine; tailgate cookbooks; white-centric culture

racial integration/segregation, 116–17

racist and ethnic caricatures, 97–98, 103–4, 112, 169*n*15

rakes, 54

*Rammer Jammer Yellow Hammer* (St. John), 117

reality series, 12

Recreational Vehicle Industry Association (RVIA), 68

recreational vehicles (RVs), 3, 16, 49–51, 67–70, 117. *See also* motorhomes

red meat. *See* meat

restaurants, 24–25

retrograde masculinity, 84, 86–89

ribs, 3, 42, 71, 74, 75, 77, 79, 80

Richards, Bruce, 134

Richards, Eugene, 17

Riggs, Harriet, 55

"rights" movements, 38

rituals and ceremonies, 55–56, 73, 134–36

rivalries and competitions, 42, 54, 63–66, 73–76, 125–36. *See also* *Tailgate Warriors*

Roberson, John and Marie, 32

Rockmaker, Tessie, 34

Roosevelt, Alice, 28

Roosevelt, Theodore, 28

rotisseries, 54, 58

*Rudy* (film), 76

## S

Sagehen's Retriever Club Tailgate Cookbook (Fleischmann), 103–4

salmon, 21, 39, 63, 64, 83, 91

San Antonio, Texas, 111

San Francisco 49ers tailgate parties and competitions: cooking equipment and gadgets, 66–67; fan participation, 40, 120; meat preparation, 75; noncompetitive position, 128; place

identity, 132; popularity, 3; special ingredients, 83, 88; televised competitions, 74, 75, 90. *See also* 3rdRail9ers
Santa Clara, California, 120
saws, 54
school buses, 40
screwdrivers, 54
seafood, 49, 65, 83, 102, 103, 134
Seattle Seahawks tailgate parties and competitions, 63, 74, 75, 90, 92, 127, 131, 132
second-wave feminism, 38
second-wave tailgate cookbooks, 100, 108–15
Section 16H Group, 142
Seismic Mike, 79–80
semi-professional football, 21–22
Sessions, Jeff, 171*n*53
sex-based segregation, 22–23
sexual innuendo, 84–87
Shanley, Timmy, 131
short ribs, 42
shovels, 54
shrimp, 62, 107, 110
sickles, 54
side dishes: gender constructs, 50, 60, 62, 127; team competition, 4, 74, 75, 92, 126–27; vegetables, 92, 127. *See also* corn
signature custom-made brand, 93
signifying ingredients and stereotypes, 98, 99–101, 103–8, 110–15, 119, 132–33
*Silver Linings Playbook* (film), 119
Simpson, Homer, 3, 5, 53, 75–76
*The Simpsons*, 12, 53, 75–76
situation comedies, 12
six-cylinder cooking, 55
sketch shows, 12
Slautterback Motor Company, 26–27
slavery, 97, 102, 117
slide-outs, 164*n*76
Sloan, Bob: ethnic cuisine, 110; football-food analogy, 88; on grilling, 52–53; on masculinity, 77, 78; misogynistic discourse, 85; on non-meat foods, 90–91; on serving fish, 83, 89
Smart-Grosvenor, Vertamae, 98

Smith, Loran, 112–14
smokers, 3, 52, 58, 66, 70, 79–80
Sobal, Jeffery, 148
social parodies, 12
soul food cookbooks, 99
*Souper Bowl of Recipes*, 107, 113
Southeastern Conference (SEC), 86–87, 114
*Southern Living: The Official SEC Tailgating Cookbook*, 84, 86–87, 114–15
*The Southern Tailgating Cookbook*, 134
Southern University, 61, 122
spareribs, 110, 120
spatial arrangements, 126, 137–39
spicy ingredients and foods, 107–8
spinning grills, 54
sport film, 76
*Sports Illustrated*, 32–33, 37
spot savers, 138–39
*Spread Formation* (Smith), 112–14
stadium construction, 18–19
stadium parking lots: charitable fund-raising, 139, 142; culinary complexity, 62–67; ethnic cuisine, 119–23; football picnics, 29–30, 33, 34–38, 42; gender arrangements, 32, 60–62; gender constructs, 14, 38–44, 50–52, 92, 127; grilling culture, 33, 38, 52–53, 57–58, 73; historical perspective, 5; meat-football relationship, 73–88; motorhomes, 49–51, 67–70; motorized vehicles, 34–36; pregame festivities, 49–52; social constructs, 10; spatial arrangements, 137–39; spectacles and performance, 3–4, 16, 56, 145–47; tailgating equipment and gadgets, 43–44, 57–58, 70; television commercials, 76–77, 86, 145; vegetarian fare, 92; visual media representations, 53, 57–58, 75–77, 86–87; white-centric culture, 119. *See also* mascots; rivalries and competitions; *Tailgate Warriors*
standardized cuisine, 97, 99, 107
Stanford Stadium, 60–61, 139
Stanford University, 25, 118, 119, 175*n*122

Stanford University tailgates, 60–61, 80, 139

station wagons, 34–36

steak: customized cooking equipment, 54; ethnic cuisine, 104, 110, 120; as gender signifier, 73, 75, 77; grilling culture, 33–34, 53, 54, 63, 78, 83, 85; mascots as culinary symbols, 134; parodies, 87. *See also* meat

stereotypes: culinary racism, 97–100, 102–6, 114–15, 117, 148, 169*n*15; food studies, 6, 39, 145–51; ghettoization and othering, 96, 97, 99, 101, 102, 103–6; immigrant and ethnic cuisine, 95, 98, 99–115, 119, 132–33; pregame festivities, 5, 32–36; race and ethnicity, 13, 97–106, 114–15, 117, 169*n*15; tailgating culture, 5, 8–14, 60–62, 71–93. *See also* femininity and cooking; gender constructs; masculinity

St. John, Warren, 117

stuffed cabbage, 101

suburban grilling culture. *See* grills/ grilling culture; outdoor cooking

suitcase grills, 31

*The Sun*, 19

*Sunset*, 33–34, 104, 108

Super Bowl, 102

Sutton, Horace, 32–33

symbolic rituals, 55–56, 73, 134–36

Syracuse University, 136

# T

taco trucks, 173*n*95

Tailgate 360 grill, 52

*The Tailgate Cookbook* (Herbert), 105, 107

tailgate cookbooks: authentic food traditions, 106, 109–10; barbecue culture, 44–45, 77–78; by-men-for-men cookbooks, 84, 88–89, 109–11; commercialization, 37; cooking equipment and gadgets, 57; cross-cultural understandings, 100–106; culinary racism, 102–6, 114–15, 117, 148; cultural significance, 11; ethnic

integration and inclusion, 108–15, 122–23, 148; ethnic revivalist period, 100–102; first-wave tailgate books, 99, 100–108, 112–13; gender constructs, 40, 41, 44–45, 56, 77–78, 84–91; ghettoization and othering, 96, 97, 99, 101, 102, 103–6; grilling culture, 52–53, 56; historical perspective, 96, 148; immigrant and ethnic cuisine, 95, 98, 99–115; mascots as culinary symbols, 134, 149; racial and ethnic diversity, 95–96, 99–115, 120–23, 148; second-wave tailgate cookbooks, 100, 108–15; suggested menus, 36

*Tailgate Cooking and Other Gastronomical Horrors*, 103

Tailgate For A Cause, 141–42

*Tailgate Parties* (Wyler), 108

*Tailgate Warriors*: communal bonds and friendships, 125, 142–43; consumerism, 65–66; cooking equipment and gadgets, 57–58, 64–66; culinary complexity, 63–66; customized cooking equipment, 53–54; gender constructs, 7, 8, 60, 65, 76, 92, 93, 125; historical perspective, 6; meat primacy, 73–75, 76; place identity and local cuisine, 131–33; purpose, 4; rivalries and competitions, 125, 126–27, 128, 131–33; signature custom-made brand, 93; special ingredients, 83; vegetarian fare, 90, 92

Tailgate With A Cause, 142

*The Tailgating Cookbook* (Sloan), 85, 88, 110

tailgating culture: charitable fundraising, 139–42, 178*n*53; commercialization, 37–38, 45; communal bonds and friendships, 125–26, 128–30, 133–43, 148–49; culinary complexity, 62–67; fan participation, 34–35, 37–41; gendered cooking, 3–6, 8–14, 33–45, 49–62, 71–93, 119, 125–36, 145–51, 176*n*15; historical perspective, 5–6, 15–25, 146–48; misogynistic discourse,

84, 85, 89–90; motorhomes, 49–51, 67–70; parodies, 87–88; place identity and local cuisine, 125–26, 131–33, 149; popularity, 37–40; portable grills, 31, 32, 33–34, 36–38; pregame festivities, 5, 32–38; prevalence, 3–6, 10, 36, 38; racial and ethnic diversity, 12, 13, 45–46, 99–115, 175n122; racist imagery, 103, 117–18, 119, 174n114; sexual innuendo, 84–87; social constructs, 8–14; southern colleges and universities, 86–87, 116–17, 134–36; spatial arrangements, 126, 137–39; spectacles and performance, 56, 63, 68–70, 73–77, 120, 146–47; team competition, 42, 54, 63–66, 73–76, 125–36; traditional cuisine, 36, 40–42, 50, 60–62, 120–22; vegetarian fare, 88–92; visual media representations, 7–8, 11–12, 53, 75–76, 86, 118–19, 129–33. *See also* pregame festivities; rivalries and competitions; tailgate cookbooks; *Tailgate Warriors*

take-out lunches, 24–25

team competition, 42, 54, 63–66, 73–76, 125–36. *See also Tailgate Warriors*

television commercials: Chevrolet, 145; gendered cooking, 11, 52, 57–58, 76–77, 91, 130; grilling culture, 52, 145; meat-football relationship, 76–77; recreational vehicles (RVs), 68; sexual objectification, 86; tailgating culture, 11, 76–77, 86; tailgating equipment and gadgets, 57–58; vegetarian fare, 91

television programming: communal bonds and friendships, 129–30; gender constructs, 12, 39–40, 73; influential role, 10, 11; meat primacy, 13, 73, 75–76, 87–88; racial and ethnic diversity, 115–16, 118–19; tailgating parodies, 87–88; televised cookery, 4, 6, 7–8, 65, 108–9, 128; white-centric culture, 13. *See also Tailgate Warriors*

tequila, 108, 111

territorialism, 126, 137–39

Texas A&M University, 87

Texas Stadium, 137

Thanksgiving Day football games, 19, 20, 23, 25, 26, 46

*The Next Food Network Star*, 8

3rdRail9ers, 3, 53, 56, 81, 128, 138

Tiger Stadium, 49–50

*Time* magazine, 39

tofu, 39, 81, 145

Tomaszewski, Joe, 40

Toyota commercial series, 130

traditional tailgating cuisine, 36, 40–42, 50, 60–62, 120–22

"Trailcooker," 42–43

tri-tip, 3, 58, 61, 64, 71, 74, 80, 132

Trump, Donald, 173n96

*Truth*, 28

turkey: burgers, 88; legs, 77; necks, 62, 71, 122; sandwiches, 107, 114

Turlock, California, 122

Tuscaloosa, Alabama, 115

Tuskegee Institute, 23

Twitchell, James, 78

Twitty, Michael, 115

**U**

United States Military Academy, 43

university athletics, 5, 16–21, 67–68, 116–17, 119

University of Alabama, 117, 134–36

University of Arkansas, 70, 114

University of California at Berkeley, 25, 27

University of Cincinnati, 113

University of Illinois, 33, 118, 174n117

University of Maryland, 136

University of Michigan, 114

University of Mississippi, 86–87, 116–17, 138

University of Nebraska, 22–23

University of North Carolina, 134

University of Oregon tailgating parties and competitions, 14, 69, 80–81, 119, 136, 175n122

University of Pennsylvania, 22

University of South Carolina mascot, 84

University of Southern California, 27

University of Tennessee tailgating parties and competitions: charitable fundraising, 141–42, 178n53; customized cooking equipment, 3–4, 58, 59–60, 78–79; immigrant and ethnic cuisine, 110, 119; white-centric culture, 119, 175n122

University of Texas, 134

University of Washington, 136

urban identification. *See* place identity

## V

vans, 69

vegetables/vegetarian fare: as gender signifier, 13, 72–73, 89–92, 119, 145; marginalization, 88–92; side dishes, 92, 127; tailgating culture, 13; vegetable-football analogy, 88, 89. *See also* corn

Vester, Katharina, 147

*Vibration Cooking*, 98

visual media representations, 11–12, 53, 75–76, 115–16, 118–19, 129–33. *See also* advertisements; film representations; television commercials; television programming

## W

Ward, Susan, 42

Watson, Graham, 135–36

Weber grills, 33, 52, 60, 61, 80

Weiner, Sally, 32

Wendy's, 42

Werblin, David "Sonny," 36

West Point, 42

wheelbarrows, 54

white-centric culture: cookbooks, 13, 96–100, 114–15, 148; ethnic food heritage and identity, 101; ethnic revivalist period, 100–102; football athletics, 17–18, 114; place identity and local cuisine, 132–33; Southern traditions, 116–17; tailgating culture, 13, 45–46, 96, 99–102, 105–6, 114–15, 117–19; television programming, 13; white privilege, 102–3, 117–18. *See also* tailgate cookbooks

white supremacy, 17, 169n15, 170n15, 174n114

Wilberforce University, 23

Williams-Brice stadium, 84

Williams-Forson, Psyche, 112

wine, 119

Wisconsin, 21–22

Witt, Doris, 116

working-class masculinity, 131–33

World War II, 30

Wyler, Susan, 108

## Y

Yahoo! Sports, 135

Yale Bowl, 5, 18–19, 26, 42

*Yale Daily News*, 21

Yale University: automobile-football relationship, 28; gameday luncheons, 21; gameday picnics, 15, 25–26, 29; stadium construction, 18–19; tailgating tradition, 5, 40, 42; Thanksgiving Day football games, 19; Yale–Princeton football game, 19, 45

York Pharmacy, 24

Yum-Yum Girls, 60

MARIA J. VERI is associate professor of kinesiology at San Francisco State University. Her research focuses on cultural and historical aspects of sport and intersections between sport and food. She is a spectacular cook.

RITA LIBERTI is professor of kinesiology at California State University, East Bay, where she is the founding director of the Center for Sport and Social Justice. Much of her work focuses on twentieth-century US women's sport history. She is a good eater.